IMAGES
of America

EAST ST. LOUIS

On the Cover: The Federal Courthouse is pictured on its dedication day. This historic image was taken by prominent St. Louis postcard photographer Henry Bregstone on October 25, 1909. He described the building as being in "gala attire" for the dedication. On the reviewing stand in front of the building was President Taft and Speaker of the House Joe Cannon. (SIUE)

IMAGES
of America

EAST ST. LOUIS

Bill Nunes and Andrew Theising

ARCADIA
PUBLISHING

ISBN 978-0-7385-8280-1

Published by Arcadia Publishing
Charleston, South Carolina

Printed in the United States of America

Library of Congress Control Number: 2010943235

For all general information, please contact Arcadia Publishing:
Telephone 843-853-2070
Fax 843-853-0044
E-mail sales@arcadiapublishing.com
For customer service and orders:
Toll-Free 1-888-313-2665

Visit us on the Internet at www.arcadiapublishing.com

Contents

Acknowledgments

This book is the product of many hands. Jeff Ruetsche of Arcadia Publishing was wonderful to work with, and the authors express their thanks to him. Sincere thanks go to the Belleville Public Library, Sr. Mary Kenan Wolff of the Diocese of Belleville, and to Bill Jacobus for his unmatched knowledge of East St. Louis geography and place.

Content for this volume has come from many sources, public and private. Some work has come from the authors' personal collections and connections (which are marked BN and AT in the photograph credits). Other work has come from private collections. Many images came from the postcard collection of Harold Fiebig and his wife, Emily, of Belleville (these are marked HF). Several images were provided courtesy of Reginald Petty (which are marked RP). The Stephens family documents were originally obtained from Betty Allen, who graciously shared her family's collection with Southern Illinois University Edwardsville (SIUE).

Finally, the Bowen Archives of Southern Illinois University Edwardsville provided both content and technical support. Most of the archival imagery came from the research collections donated by Andrew Theising, Raymond "Sandy" Peters, and Reginald Petty. Dr. Steven Kerber, university archivist and special collections librarian, supervised the scanning process, and provided both access to collections and timely digital processing. He was assisted in this work by digital imaging specialist Ginger Strickland and Amanda Bahr-Evola, archives specialist. This project had the full support of the Lovejoy Library and Dean Regina McBride, for which the authors are grateful.

The SIUE Institute for Urban Research managed the assembly of the book. Vamsi Kammili converted the images for publication. The project received the support of other IUR staff members, including Hugh Pavitt, Rhonda Penelton, and Delia Major. This project enjoyed the support of Deans Stephen Hansen and Jerry Weinberg of the SIUE School of Graduate Studies and Research.

The authors extend thanks to these and the many other people who provided content and assistance for this book. We apologize for any errors or omissions, responsibility for which is solely ours.

—Bill Nunes and Andrew Theising

INTRODUCTION

The municipality called East St. Louis, Illinois, was officially established on April 1, 1861. The small town soon grew to a bustling city at the center of the booming St. Louis economy (St. Louis would be the fourth largest city in the United States by 1870). East St. Louis was home to major factories, endless railroads, and extensive river commerce. It was home to expansive parks, stout churches, and high-quality schools. Called the "Pittsburgh of the West," the metropolis of 80,000 was named an All-American City in 1960 and proudly celebrated its centennial in 1961. It was also home to colorful politicians, one of the country's most infamous red-light districts, and an abundance of saloons—the 1912 directory lists 309 of them.

The people of East St. Louis were as colorful and varied as they come. They arrived here from across the United States and Europe, lured by the promise of employment. East St. Louisans worked hard, and as the WPA writers noted in 1940, "on the faces of the people is written the strife and strain of the factories." They called it "a rough, alien land of many races, a melting pot of steel and bone." Politicians may have run the city by day, but organized crime ran the city at night. There were no closing times here. East St. Louis was a party that ran all night long.

On one tragic day, the city exploded with violence. July 2, 1917, was the day when whites took up arms against blacks and blood was spilled in the streets. Innocent people were killed, and justice was never served. People around the country were appalled at what happened. William Edward Burghardt, or W.E.B., DuBois came to investigate personally. Congress investigated. Theodore Roosevelt and Samuel Gompers got into a shouting match at Carnegie Hall over the incident. Prof. Eugene Redmond, the city's poet laureate, said to Harper Barnes that there's "never been a time" when the riot was not present. It remains a scar on the city's history.

Despite the struggles, the people persevered. Amazing talent came from here—world-class musicians (Miles Davis, Ike Turner), professional athletes (Hank Bauer, Bryan Cox, Jimmy Connors), and Olympic champions (Jackie Joyner-Kersee, Dawn Harper), as well as scholars and statesmen. Katherine Dunham, renowned dancer, actress, and anthropologist, called this place home, as did Lillian Gish, star of the silent screen. Chuck Berry got his start here, and the great Chief Pontiac met his end here. W.C. Handy and Duke Ellington both wrote songs about the city, Charles Dickens wrote how unimpressed he was by what he saw here, and Walt Whitman was struck by the magnitude of the stockyards. Some say that more talent intersected in this small city than any other of its size.

Over time, it all seemed to have slipped away. The factories closed, smokestacks no longer poured, and the slaughterhouses fell silent and the animal pens emptied. Families moved as school and church buildings fell in the path of interstate highways. Jobs were gone. The city that had doubled its population with each census before World War II started losing all that it had gained. The Aluminum Ore plant was first to cut back in 1954. Other plants followed suit—Swift, American Zinc, Armour meatpacking, Obear-Nester. Familiar names disappeared. The city knew pain all over again. Unemployment, poverty, and vice filled the streets. In some respects, they never left.

The city now enters its 150th year. Physically, it looks very different today than it did a century ago. So much is gone. The grass and trees cannot tell the stories of what happened on the now-vacant lots. The facades of old buildings do not speak of the joy and pain they have witnessed. Photographs and memorabilia are the final remnants that document that history. This volume captures the early history of this place called East St. Louis—the history of a city on an upswing.

One

LANDMARKS

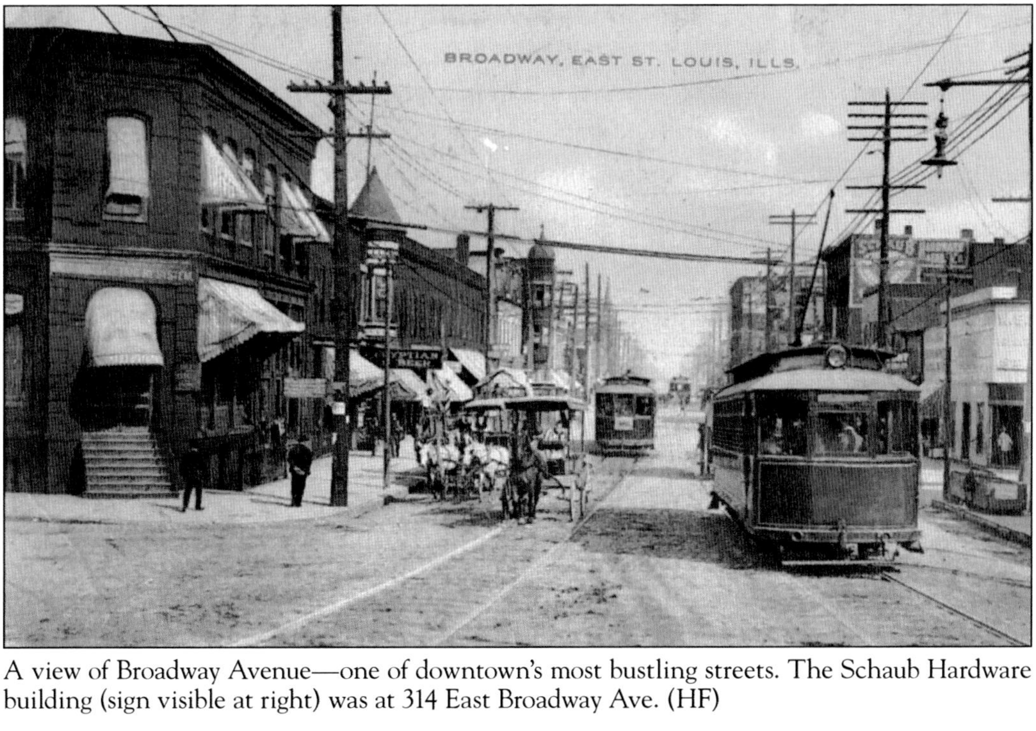

A view of Broadway Avenue—one of downtown's most bustling streets. The Schaub Hardware building (sign visible at right) was at 314 East Broadway Ave. (HF)

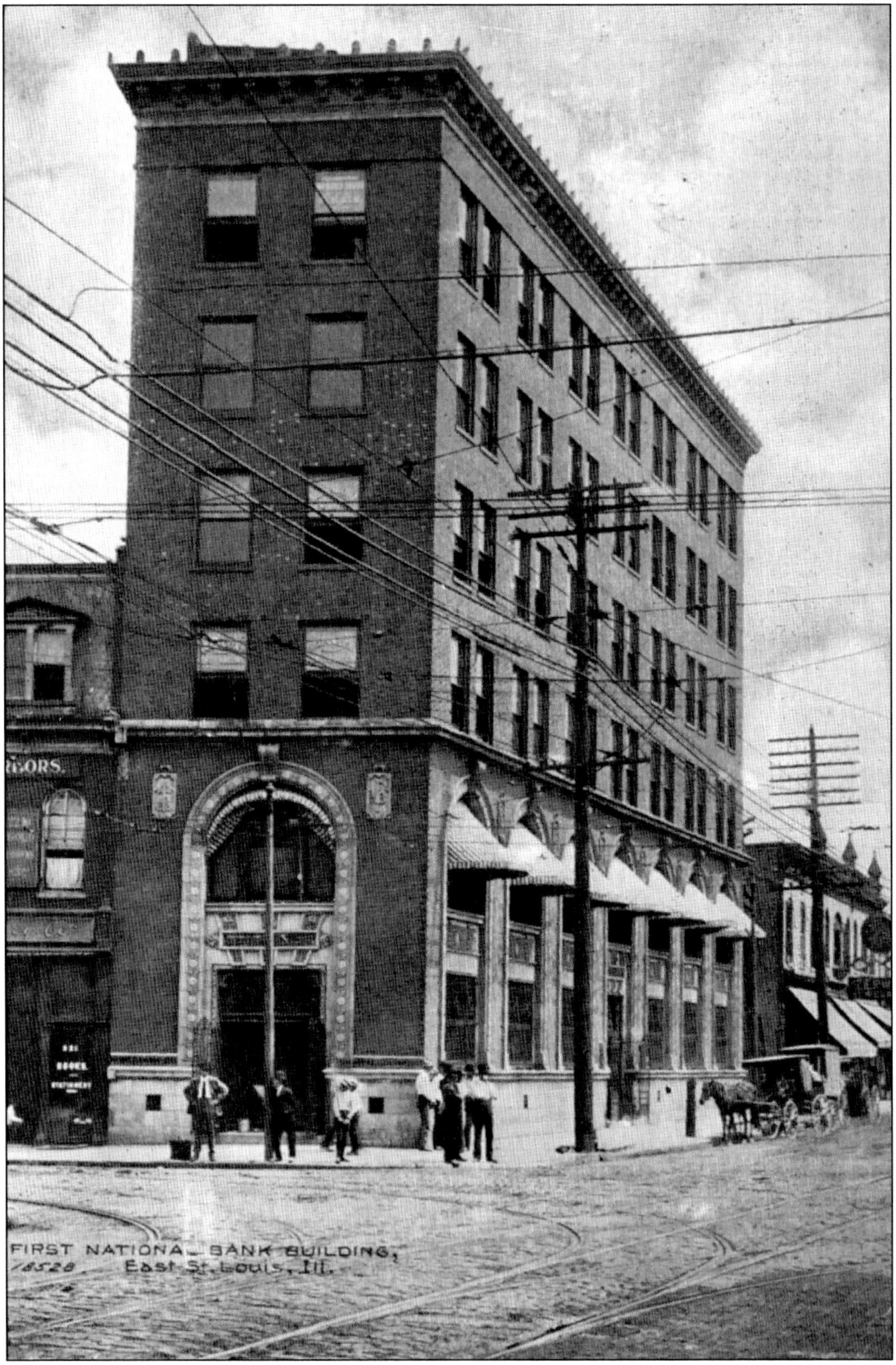

The Cahokia Building, at the northwest corner of Missouri and Collinsville Avenues, was the first six-story building in East St. Louis. Its main level became home to the First National Bank of East St. Louis, noted for its clock on the corner. The building also had a basement. It is a tall, narrow building in this image; it was later tripled in size toward the north. It still stands and currently houses its successor bank. (HF)

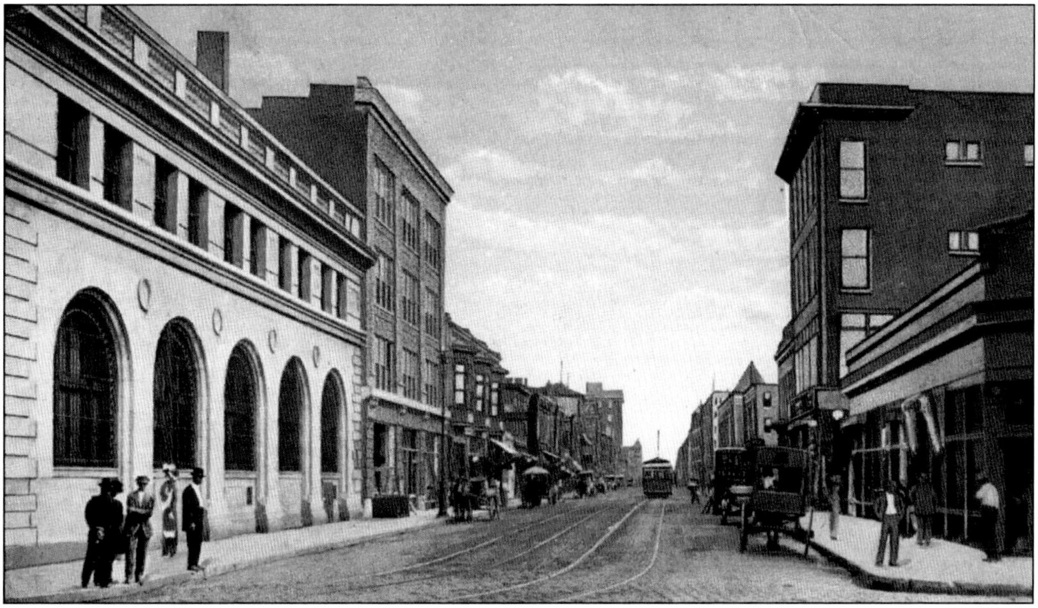

This is a view of Collinsville Avenue looking north from Broadway Avenue. On the immediate left is the Southern Illinois Bank (torn down in the 1990s). Next to it are the offices of East St. Louis Light and Power Company. The four-story building on the right was later home to the Slack Furniture Company, which also had a location in St. Louis. "Uncle Dick" Slack referred to himself as the "Jolly Irishman." (HF)

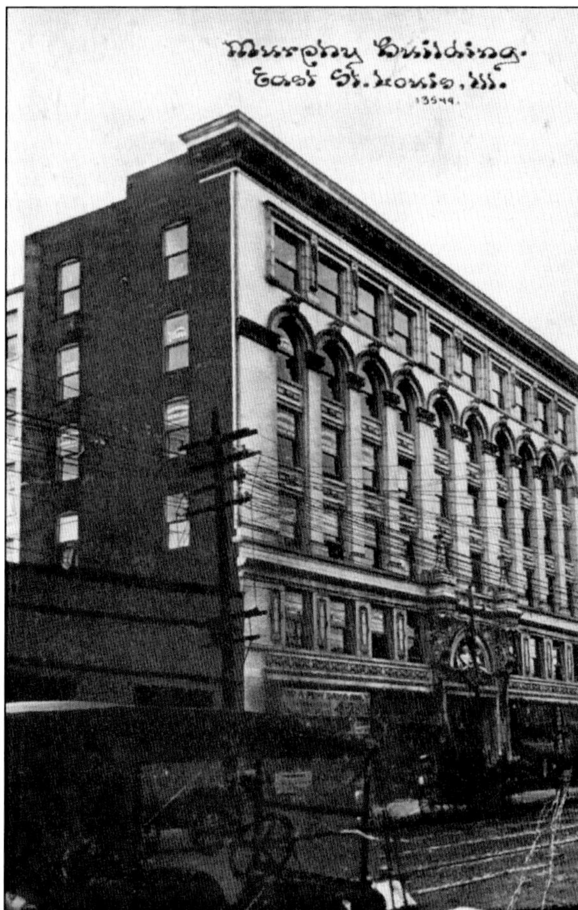

The Murphy Building on Collinsville Avenue, completed in 1904, was adjacent to the Majestic Theater. It featured two nude female statues that flanked the top corner on each side of the entrance. The building contained a pharmacy and was home to a number of doctors, lawyers, insurance companies, and real estate offices. Dr. West started out in the Murphy Building on the fourth floor. The facade still stands, but the rear of the building is collapsing. (SIUE)

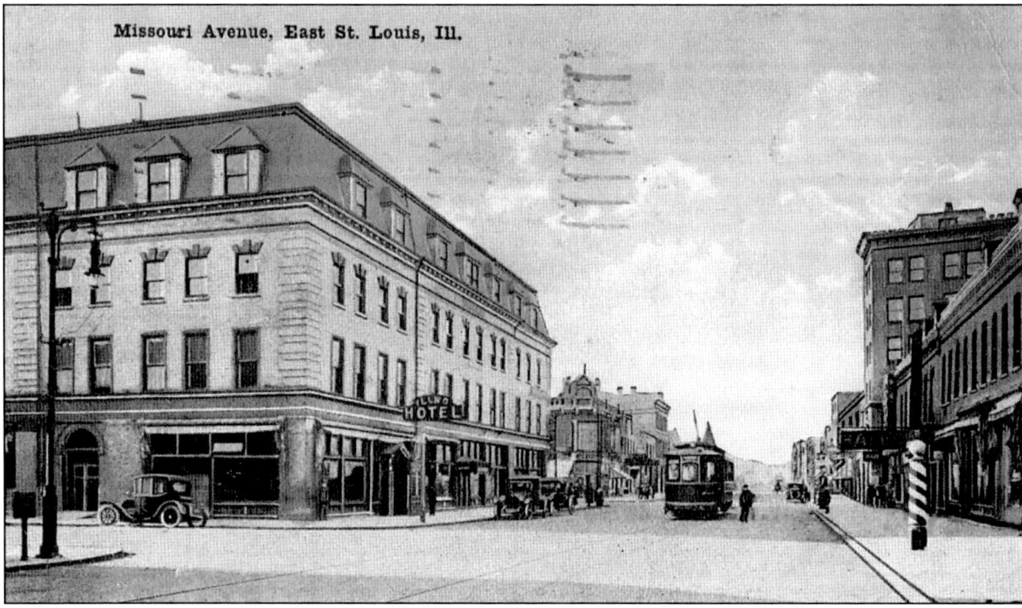

The Ill-Mo (Illinois-Missouri) Hotel on the southeast corner of Missouri and Collinsville Avenues was destroyed by fire in 1927—not long after this image was illustrated. It was replaced by the Goldman Building, which housed the second oldest Walgreens store in the state of Illinois. Walgreens was quite distinctive because it was topped by a Norman tower on the corner of the building. During the holiday season, Christmas music was piped from the tower to shoppers on the streets below to enliven their spirits. (HF)

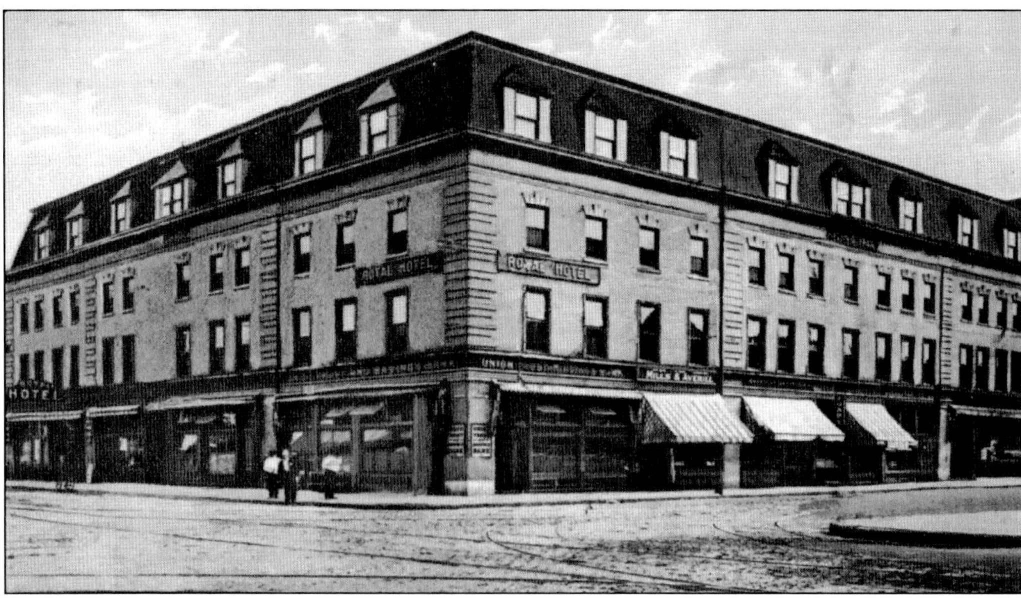

The Royal Hotel, later the Ill-Mo, covered the entire block of Missouri Avenue from Collinsville Avenue to Fourth Street. Century Cigar was originally located in the basement of this building. The building was erected by George Diehl in 1900, and was called the Diehl Hotel until 1903. This image shows the intersection of Collinsville Avenue and Missouri Avenue. The historic Cahokia Building would have been to the photographer's back. (HF)

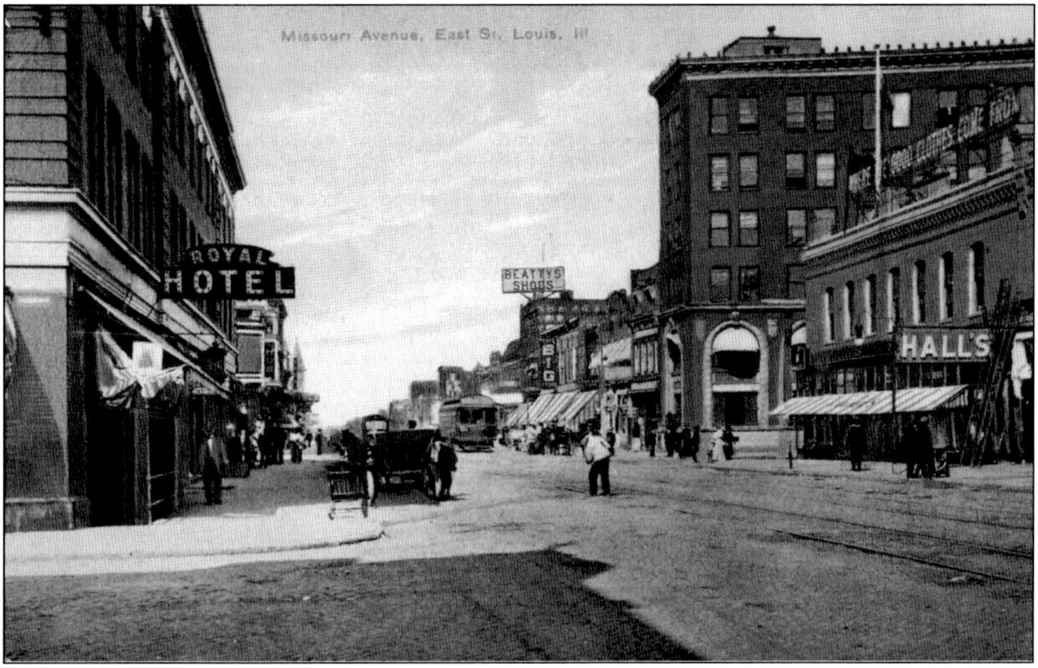

This photograph of Missouri Avenue, similar to the Ill-Mo Hotel street scene, was taken at the corner of Fourth Street. It is an older photograph and shows the hotel when it was the Royal. The tall and slender Cahokia Building stands on the right, where Collinsville Avenue crosses. All of the buildings beyond the Cahokia Building have been demolished over the years. (HF)

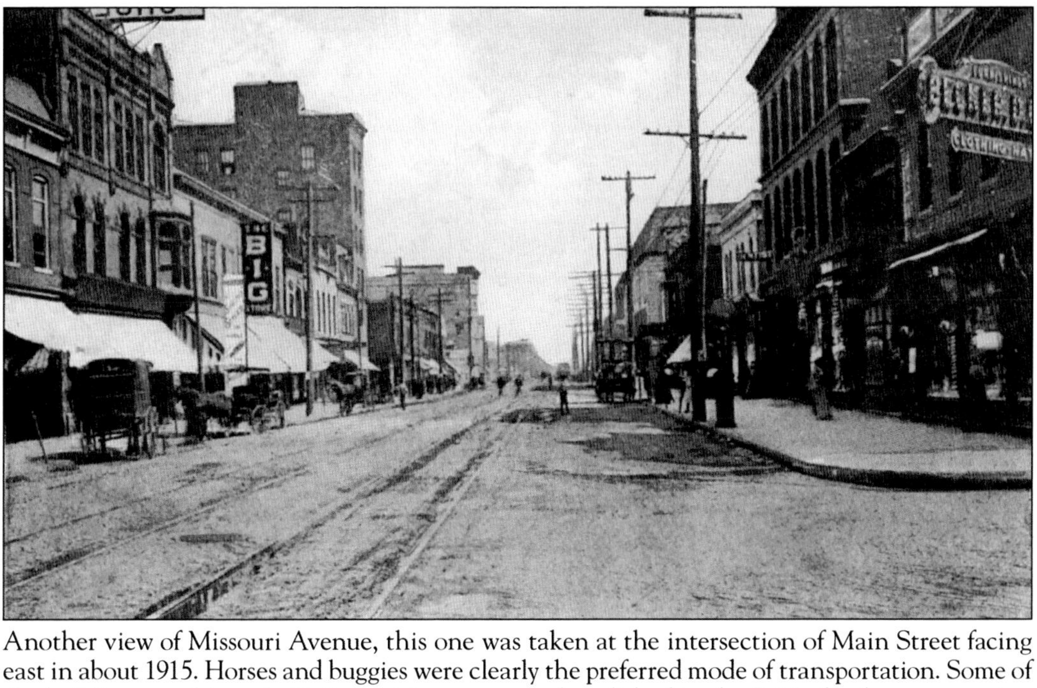

Another view of Missouri Avenue, this one was taken at the intersection of Main Street facing east in about 1915. Horses and buggies were clearly the preferred mode of transportation. Some of the buildings on this end of Missouri Avenue were demolished in the 1960s for the construction of Interstates 64/55/70. (HF)

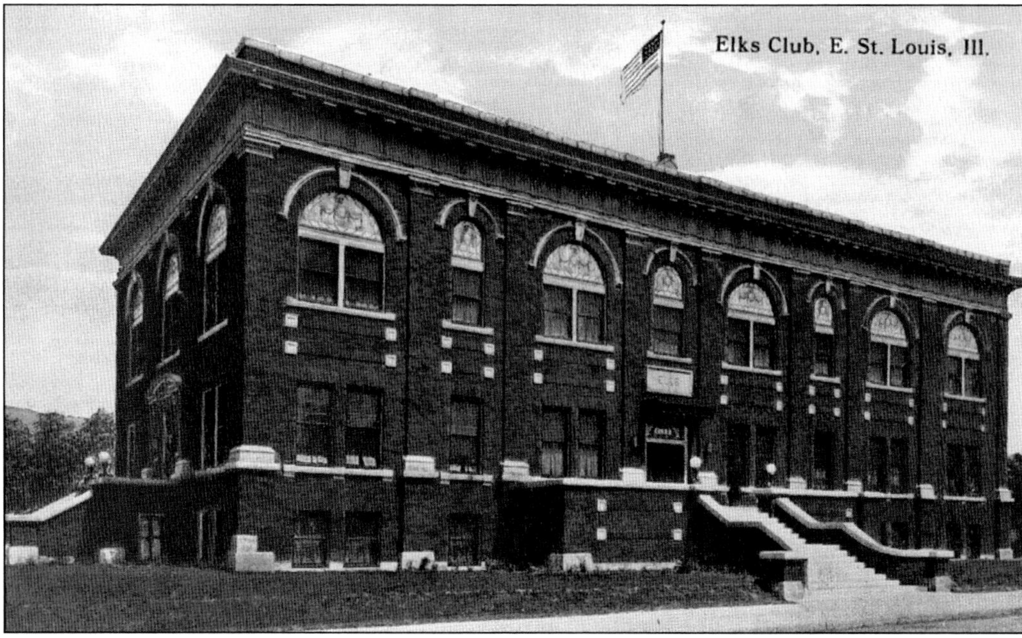

The Elks Building still stands at the corner of Ninth and State Streets. The Library Board purchased the building in 1927 for the price of $150,000. It was located not far from the Beulah Club and the high school. Lyon Woodruff was the head librarian at that time. The Elks Club moved to a smaller location above the Greyhound Bus Station, across from City Hall Park. For years, it housed the bronze bust of John Bowman, the founder of both the city and the library. A new one-story library was built in 2001 at 5320 State Street, and this building has remained largely vacant since. (HF)

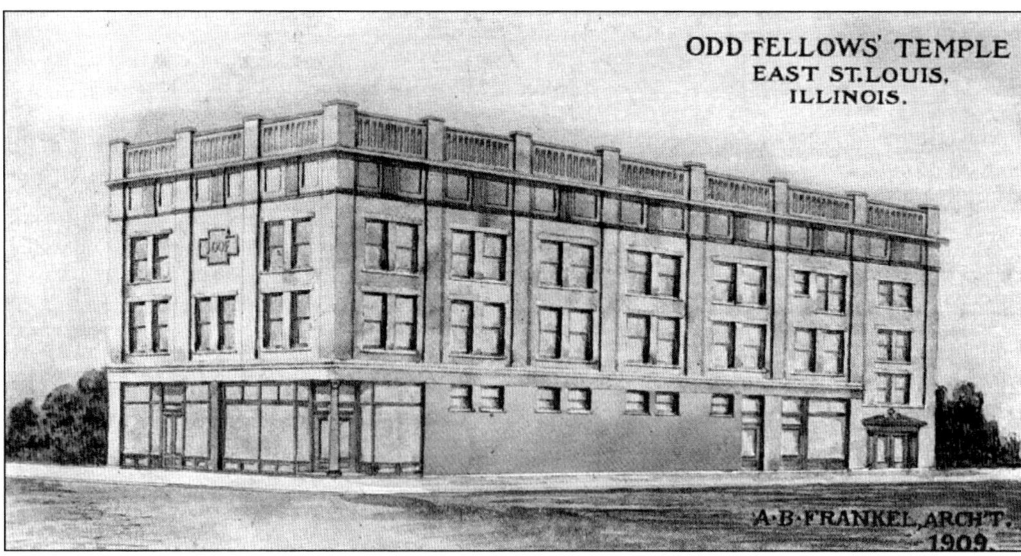

The International Order of Odd Fellows, Lodge no. 374, was located in this building at 242 North Seventh Street. By the 1940s, the group was meeting on the second floor of a building on the 700 block of St. Louis Avenue. The IOOF started in England in the 18th century and came to the United States in 1806. (HF)

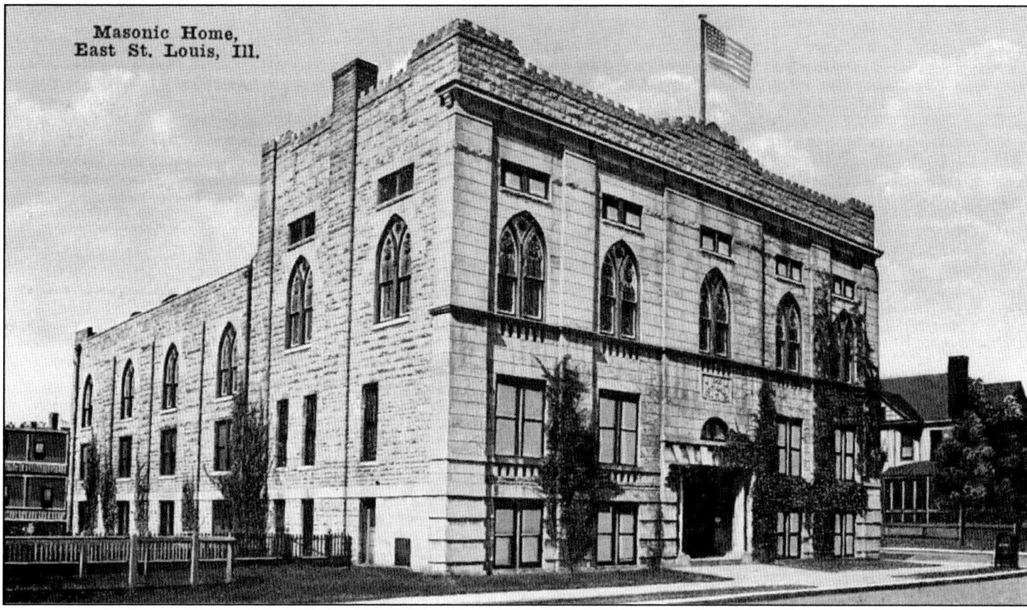

The Masons were first organized in East St. Louis in 1912 for the "betterment of family, friends, and community." They devoted their work to helping sick or needy children and held an annual picnic and a circus to raise money for that cause. Depicted here is the Scottish Rite Temple on 14th and College. The building was destroyed by fire in 2005, but the stone facade still stands. (HF)

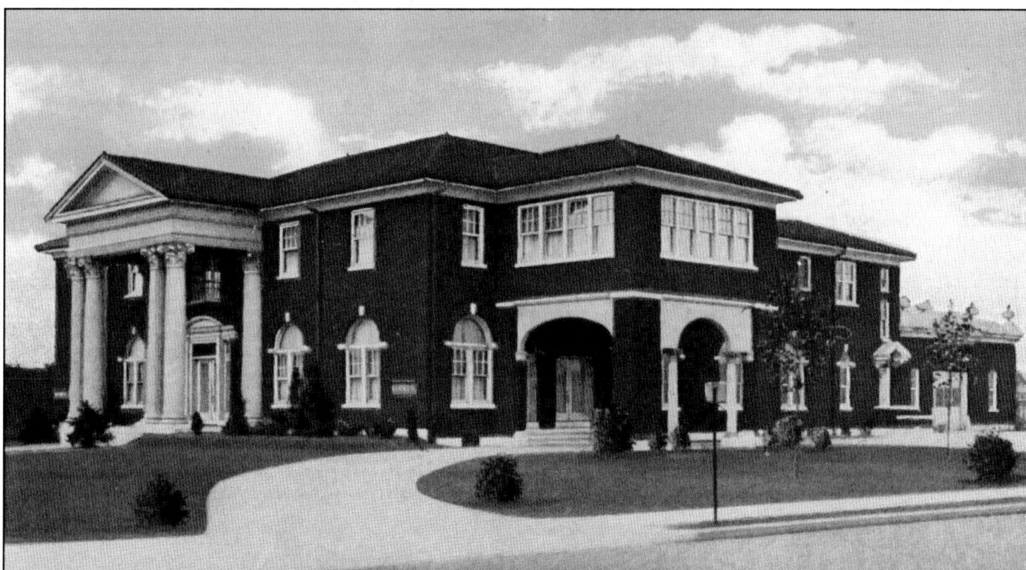

Kurrus Funeral Home, with its stately Greek columns, was one of the largest in the city. It was originally on Third Street, but later moved to 25th and State Streets, where this image was taken. Today, the funeral home is located in Belleville on Frank Scott Parkway. Other funeral homes included Sedlack, Kassly, Holten (76th and State Streets), Julius Marshall (3205 Missouri Avenue), Nash Brothers (111 North 13th Street), Brichler (22nd and State Streets), R.M.C. Green (1318 East Broadway Avenue), Robbins (8th Street), Officer (20th Street and Missouri Avenue), Degan (611 North Ninth Street), Walsh (201 Illinois Avenue), and Woodside (709 St. Louis Avenue). (HF)

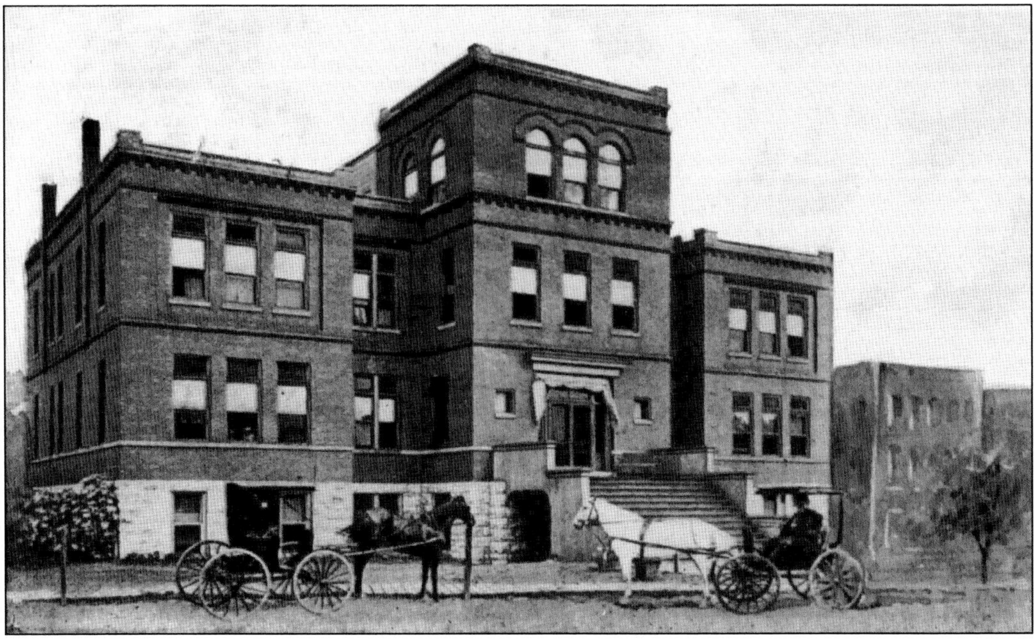

The Henrietta Hospital at 1509 Illinois Avenue, a four-story brick and stone structure, was built in 1897. It subsequently was known as Deaconness Hospital, eventually becoming Christian Welfare Hospital. It was regarded as the Protestant hospital, with most Catholics going to St. Mary's. (HF)

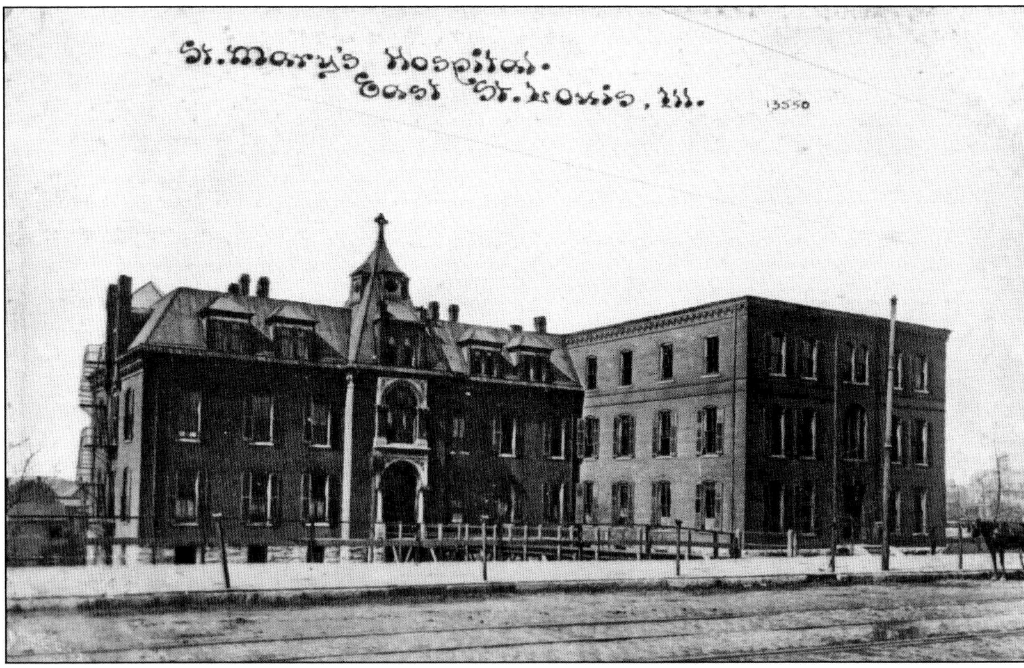

St. Mary's Hospital, shown here about 1911, was the Catholic hospital serving East St. Louis. It was expanded over the years and remains a hospital, though no longer operated by the Sisters of Mary. Note the long walkway leading to the entrance. This was required since the streets of downtown were raised high above the lots to protect the city from floods. (SIUE)

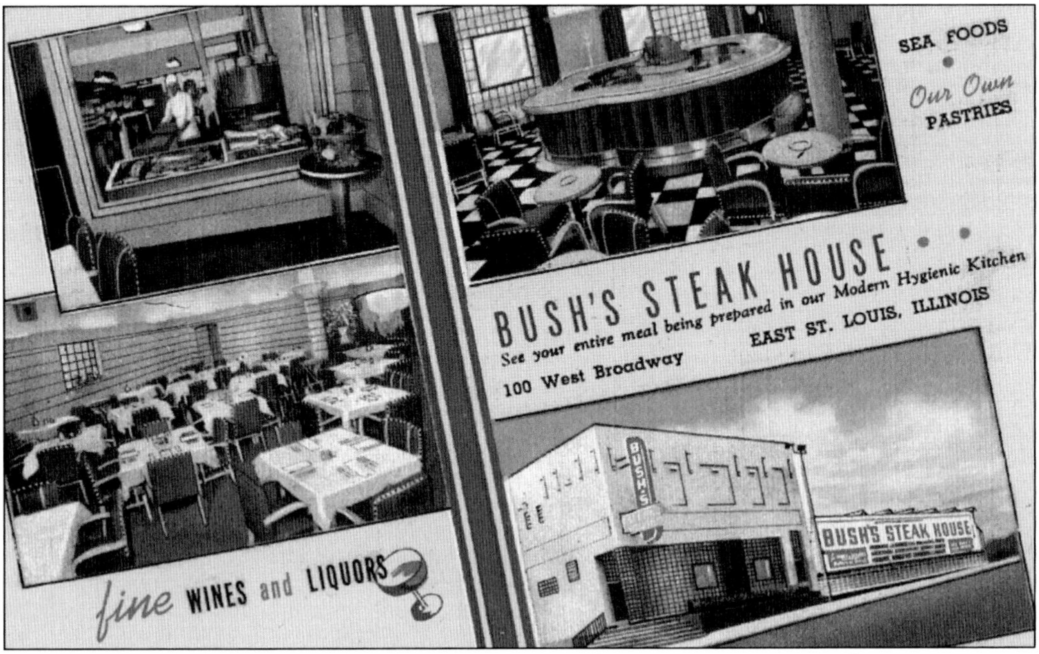

Bush's Steak House, later operated by Ed and Jack English, was at 100 West Broadway Avenue near the foot of the Eads Bridge on what was referred to as the Island area. It drew many customers from St. Louis, due to its proximity to the bridge and the fact that St. Louis had blue laws. This meant that nightclubs and restaurants had to close by 1 a.m. and restaurants could not serve liquor on Sundays. Bush's Steak House thus came to be frequented by notable athletes such as Lou Thesz and Red Schoendinst, who often dined in East St. Louis on Sundays. (HF)

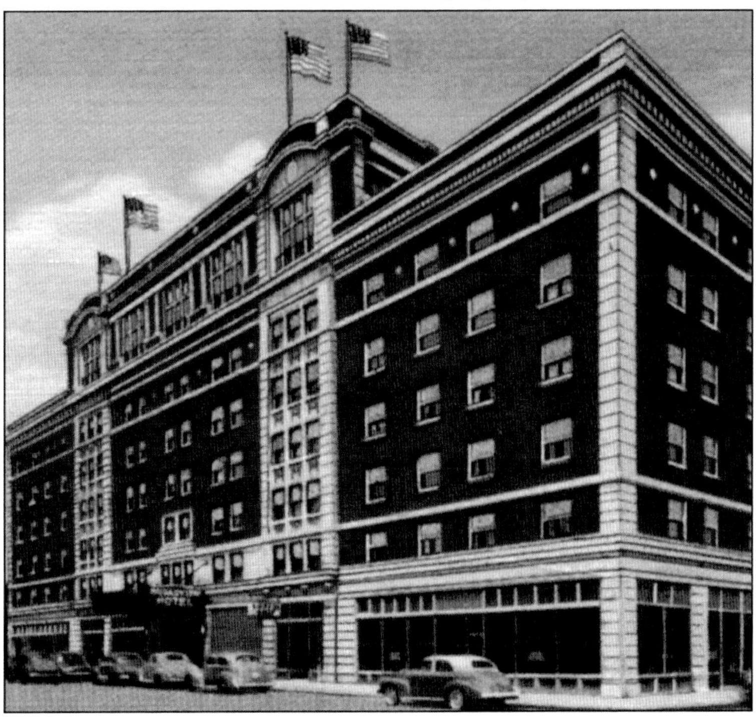

The Broadview Hotel was built in 1927 on East Broadway Avenue, between Fourth and Fifth Streets. The cost was $1,225,000. The mezzanine level housed the radio station WTMV, whose call letters stood for "Watch The Mississippi Valley." Joe Taylor was the original manager. The seventh floor at the top featured a spacious ballroom. For years, it was home to the East St. Louis branch of Southern Illinois University Edwardsville. The building still stands, and the city has plans for its renovation. (SIUE)

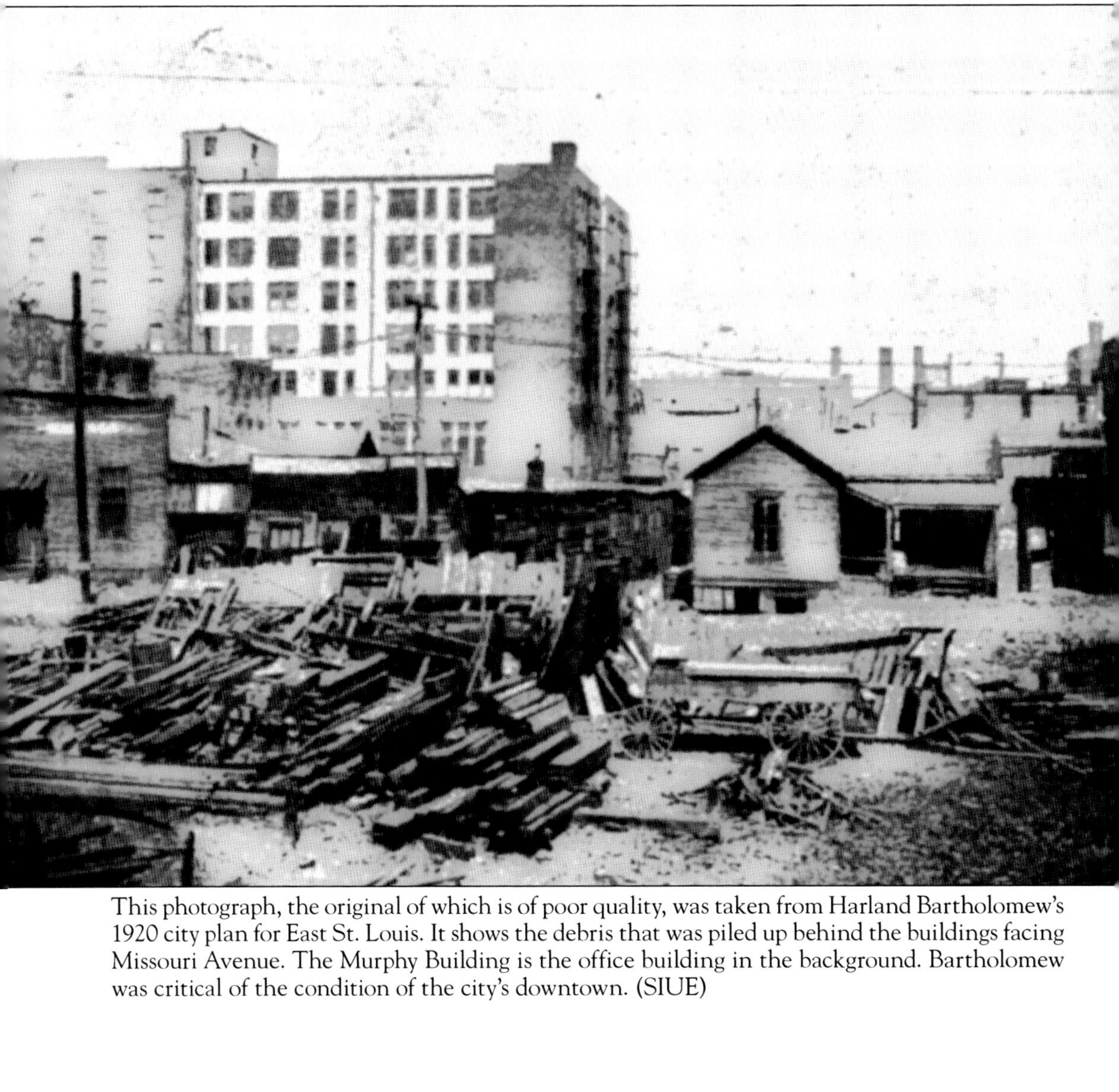

This photograph, the original of which is of poor quality, was taken from Harland Bartholomew's 1920 city plan for East St. Louis. It shows the debris that was piled up behind the buildings facing Missouri Avenue. The Murphy Building is the office building in the background. Bartholomew was critical of the condition of the city's downtown. (SIUE)

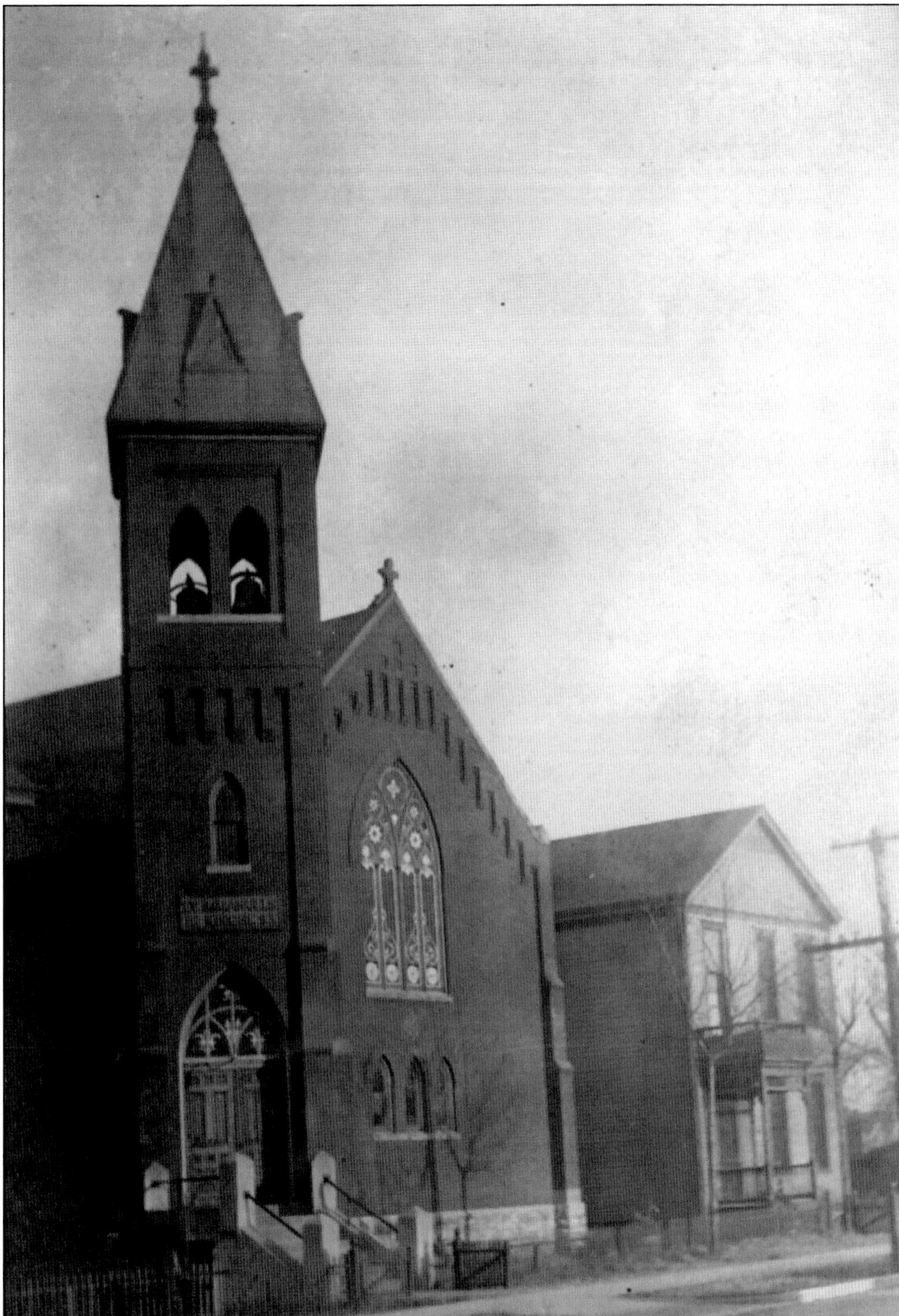

The Emmanuel Church on 14th Street, about a block south of State Street, originally sponsored the Henrietta Hospital. The churches of East St. Louis were far more than places of worship. They were critical social institutions that provided services to the working-class population of East St. Louis. Hospitals, schools, recreation programs, and social clubs have been affiliated with various churches in the city from the very beginning, continuing to this day. (SIUE)

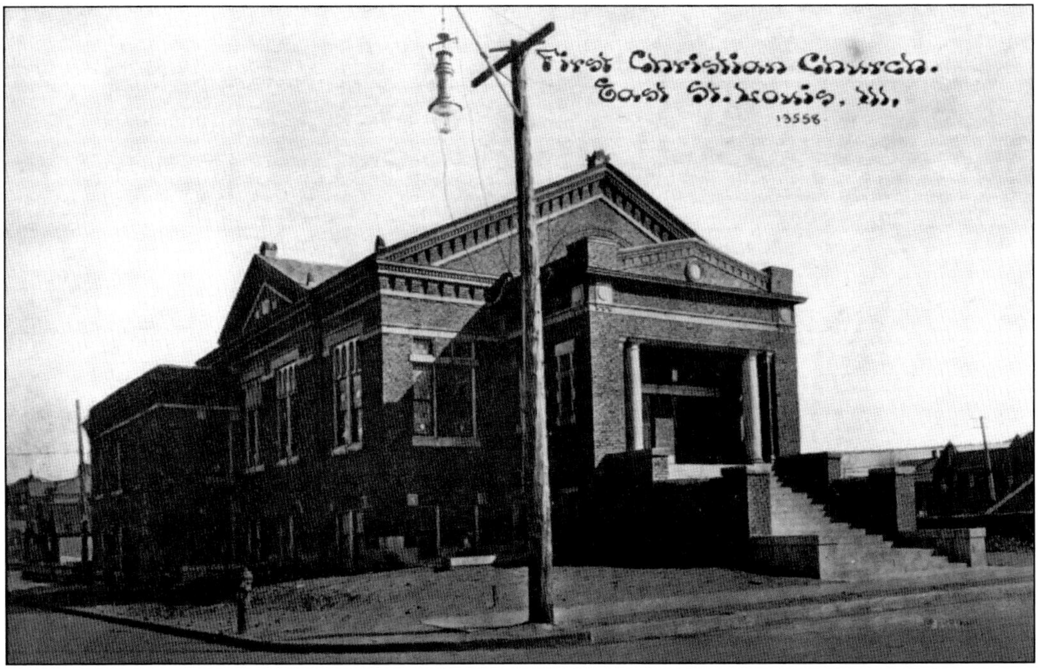

The First Christian Church was located at 518 Washington Place at State Street. This image was produced in about 1911. The building still stands and is home to the Community Mission Church of God in Christ. (HF)

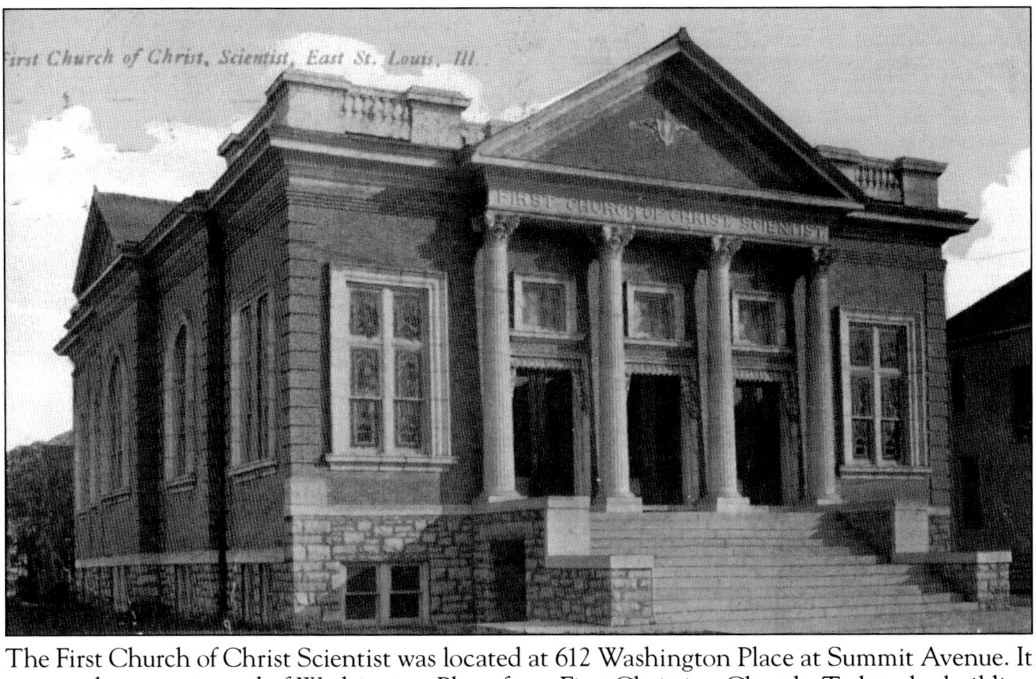

The First Church of Christ Scientist was located at 612 Washington Place at Summit Avenue. It was on the opposite end of Washington Place from First Christian Church. Today, the building is home to Mount Olive Baptist Church. Washington Place had many prominent residents over time, including politicians Silas Cook, Fred Gerold, and Locke Tarlton. (HF)

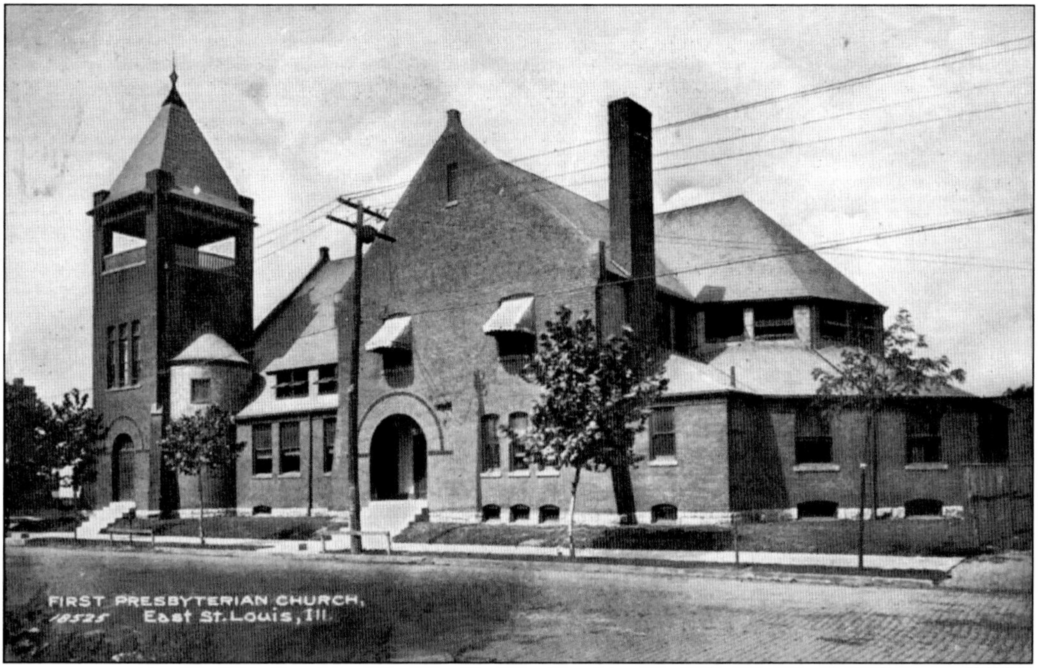

The First Presbyterian Church, located at 13th Street and Gaty Avenue, originally started out as the First Uptown Church on Collinsville Avenue. It later moved to State Street, across from the Greek Temple. The church is now located on Route 161 near Royal Heights Road in Belleville. The Live Wires, a Sunday school class here for young men with over 1,000 members, was the largest in the United States in 1912. (HF)

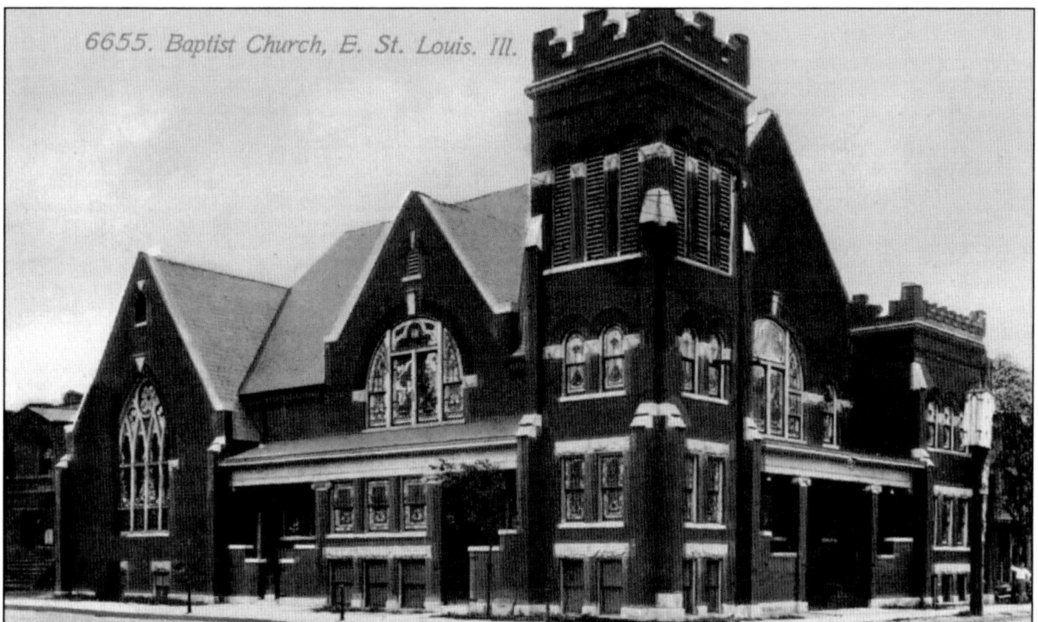

The First Baptist Church was at 1101 State Street next to the Sears parking lot. State Street, which stretches the entire length of East St. Louis, was a major commercial thoroughfare and was also home to churches, public schools, apartment buildings, and stately homes. (HF)

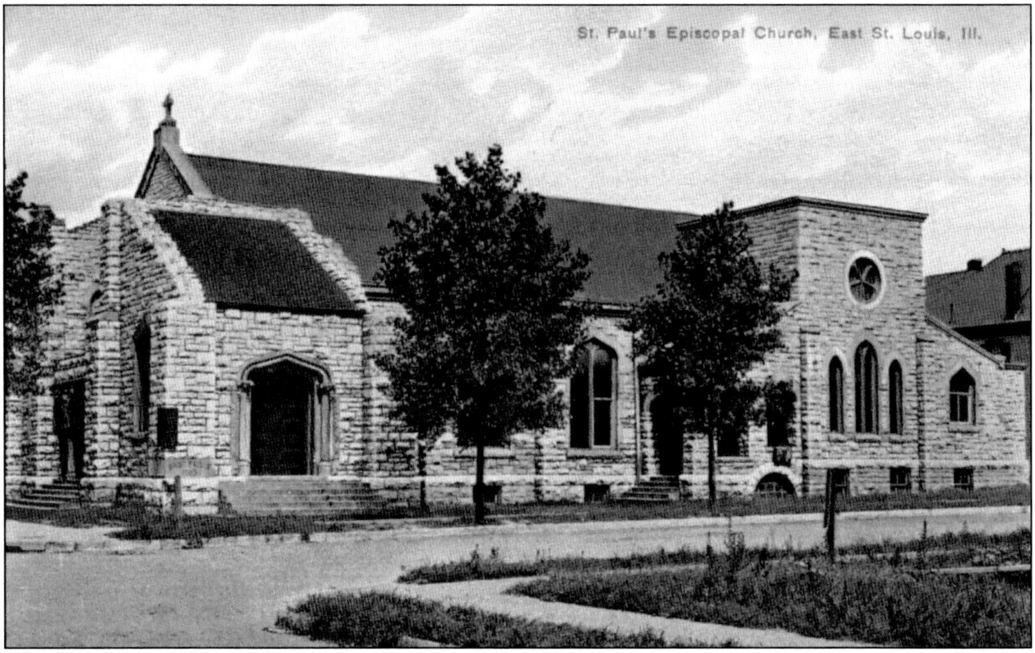

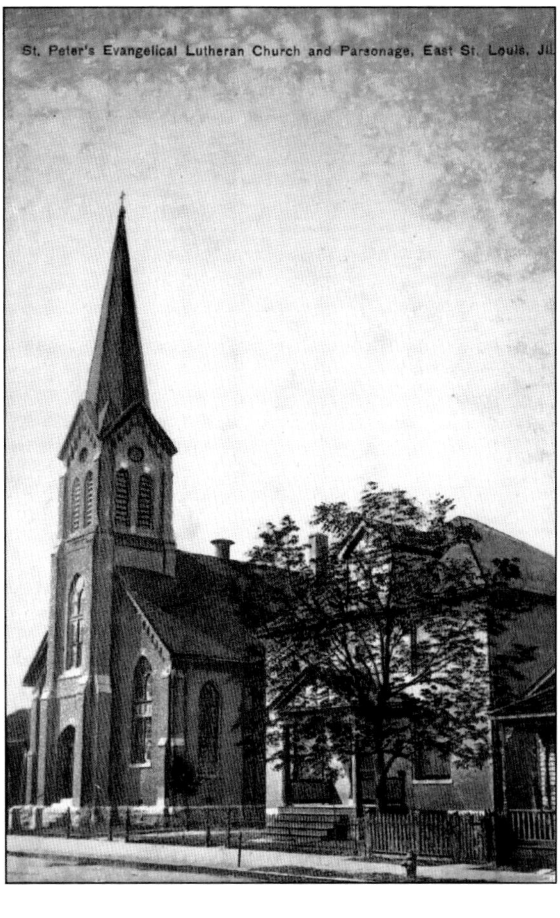

St. Paul's Episcopal Church, made of light gray limestone, was on Ninth Street and Summit Avenue across the street from Rock Junior High. It was one of the most popular churches in the city because it hosted semipro wrestling matches in its annex, better known as the Social Center. Lou Thesz, considered one of the greatest wrestlers in the history of the sport, had his first professional match here in 1935, earning the grand sum of $3. He told Bill Nunes that his actual pay was $2 and he was given an extra dollar for setting up and taking down folding chairs for the audience. The building still stands, though the interior of the half that is shown here has collapsed. (HF)

Saint Peter's Evangelical Lutheran Church and parsonage was located on Eighth Street between Illinois and St. Louis Avenues. The back rooms of the church, with a side entrance on Illinois, were used for elementary school education. Northern Germany was mainly Lutheran while Southern Germany remained Catholic. St. Henry's on East Broadway Avenue was the German Catholic Church. (HF)

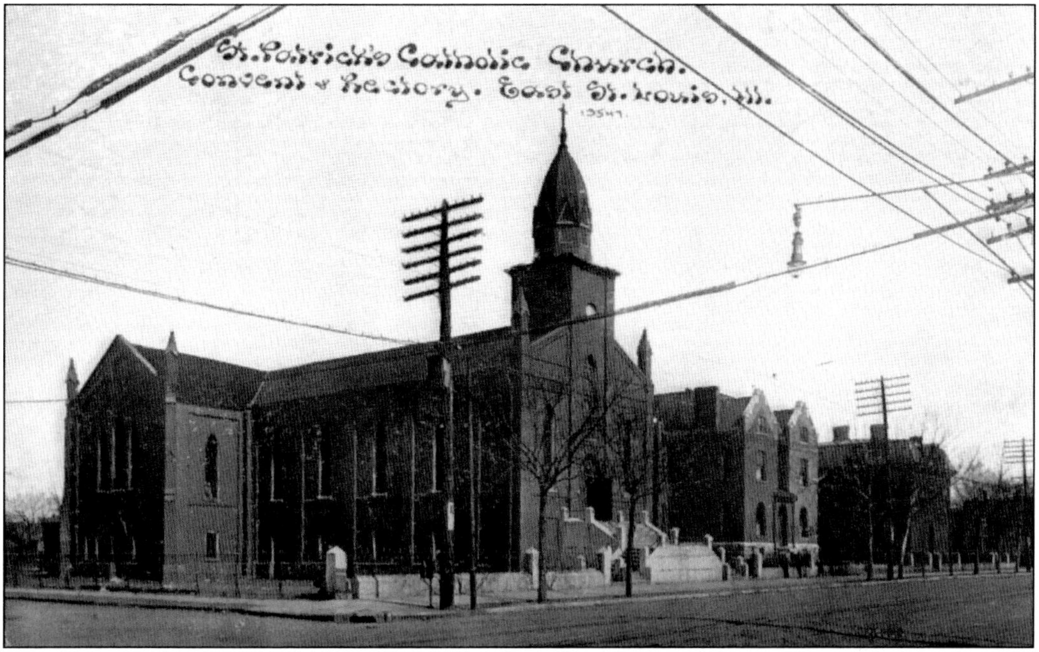

St. Patrick's Catholic Church, founded in 1841, was one of the earliest Catholic parishes in the city. This photograph is from 1911. The building was deemed unsafe in 1930 and demolished. The first pastor of St. Patrick's was Jean Francis Regis Loisel. Two neighborhoods bear the pastor's name today: Loisel Hills and Loisel Park. (HF)

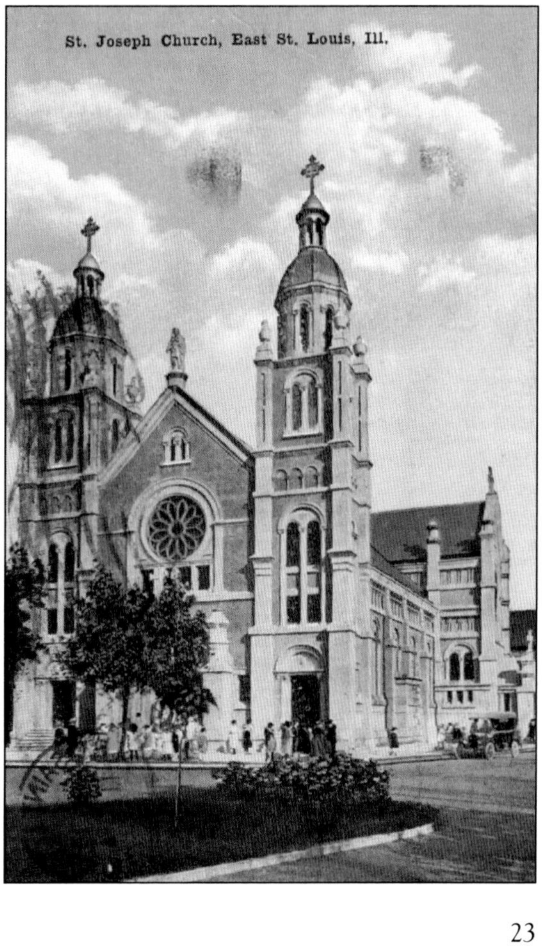

Shown at right is St. Joseph's Parish on the corner of Columbia Place and Illinois Avenue. Monroe School was about a block farther east on Illinois Avenue on the other side of the street. The church was organized in 1902 and closed in 2006. The Italian Renaissance–style building prominently featured twin towers. St. Joseph's Elementary School was nearby. (HF)

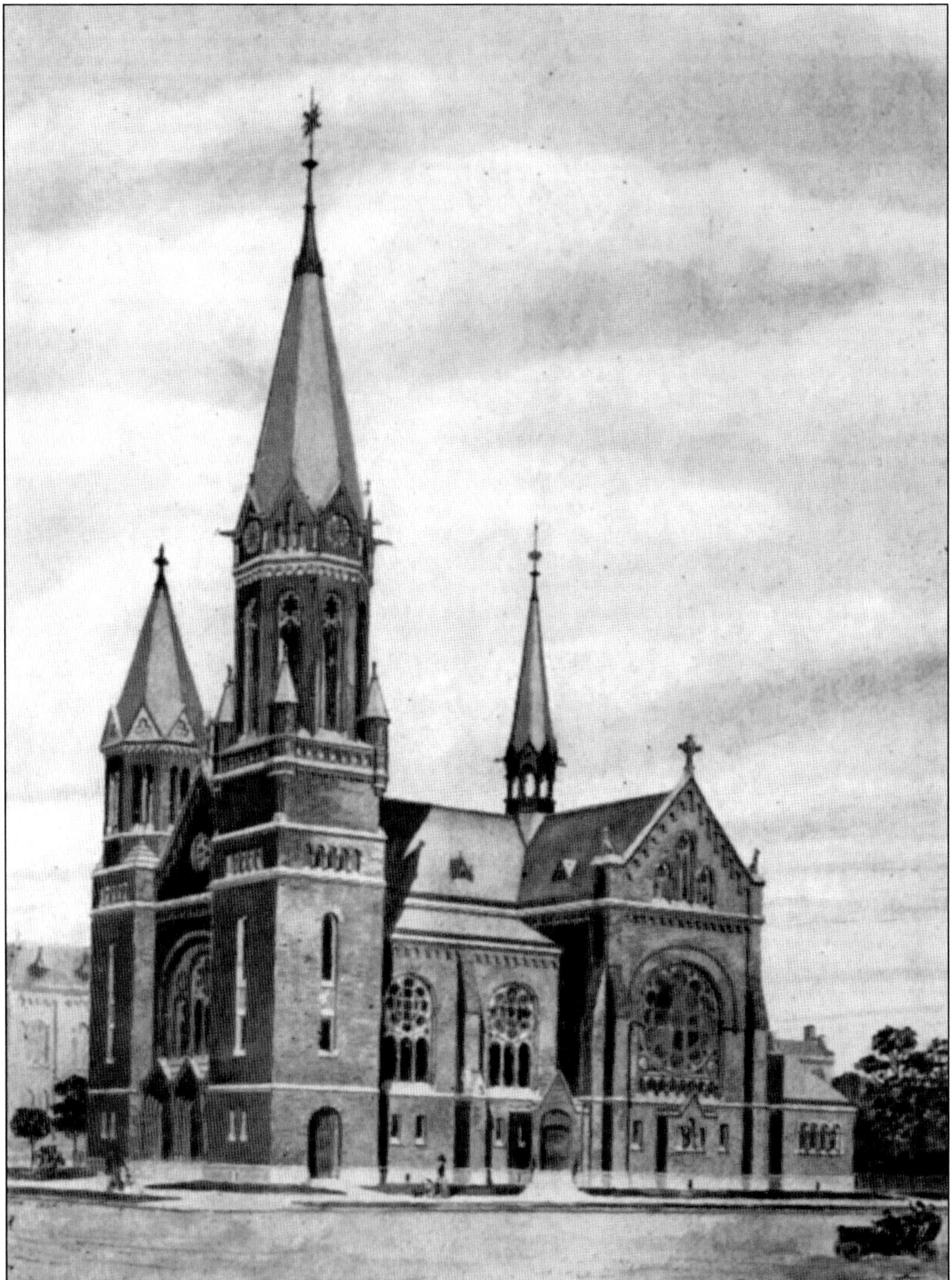

Sacred Heart Catholic Church, noted for its imposing clock and bell tower, was located at Eighth Street and Baugh Avenue and opened in 1902. It was torn down when Interstate 64 was built. Its longtime pastor was Msgr. Charles Gilmartin. The congregation merged with St. Adalbert's, the Polish church at 701 Summit. Eastern Europeans who lived in the Goose Hill area attended this church. (HF)

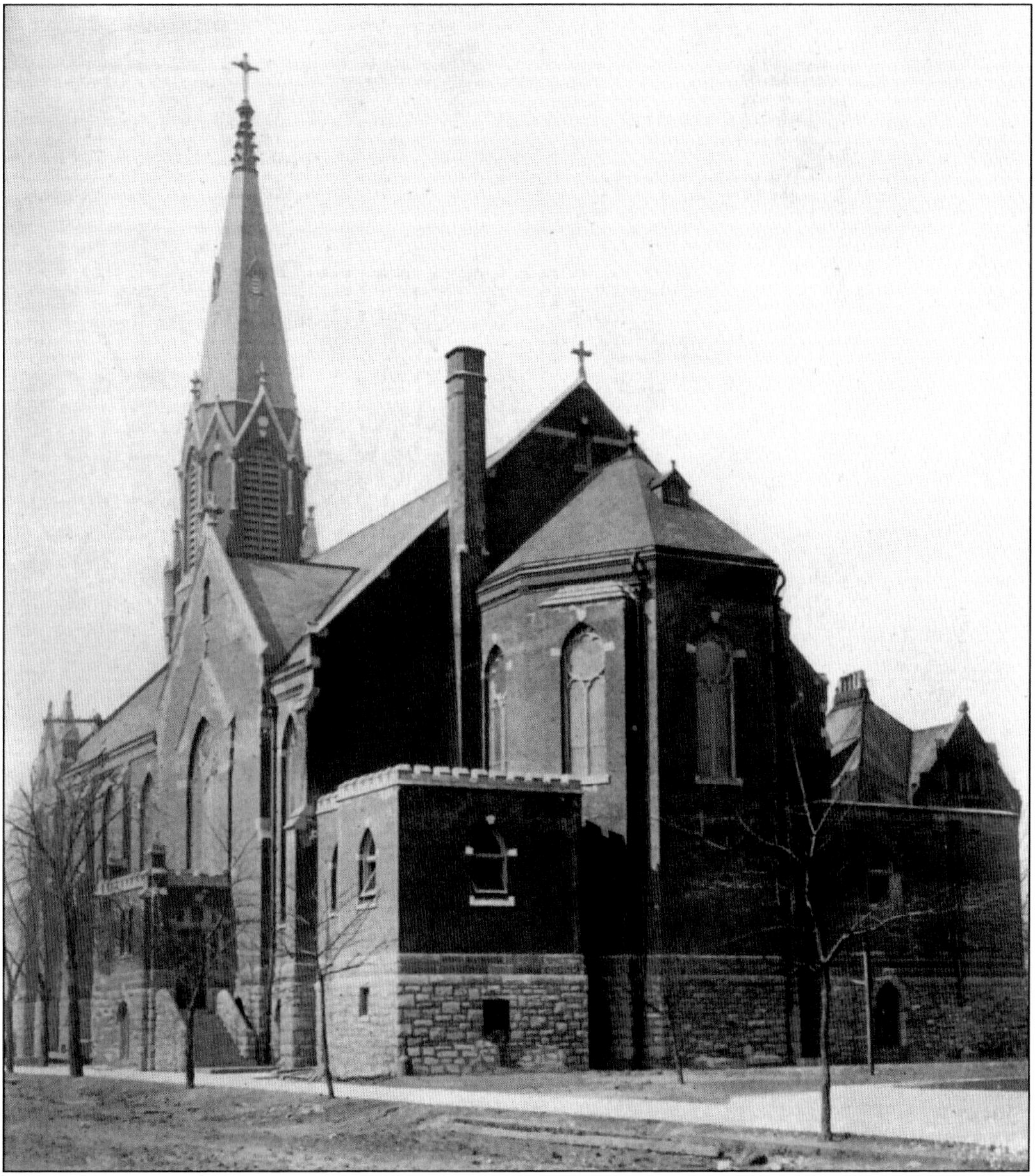

St. Elizabeth's Church, on 25th Street and Ridge Avenue, served the Winstanley area of East St. Louis. St. Teresa's Academy for girls was just north of the Catholic Church. The parish was established in 1894 and this imposing structure was completed in 1912. It closed in 1964 when it was merged with St. Joseph's. Elizabeth Winstanley, a parishioner, donated money for the stained glass window that depicted St. Elizabeth of Hungary, who dedicated her life to helping the poor. (SIUE)

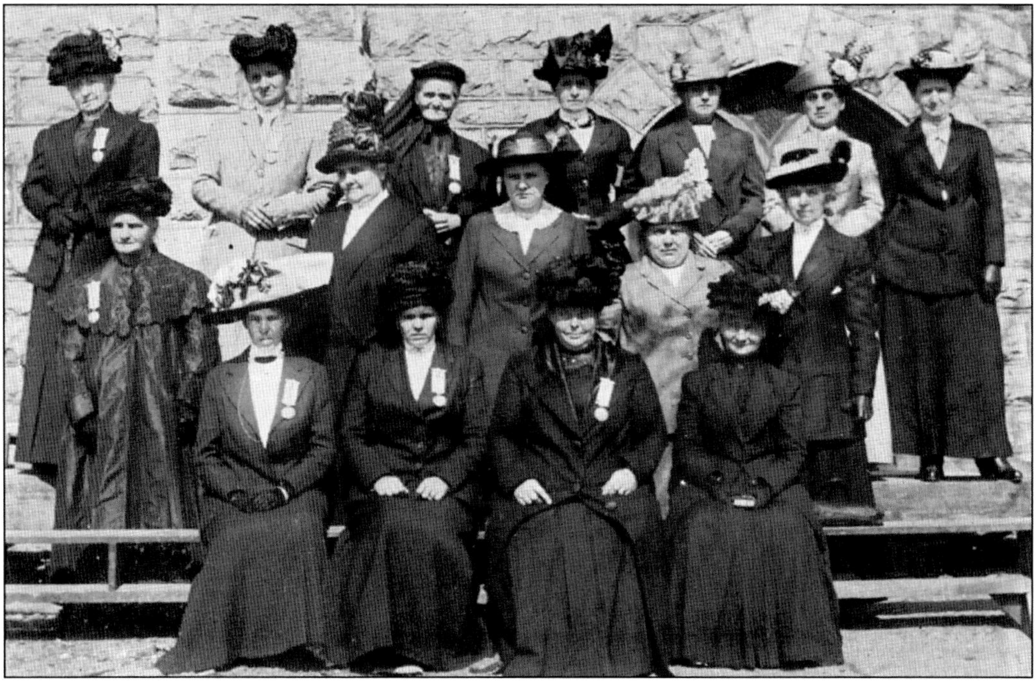

Seen here is the Altar Society of St. Elizabeth's in 1912, when the new church building was erected. The building had one main altar flanked by two side altars. This image was taken from the souvenir booklet prepared for the church's dedication in 1912. (SIUE)

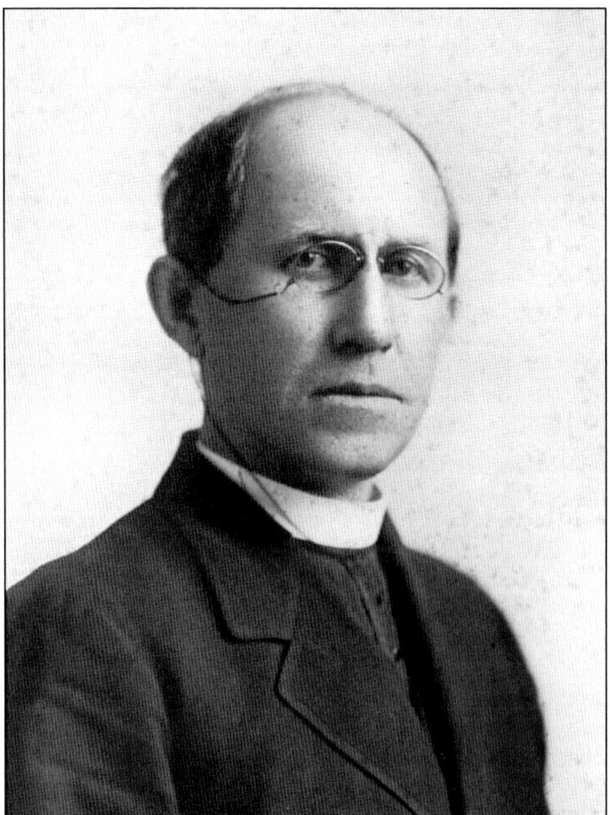

The Reverend Peter Engel was the rector of the new St. Elizabeth's Church. He was assigned to St. Elizabeth's in 1908 and served there until 1940. He guided the parish through some very difficult times in the city: the 1917 riot, World War I, and the Great Depression. (SIUE)

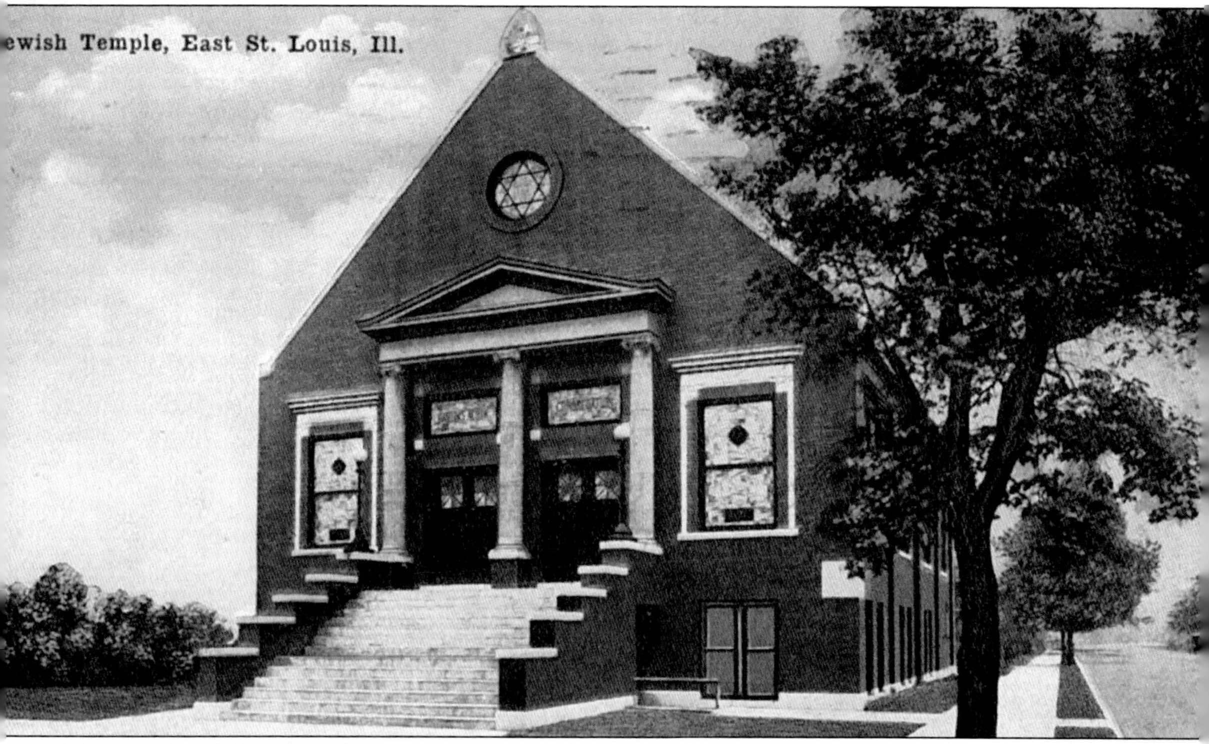

The Agudas Achim Jewish Synagogue, located on Ninth Street and Pennsylvania Avenue, was built in 1916. Abraham Lassen was the first rabbi, and the congregation was made up of about 300 members. It was located in one of the city's finest neighborhoods, where there were several houses of worship within a few blocks in all directions. No synagogues remain in East St. Louis today. (HF)

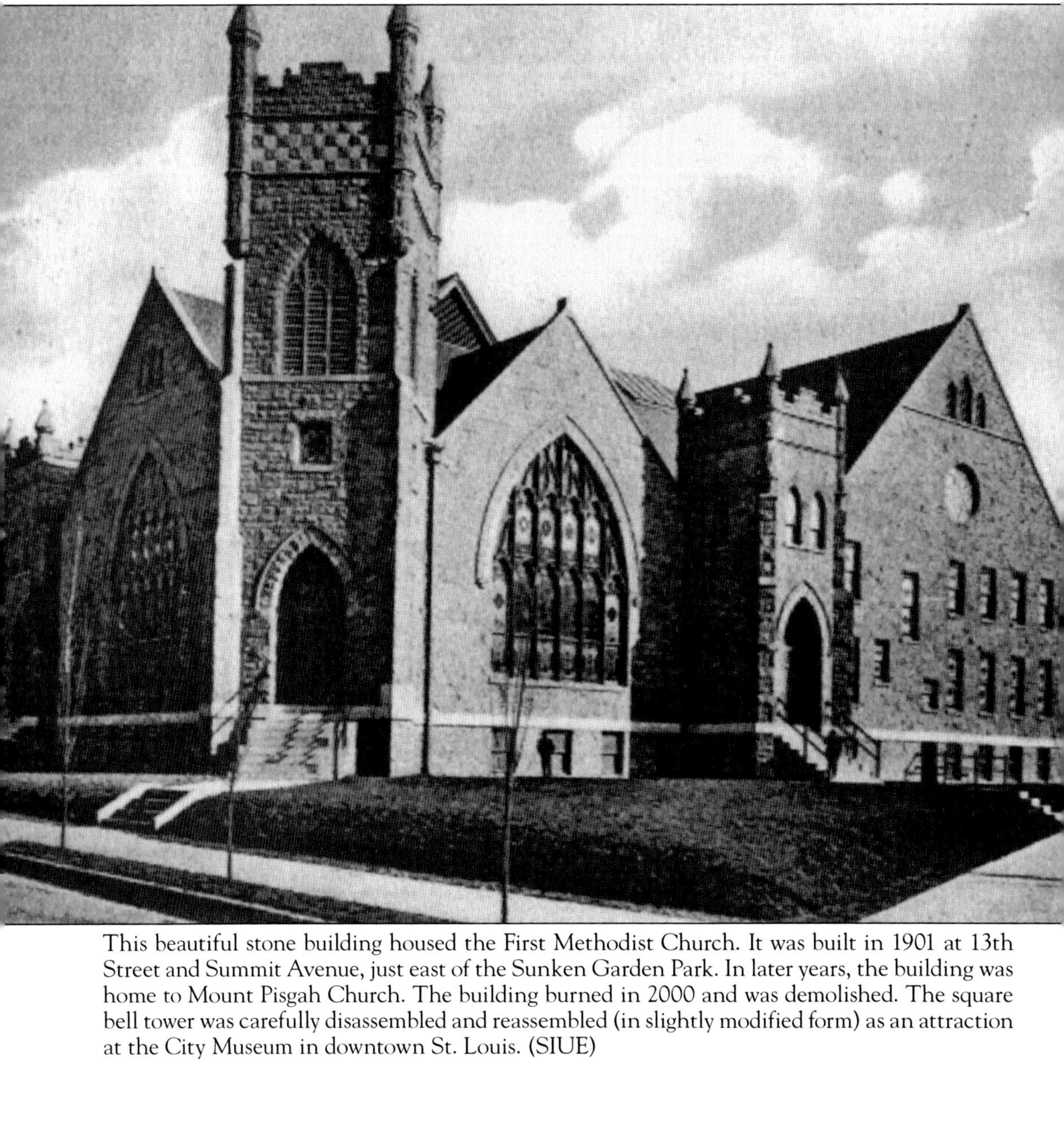

This beautiful stone building housed the First Methodist Church. It was built in 1901 at 13th Street and Summit Avenue, just east of the Sunken Garden Park. In later years, the building was home to Mount Pisgah Church. The building burned in 2000 and was demolished. The square bell tower was carefully disassembled and reassembled (in slightly modified form) as an attraction at the City Museum in downtown St. Louis. (SIUE)

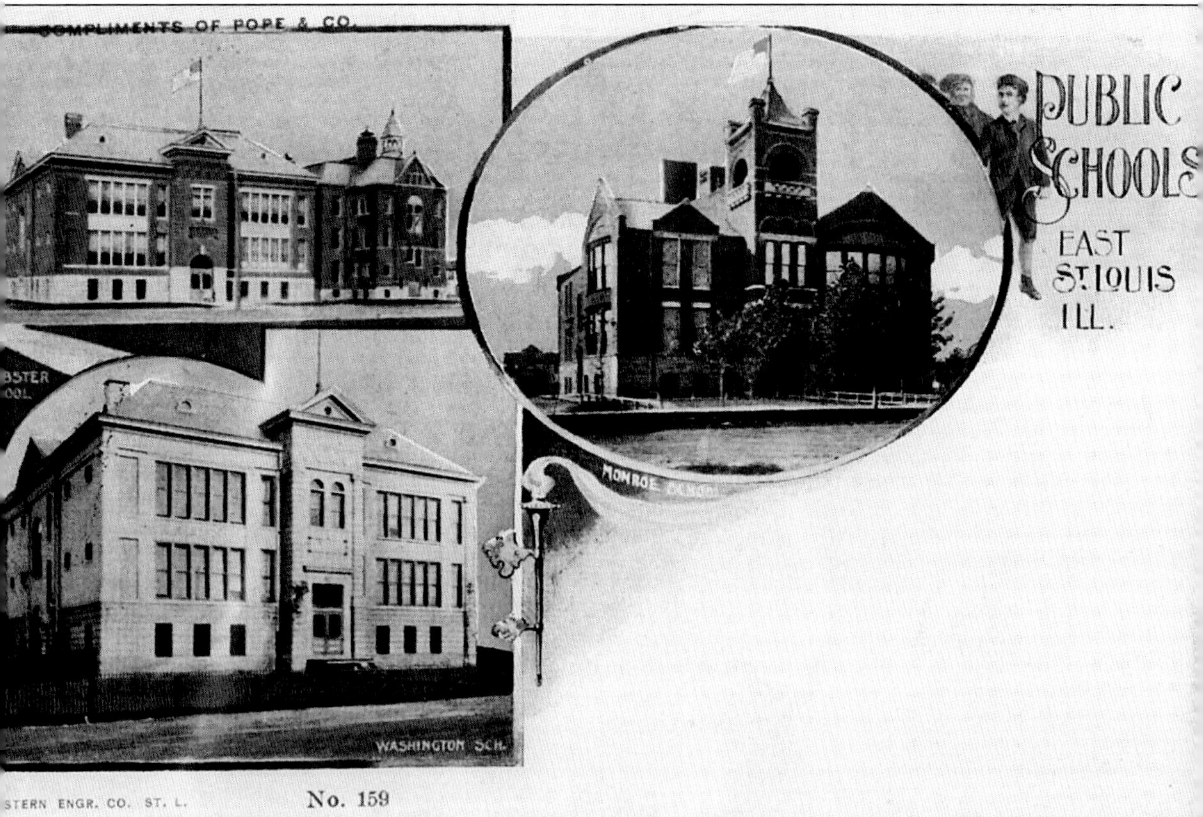

This is a very special postcard known as a Private Mailing Card, or PMC. These kinds of cards were produced from 1898 to 1901, and several exist for East St. Louis. This PMC shows (clockwise from top left) Webster School (10th Street and St. Louis Avenue), Monroe School (1600 Illinois Avenue), and Washington School. Many new schools were constructed in the early 1900s, as the city's population began to grow at an astonishing rate. The population nearly doubled for every census period through World War II. (SIUE)

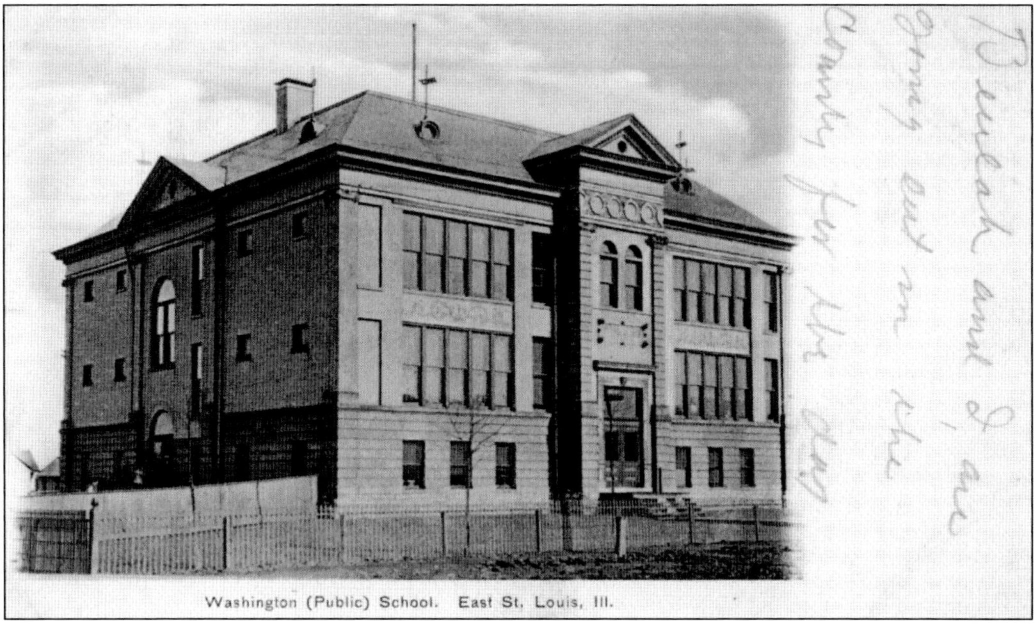

The Washington School was one of the very early school buildings in East St. Louis. In 1912, John W. Huddle served as the principal of both Washington and Irving Schools. That year, the city directory boasted, "go into any school building in the city and the interest manifested on the part of the teachers will convince the most skeptical that the children of this young metropolis are indeed fortunate in their educational environment." (SIUE)

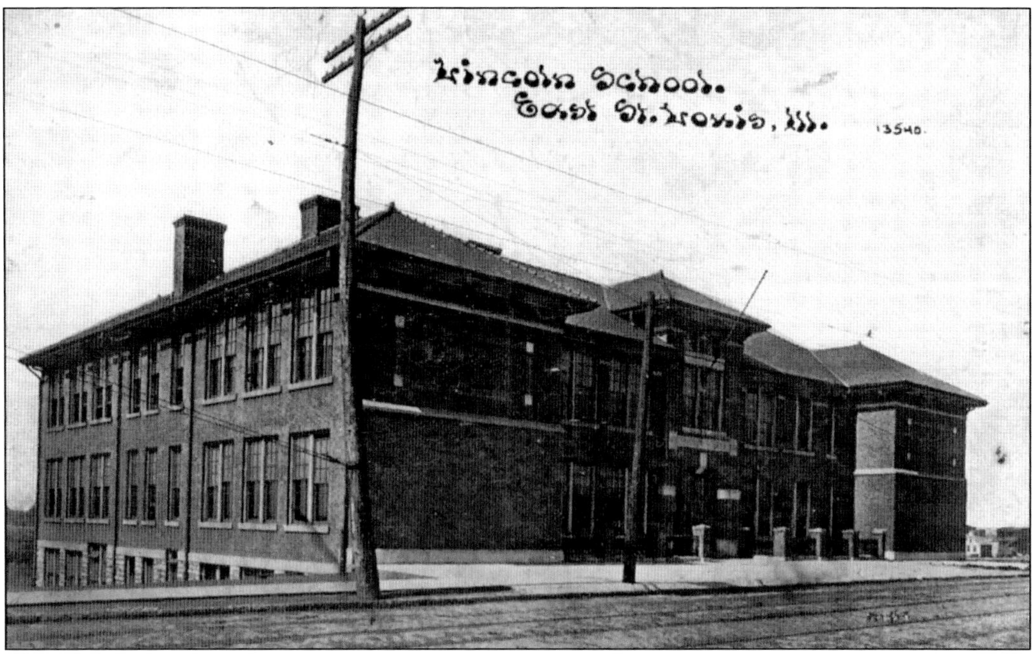

This Lincoln School (the second iteration of that name) stood at 11th Street and Broadway Avenue. Schools were segregated in East St. Louis, even though Illinois state law prohibited segregation. This de facto segregation continued until 1950, when the high school was integrated. (SIUE)

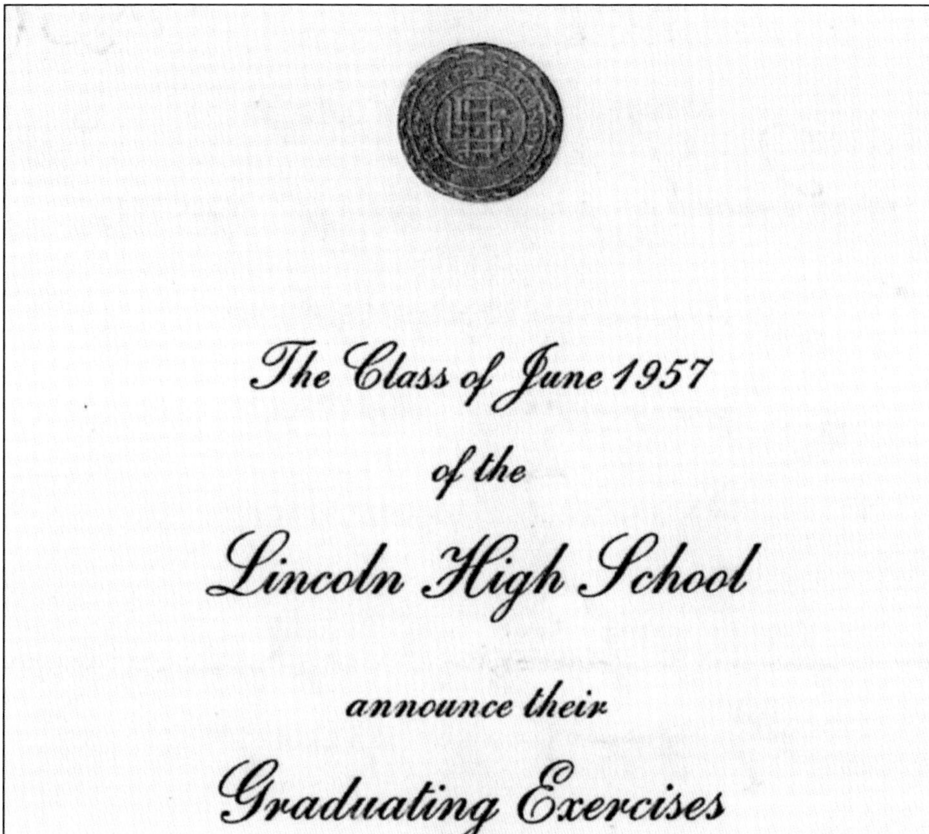

The Class of June 1957

of the

Lincoln High School

announce their

Graduating Exercises

Thursday, June thirteenth

at eight o'clock in the evening

Lincoln High School Gymnasium

East St. Louis, Illinois

No flowers — Admission by ticket

This is a commencement invitation from the 1957 graduating class of Lincoln High School (the third iteration of that name), which stood at 1211 Bond Avenue. It was this Lincoln School that the family of Miles Davis attended, as well as Olympic athlete Jackie Joyner-Kersee. The building still stands today, but a new Lincoln School (now a middle school) has been constructed at South 10th Street and Broadway Avenue. (SIUE)

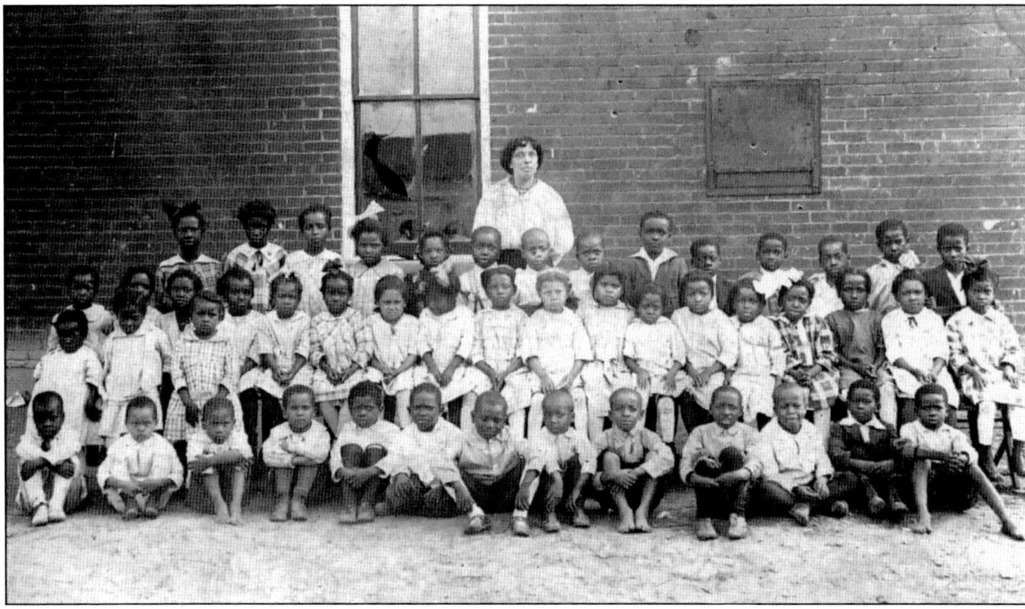

African American school children pose outside an unidentified area school, probably around 1920. As indicated by this photograph, African American schools generally had a higher student-teacher ratio (here, 48:1) and buildings were not kept in repair (as evidenced by the broken window). (RP)

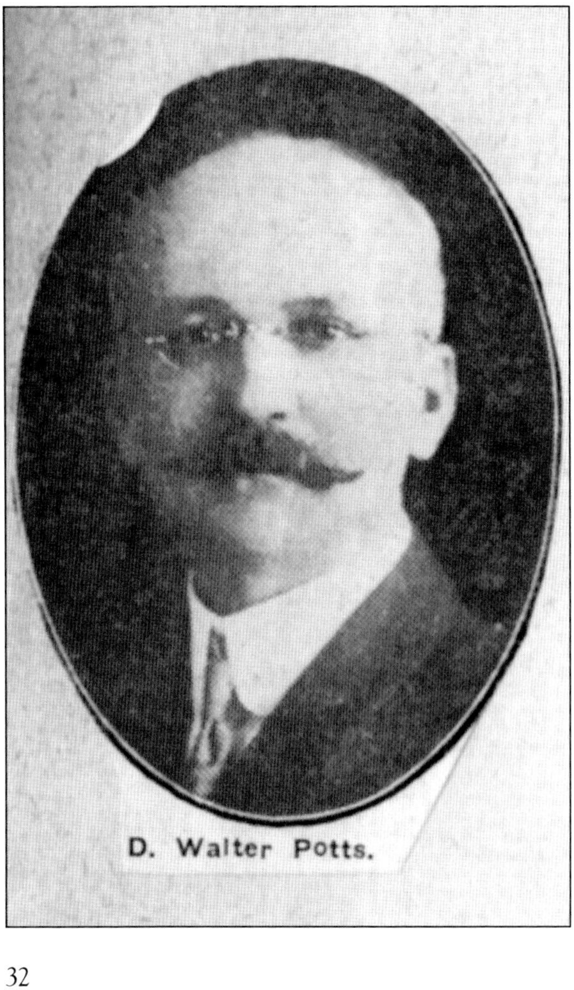

D. Walter Potts was the longtime superintendent of schools in East St. Louis. This image is from 1917. By this time, Potts oversaw a school system of 8,000 students, 185 teachers, and 30 different buildings—including manual training centers for boys, which operated on Saturdays and after regular school hours. (SIUE)

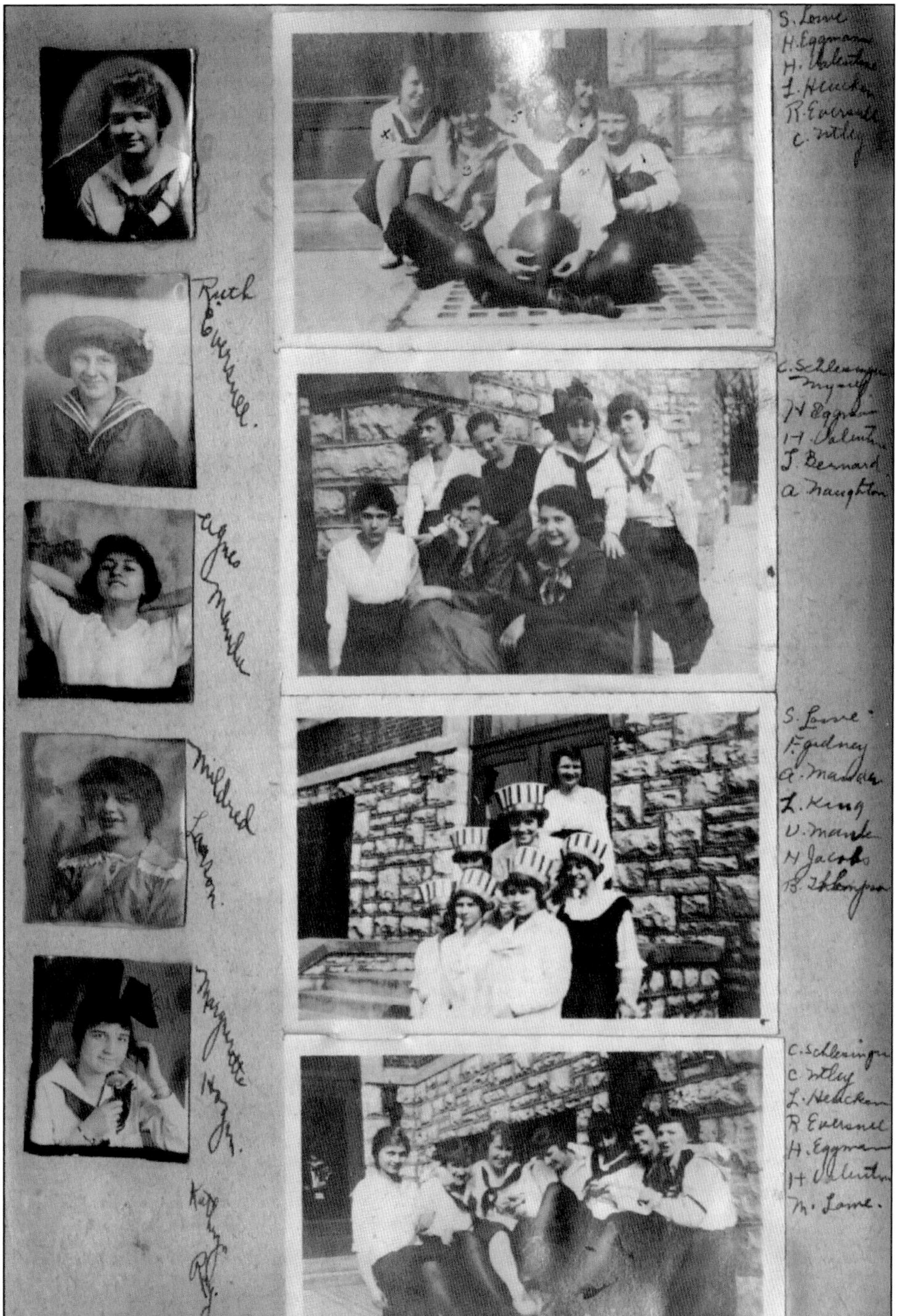

This is a page from a Rock High School student's 1917 scrapbook. She identifies many of her friends by name. At left, top to bottom, are: unidentified, Ruth Eversull, Agnes Mandu, Mildred Larson, and Margueritte Hogan. The photo of Kathryn Ray is missing. On the right, groups of girls pose by the building's familiar rock foundation. One of them is Hortense Eggman, whose father, Horace, served on the school board. (SIUE)

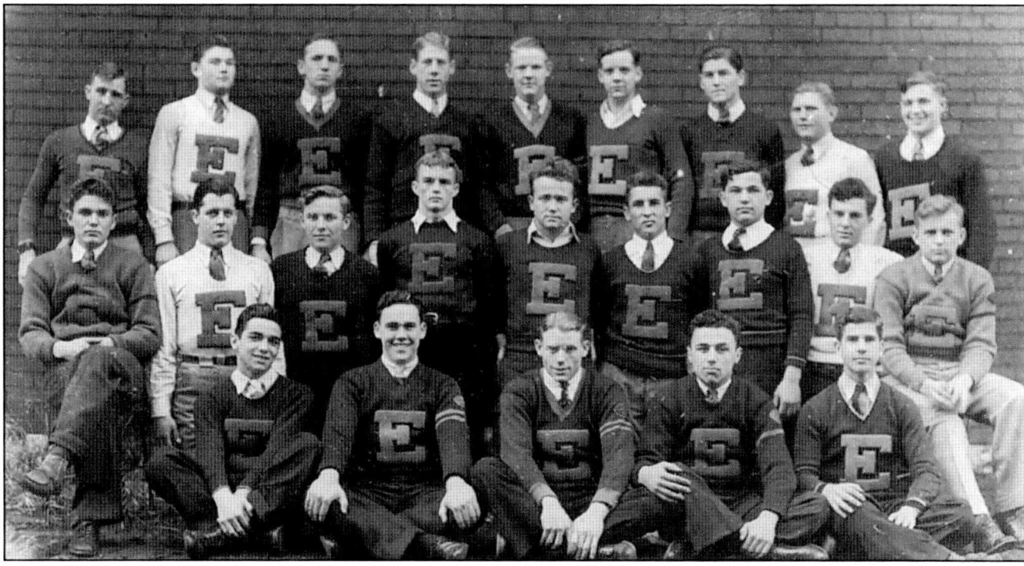

This unidentified team is from East St. Louis High School. The city was quite proud that the school system employed a supervisor of physical education. According to an early city directory, "not only is the physical body preserved and strengthened, but mental power is also developed." (SIUE)

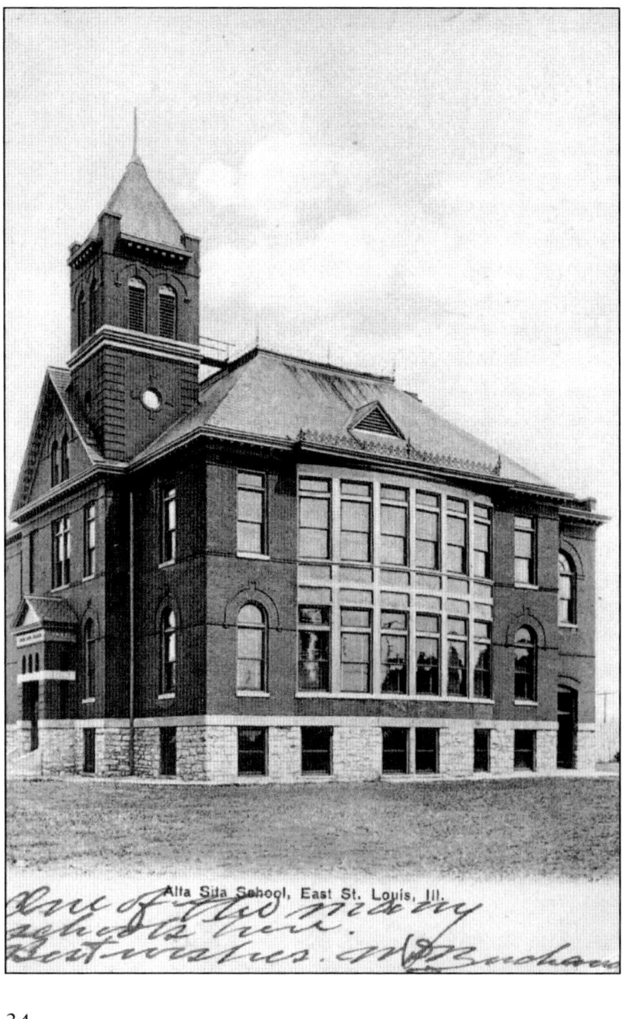

The old Alta Sita school stood at 26th and Bond. This image is from about 1910. The building has a design very typical of other East St. Louis schools, with a tall tower, a section of bowed windows, and a high-pitched roof. Monroe School had very similar architectural elements. (SIUE)

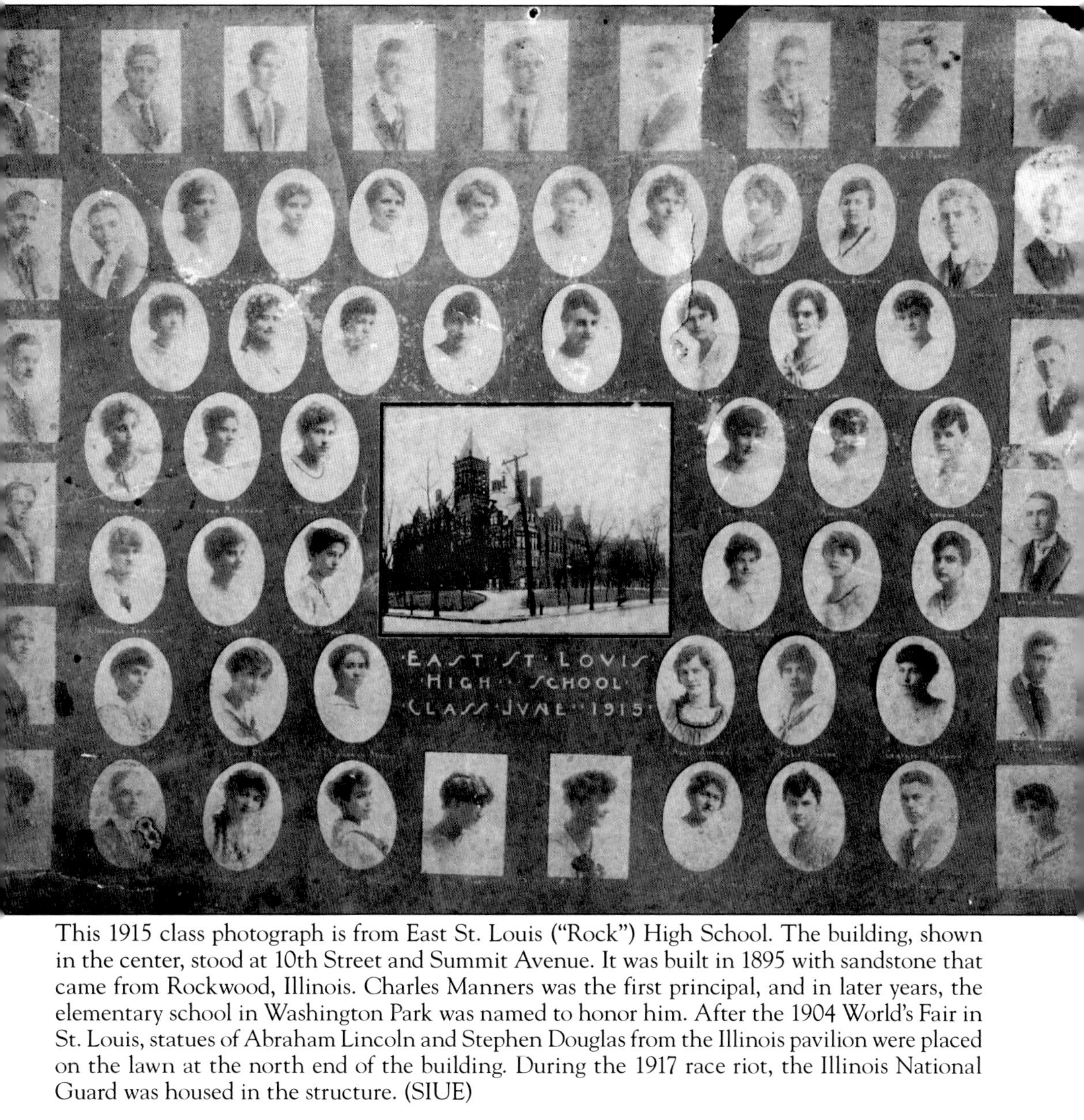

This 1915 class photograph is from East St. Louis ("Rock") High School. The building, shown in the center, stood at 10th Street and Summit Avenue. It was built in 1895 with sandstone that came from Rockwood, Illinois. Charles Manners was the first principal, and in later years, the elementary school in Washington Park was named to honor him. After the 1904 World's Fair in St. Louis, statues of Abraham Lincoln and Stephen Douglas from the Illinois pavilion were placed on the lawn at the north end of the building. During the 1917 race riot, the Illinois National Guard was housed in the structure. (SIUE)

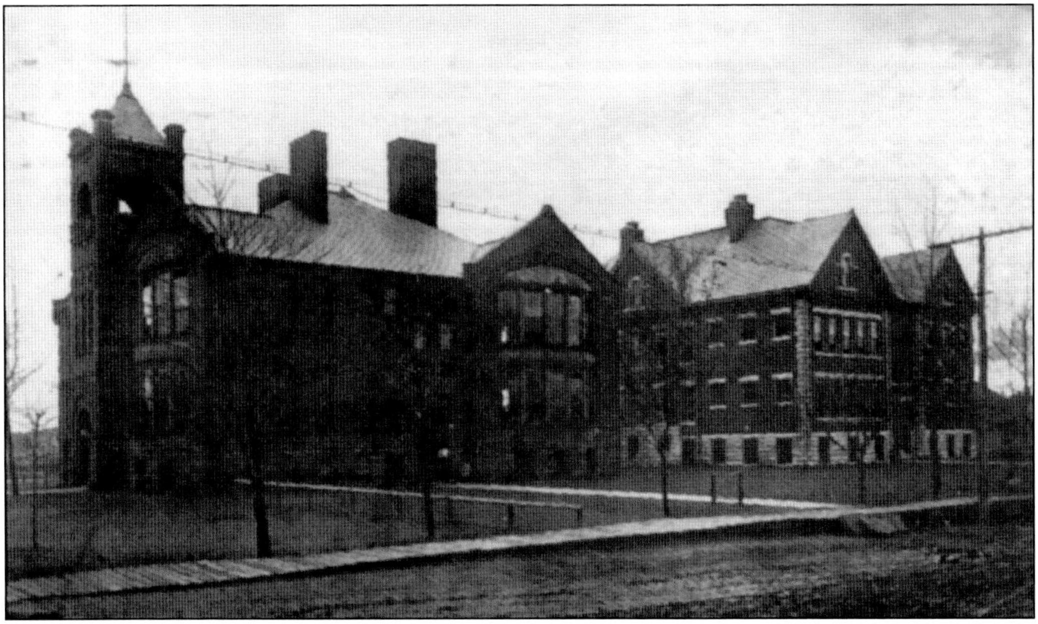

Monroe School, located at 1600 Illinois Avenue, was really a complex of a school (on the left side of the image) and an annex (on the right). Additional buildings like the Monroe Manual Training Center stood nearby. These buildings still stand today and some are in use. (SIUE)

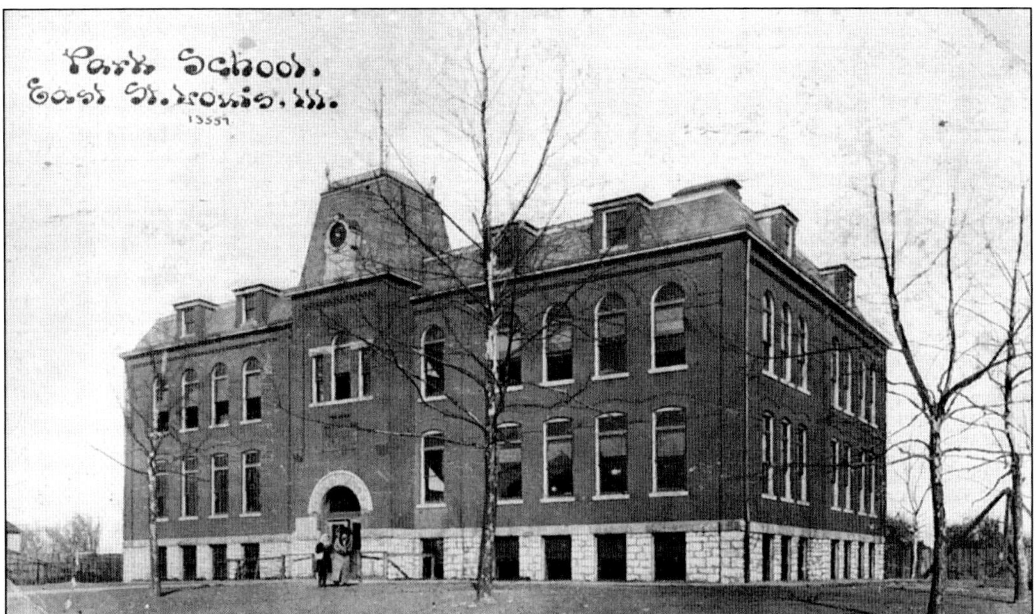

Park School, as seen above, stood at 27th Street and Henrietta Avenue. The school buildings were described in 1912 as "modern, well-equipped, well-lighted, well-seated with double adjustable desks; in fact, every convenience [is] provided." This image dates from 1911. (SIUE)

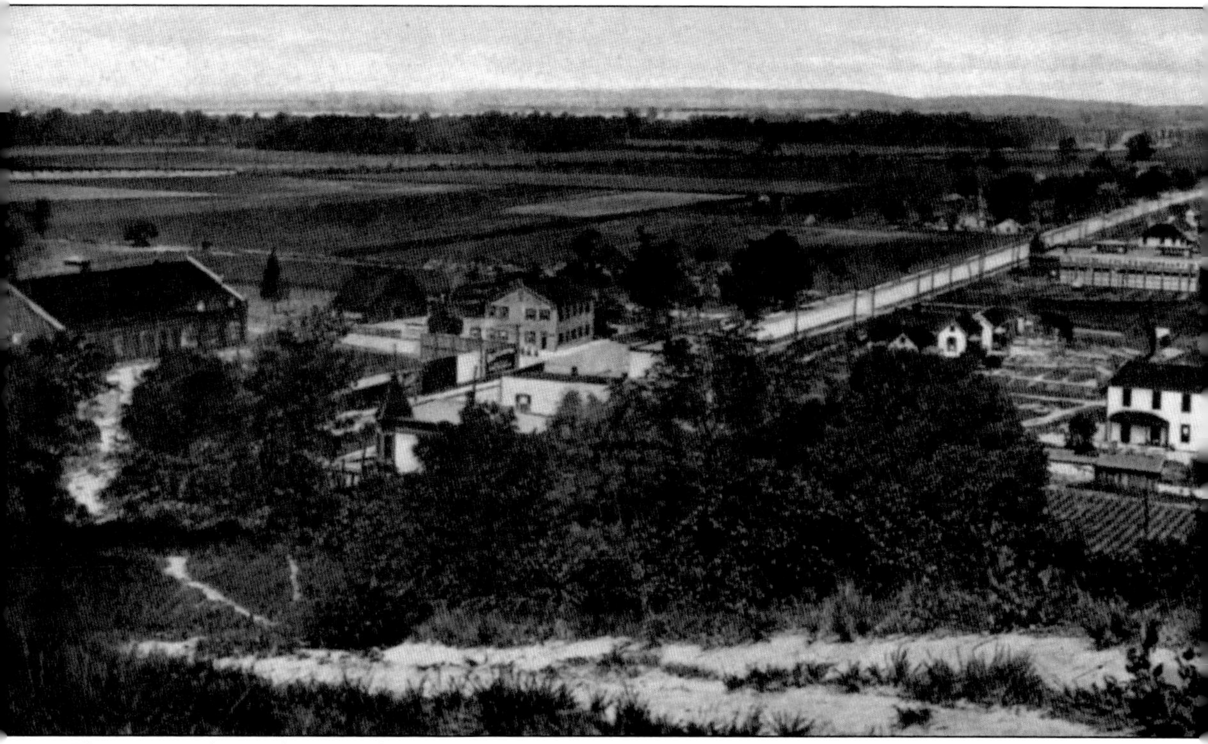

This image shows the view from Signal Hill (once used by Native Americans to send smoke signals) near Lake Park and between the cities of East St. Louis and Belleville. The Signal Hill neighborhood today is a close-knit community of historic homes. Lake Park is now Frank Holten State Park, named for the long-time state representative from East St. Louis. (HF)

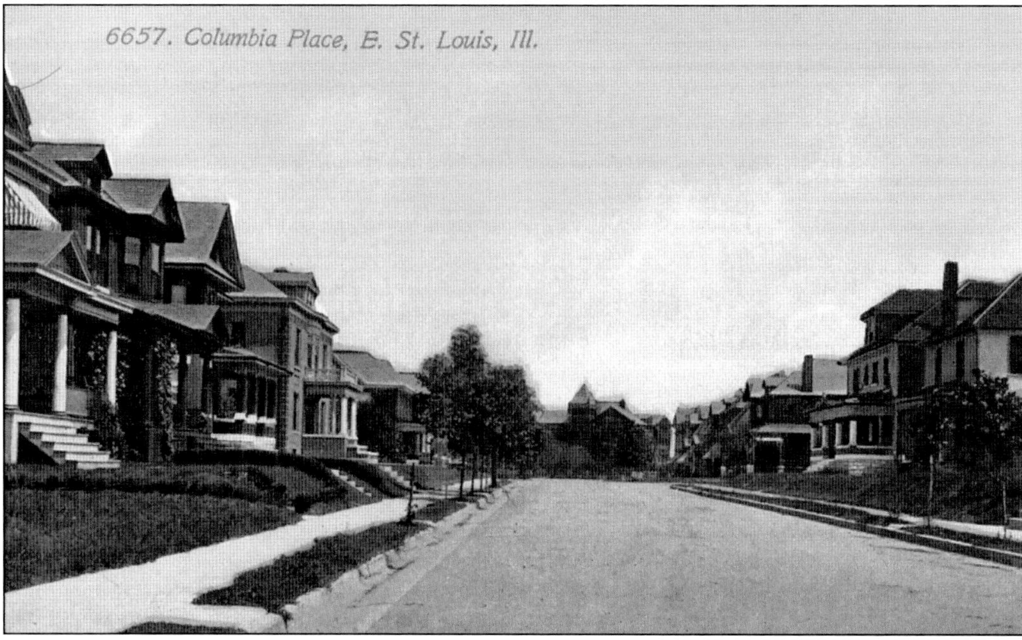

Columbia Place (400 block) was a nice neighborhood located between Illinois Avenue and State Street. Washington Place (500 block) was nearby, just north of State Street. (HF)

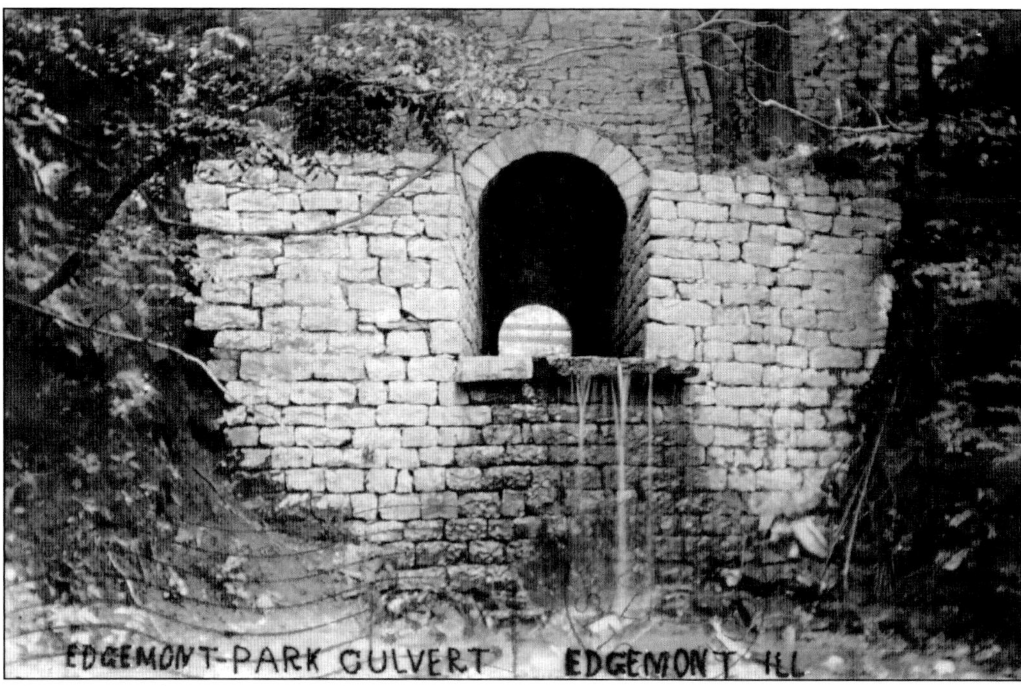

This image is from Edgemont, the East St. Louis neighborhood annexed in the early 1900s and located near the 7000 block of State Street. This culvert is one of many floodplain improvements made in the East St. Louis area. The notation on the postcard reads, "culvert where poor Bert was found." (SIUE)

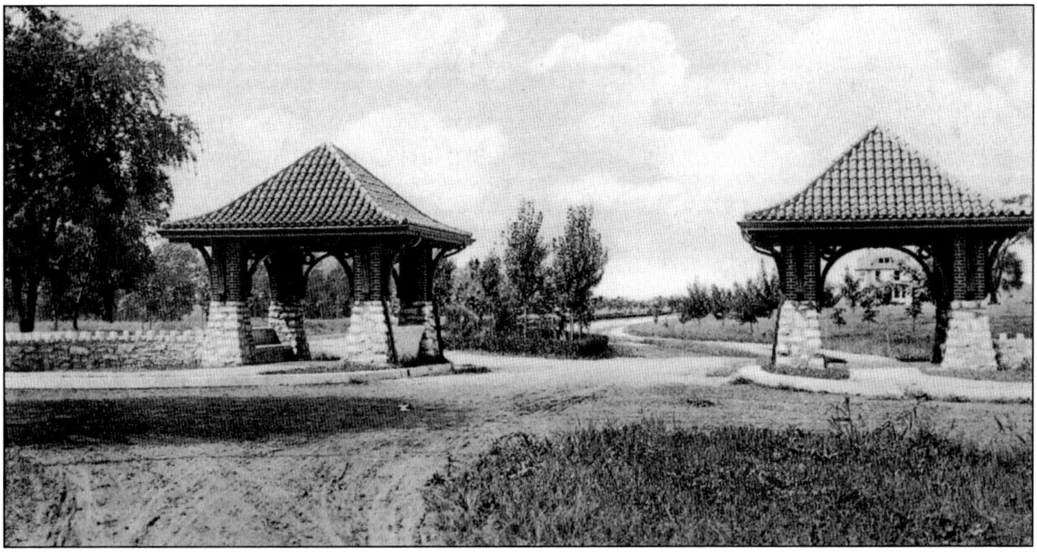

The Alta Sita neighborhood enjoyed a stately gated entrance when this image was produced in about 1910. Obviously, the neighborhood was still being developed. (HF)

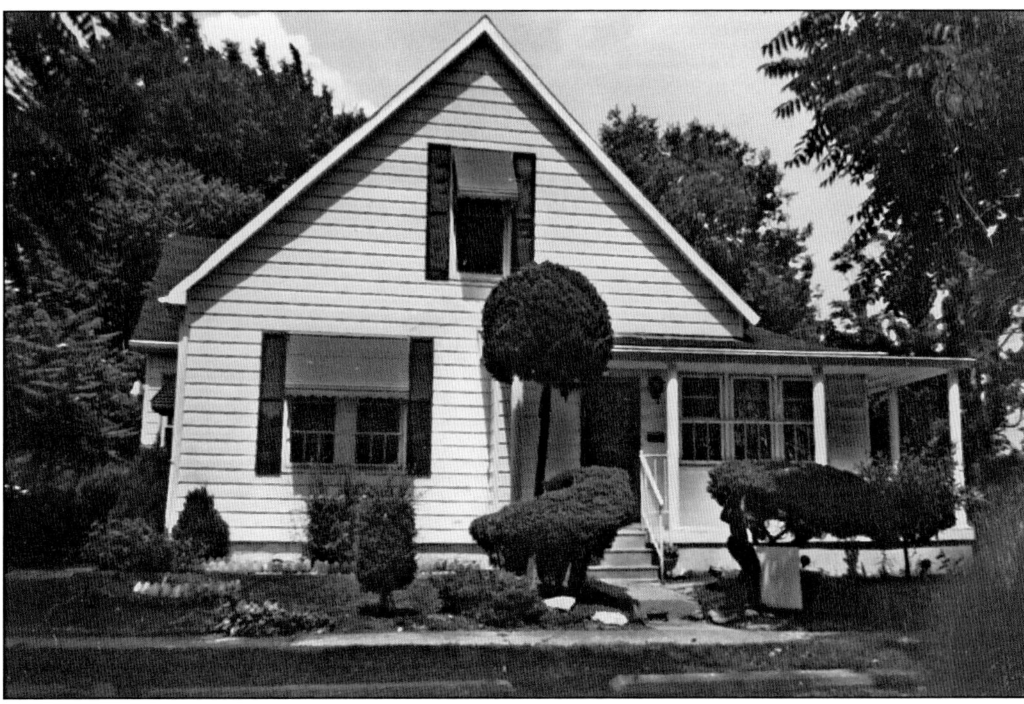

Miles Davis grew up in this house at the corner of 17th Street and Kansas Avenue. He was born in Alton in 1926, but his father moved the family to East St. Louis when young Miles was about seven years old. This image was captured in 2000. The house still stands, and some hope it will help the city become a tourist destination. (AT)

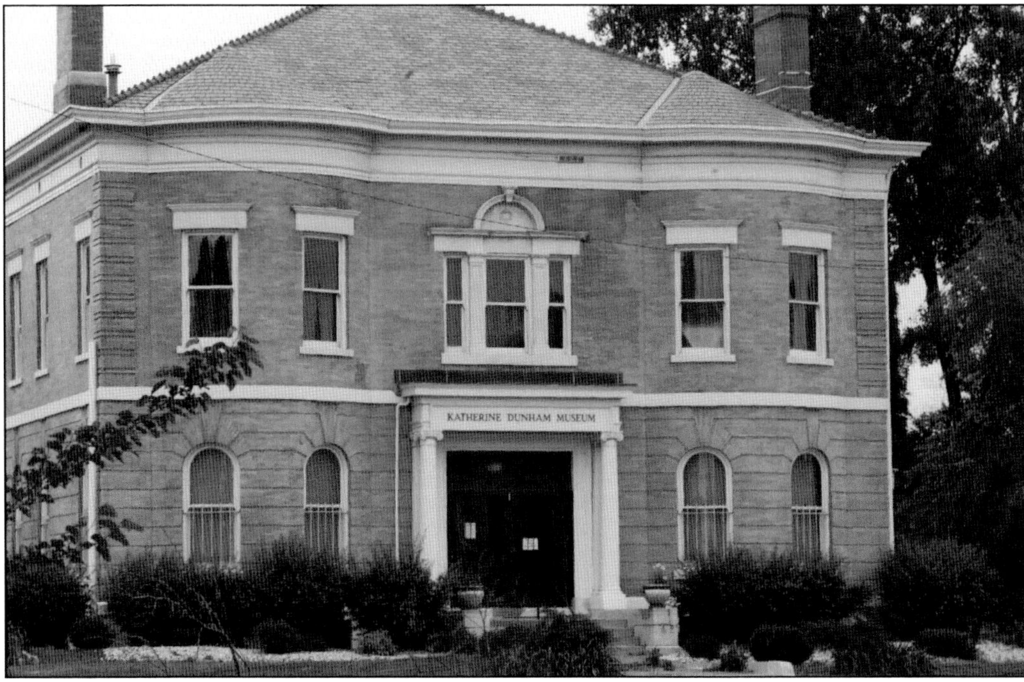

This impressive two-story structure at 1005 Pennsylvania Avenue was the home of Maurice V. Joyce, son of Mayor Maurice Joyce, also a longtime city attorney and judge. It was designed by prominent East St. Louis architect A.B. Frankel. Joyce was a candidate for mayor in 1909. In the 1940s and 1950s, it housed the YWCA, which had previously been located in the Beatty Building at 317 Missouri Avenue. Since the 1970s, the building has served as the home of the Katherine Dunham Museum. It is beautifully restored and open to the public. This photograph was taken in 2000. (AT)

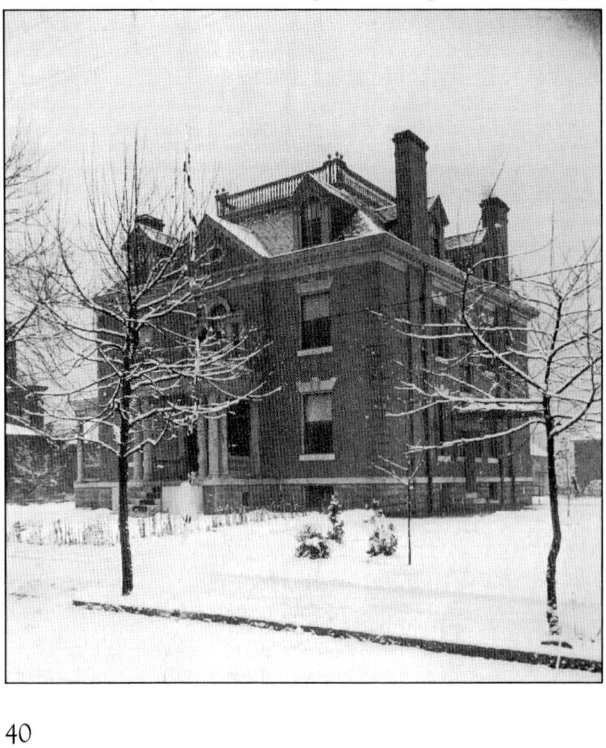

This stately building at 1010 Pennsylvania Avenue was typical of the mansions that lined this street. It was built in 1902 by Mayor M.M. Stephens (who had just been voted out of office) and, ironically, stood across the street from Maurice V. Joyce, who was his political nemesis. Shortly after Stephens died in 1928, the family sold the home. It was the Ogonoski Funeral Home for many years, but it is now demolished. (SIUE)

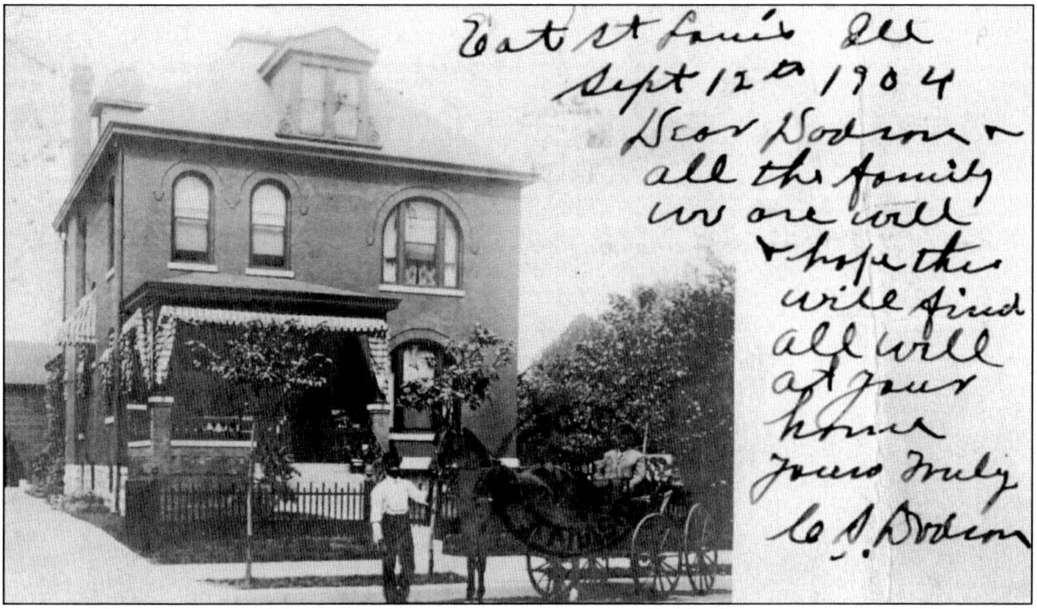

Above is a photograph postcard from C.S. Dodson. "We are well," he writes in 1904. The large home, as well as the fine horse and buggy, is a reminder that East St. Louis had a prosperous and professional African American community in the early 1900s. (SIUE)

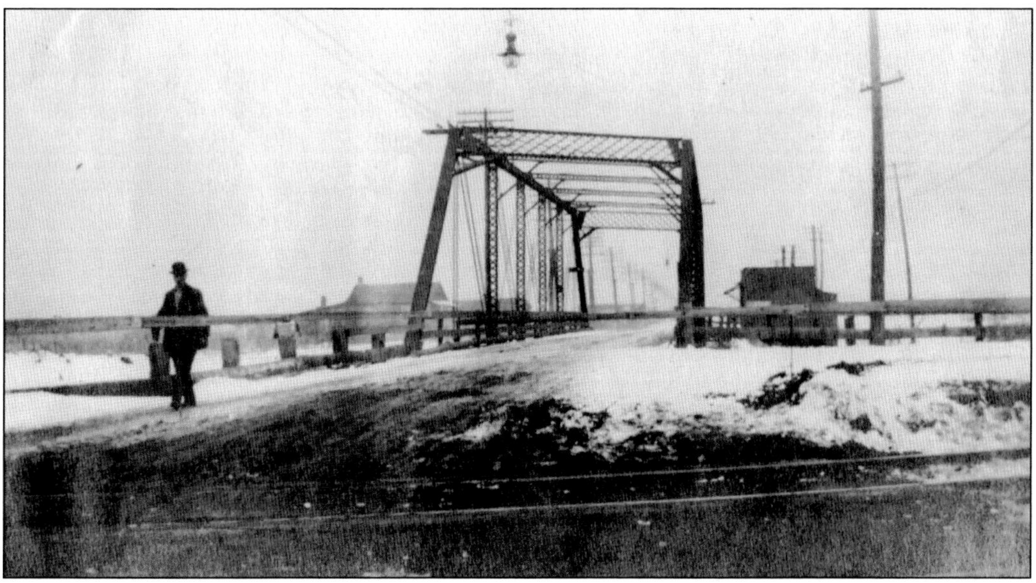

This photograph from 1914, taken northwest of the National Stock Yards, is simply marked "Black Bridge." The National Stock Yards site was located on 600 acres just outside of the East St. Louis city limits. This was one of several ways to enter the property. (SIUE)

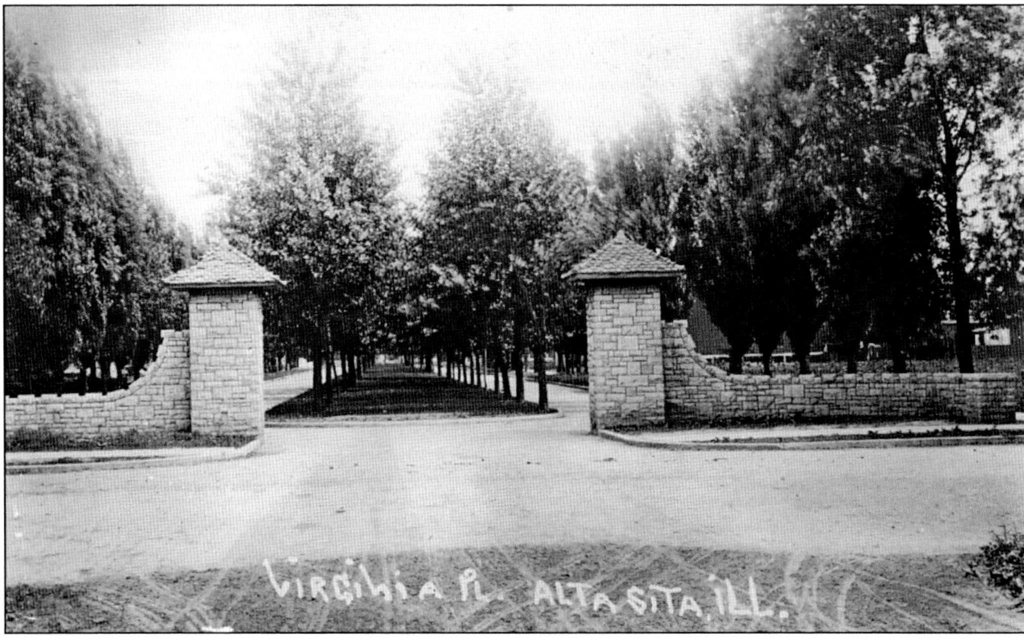

The image above shows the beautiful entrance to Virginia Place located within the upscale Alta Sita neighborhood in the southeast part of town. Alta Sita started at 21st Street and extended to 36th Street, off of Bond Avenue. (SIUE)

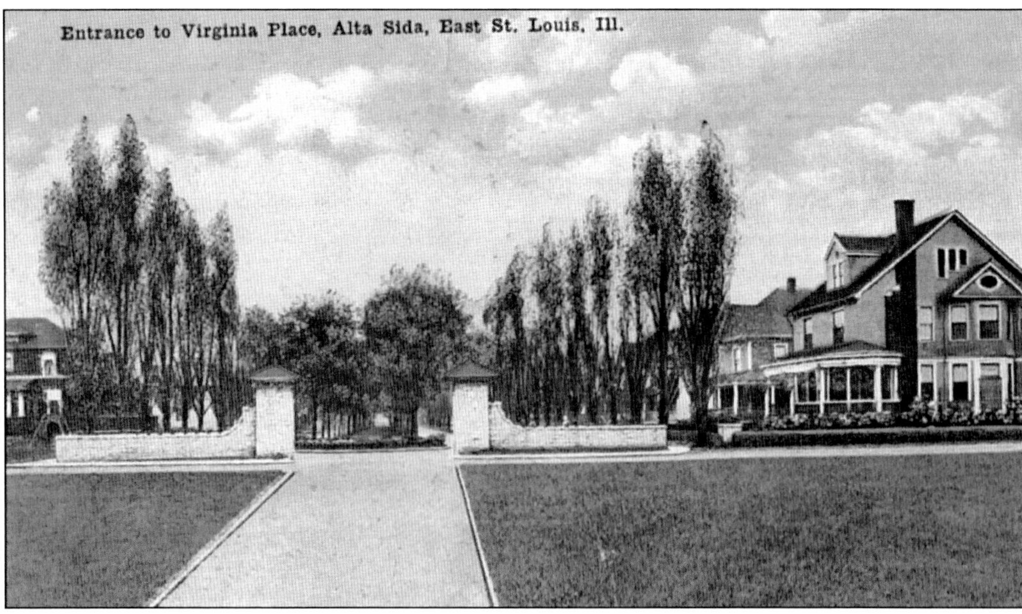

This view of Virginia Place shows some of the fine homes that were constructed in the subdivision. Around 1958, Ike and Tina Turner moved into a house several doors down from the home seen at right. (HF)

Two

EVENTS

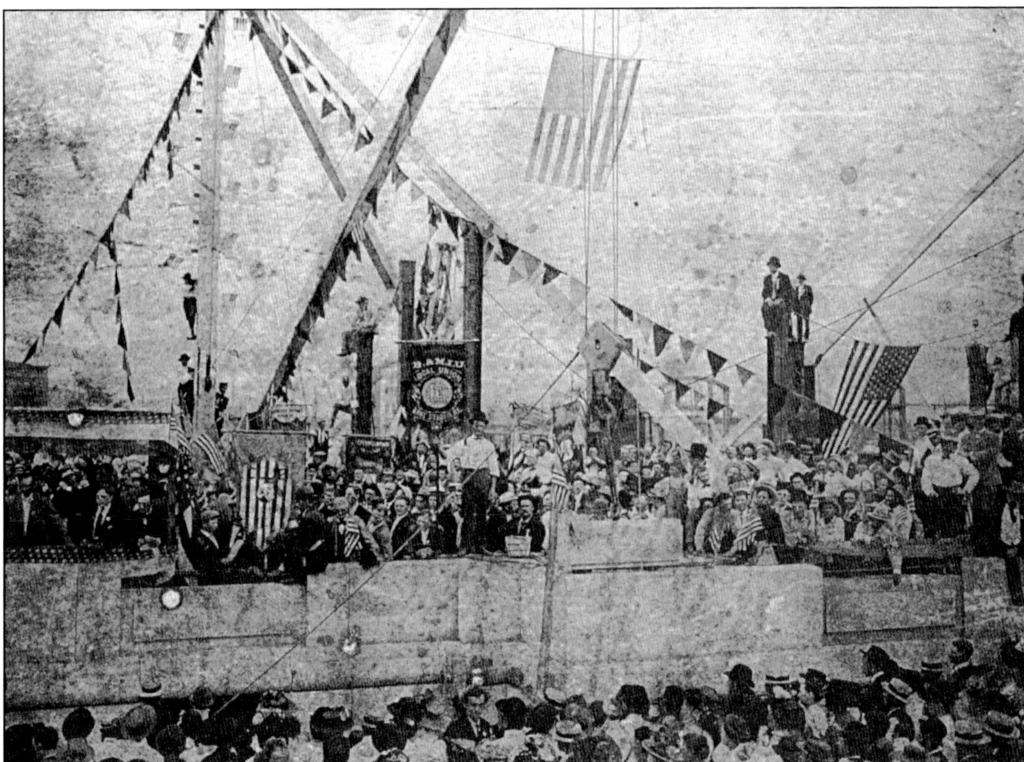

October 25, 1909, was a great date in the history of East St. Louis. It was the day when the new federal courthouse was dedicated. Government officials had worked a long time to secure the building for the city. This rare photograph, probably taken in 1908, shows the cornerstone ceremony at the start of the federal courthouse construction. Laborers and their union banners are visible throughout the building's foundation, which is decorated festively. (SIUE)

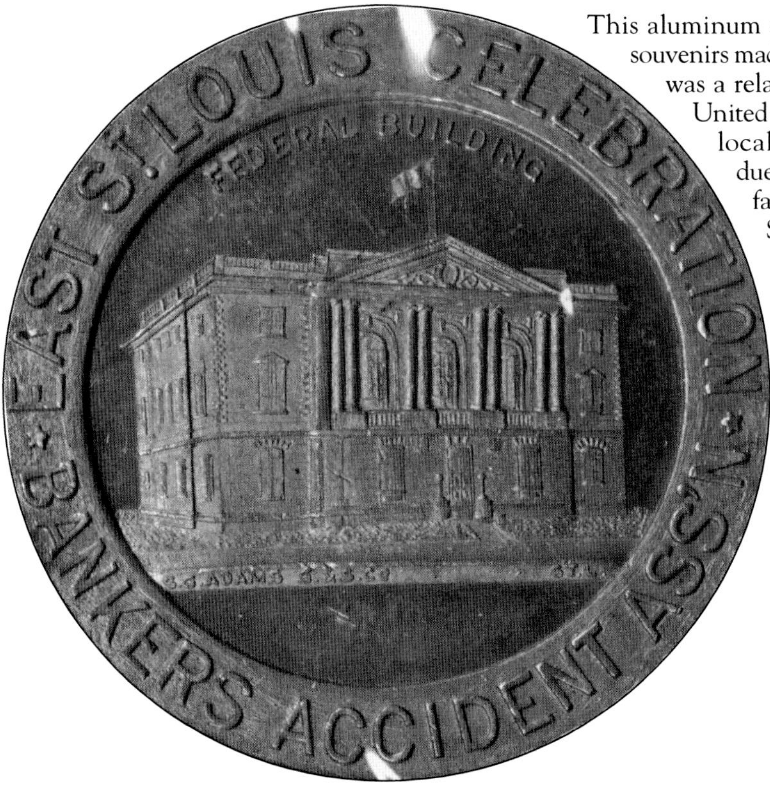

This aluminum coin was one of several souvenirs made for the day. Aluminum was a relatively new metal in the United States at this time. It was locally prominent, though, due to the Aluminum Ore factory that opened in East St. Louis in 1902 and the metal's prominence at the 1904 World's Fair. (SIUE)

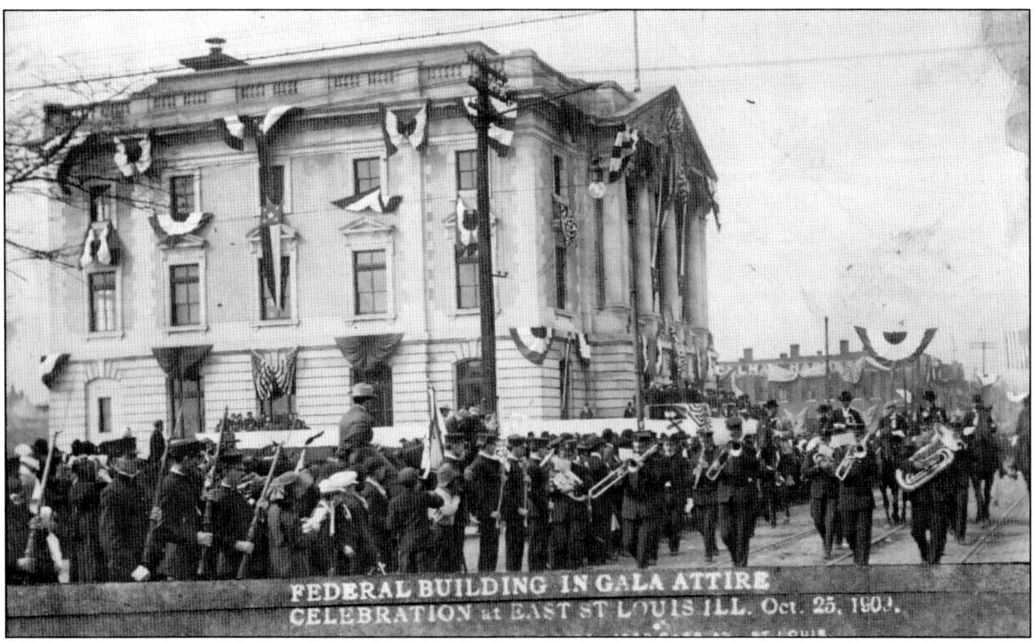

A marching band passes before the dignitaries as the Celebration Day parade works its way down Missouri Avenue. Congressman William Rodenberg shepherded the project through Washington and secured the attendance of President Taft and House Speaker Joe Cannon. The building is decorated in "gala attire" for the president's dedication. (SIUE)

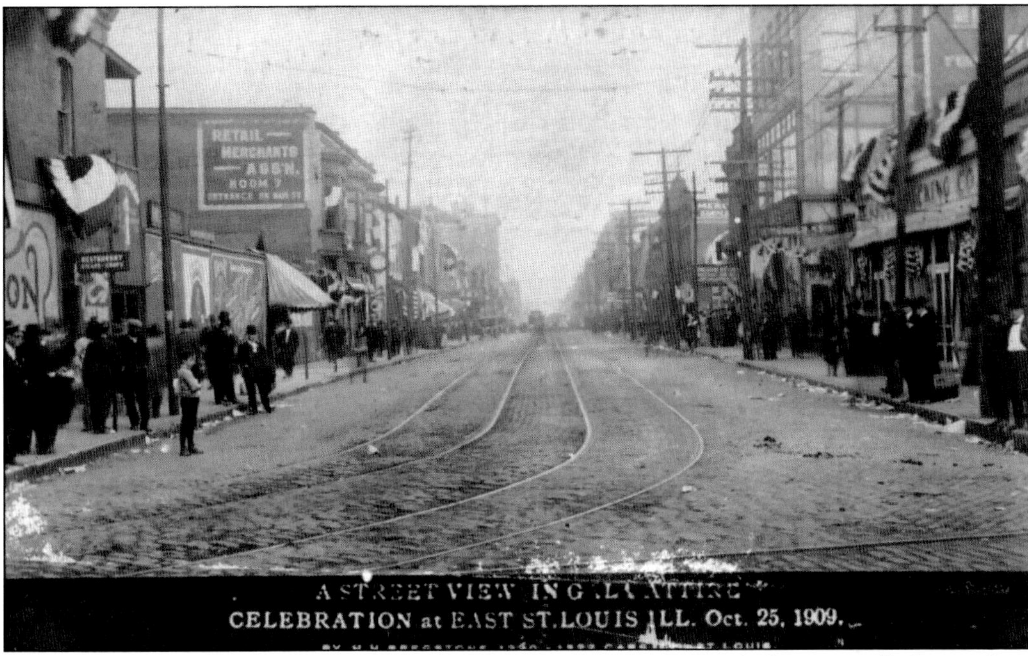

The highlight of the day, aside from the president's visit, was a parade featuring all the products made in East St. Louis. Photographer Henry Bregstone captured the day in a collection of images now housed in the SIUE Archives. Citizens lined up early to view the parade. (SIUE)

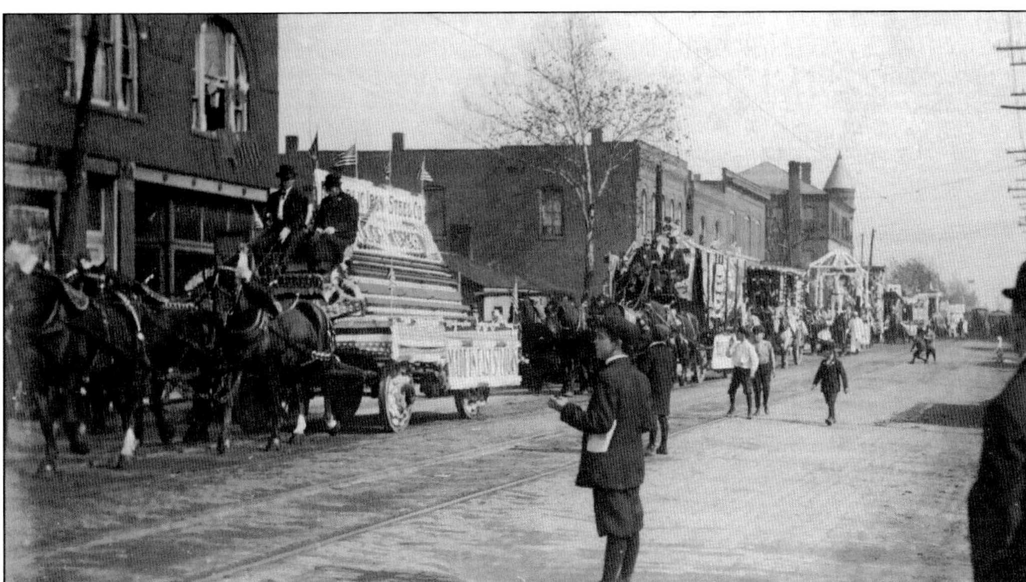

Above is a view of the parade moving along the route. The float that features a horse is from Mollman Harness Company, and future mayor Fred Mollman is presiding. The Mollman Harness Company was just north of the new courthouse. (SIUE)

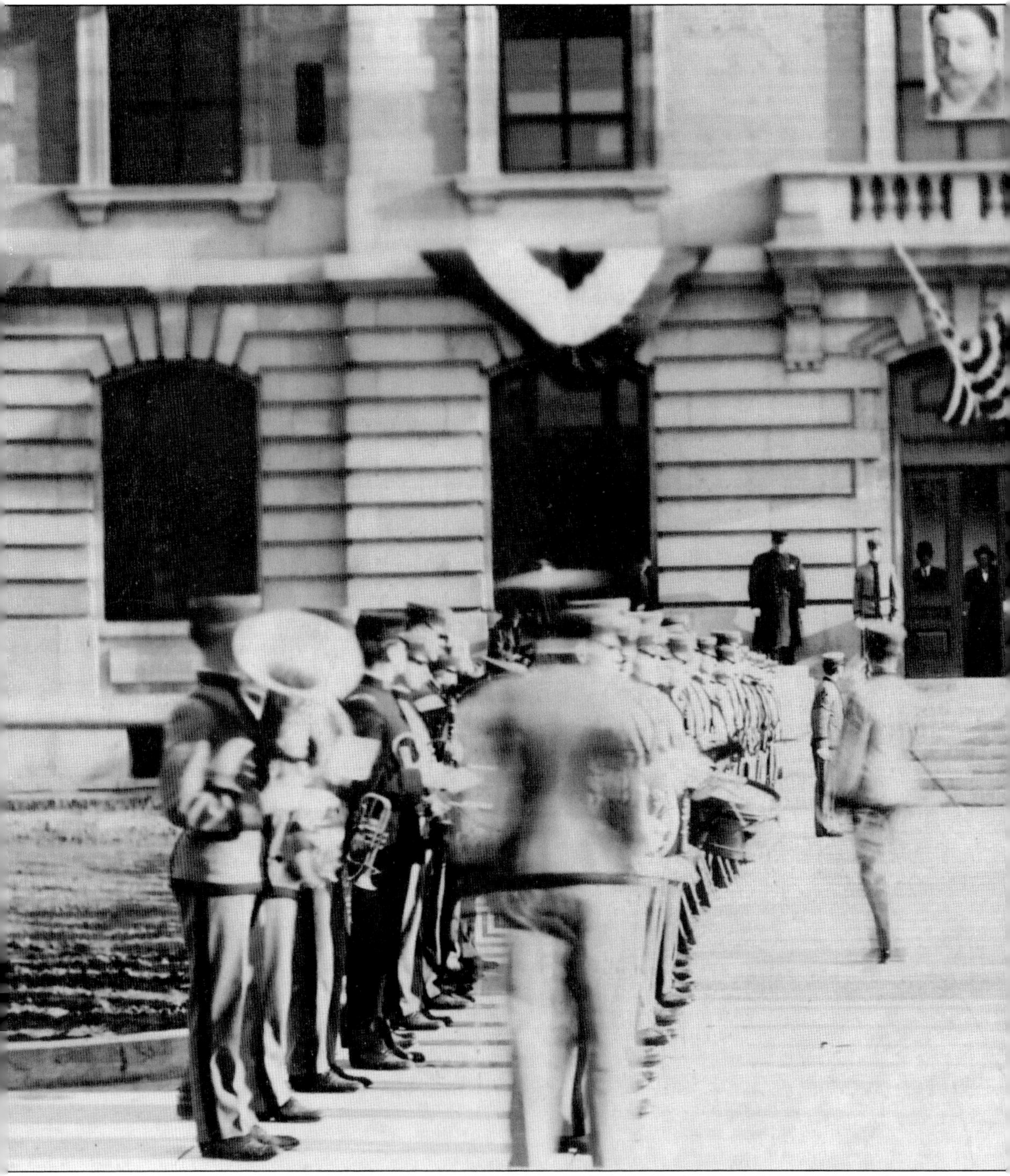

A group of military cadets await the president's arrival. Notice the president's portrait hanging over the balcony. This photograph probably was taken at a side entrance that no longer exists. Within ten years, wings were constructed on both sides of the building, almost doubling the size

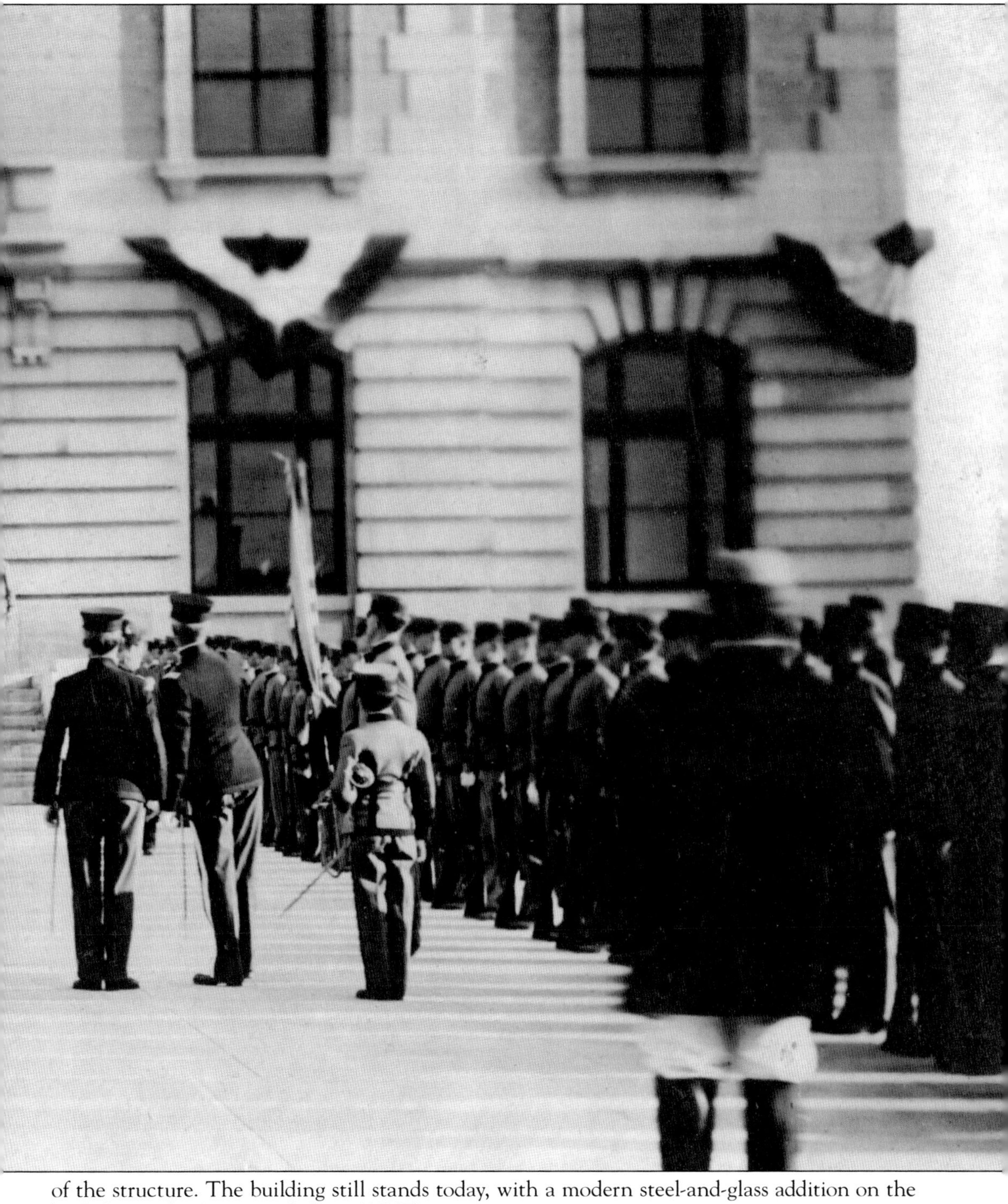

of the structure. The building still stands today, with a modern steel-and-glass addition on the back facing the St. Louis skyline. (SIUE)

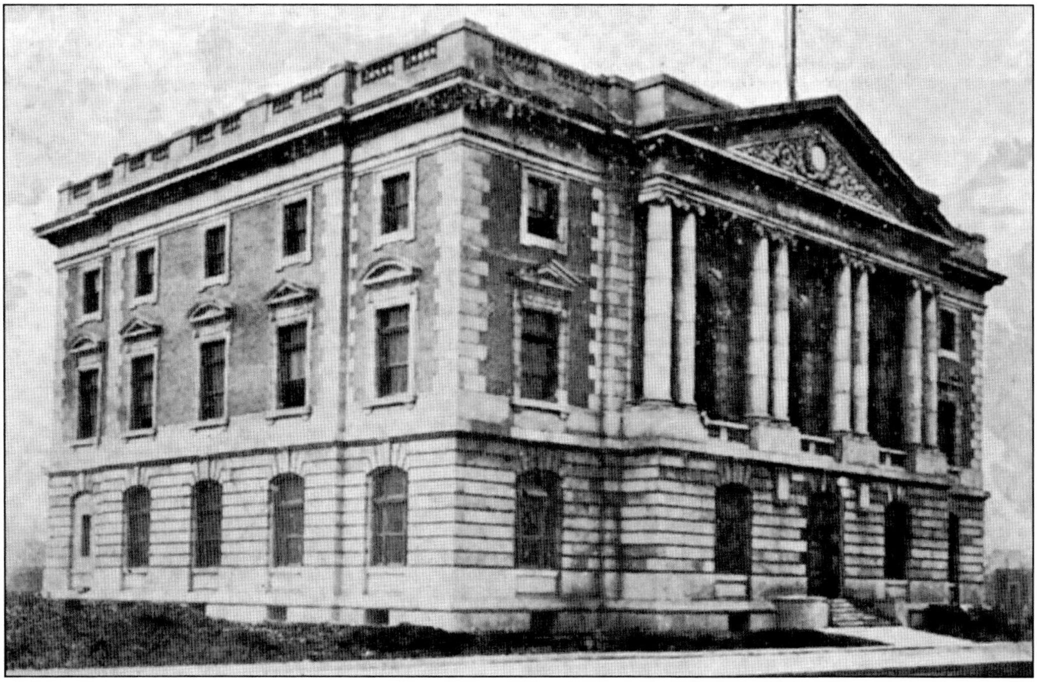

This image is from a special postcard that was distributed at the dedication ceremony. The new courthouse was a point of pride for the city, and housed the post office as well as other federal offices. Today, it houses the Federal District Court for Southern Illinois. New buildings next door to the courthouse on Missouri Avenue house the post office and other federal offices. (SIUE)

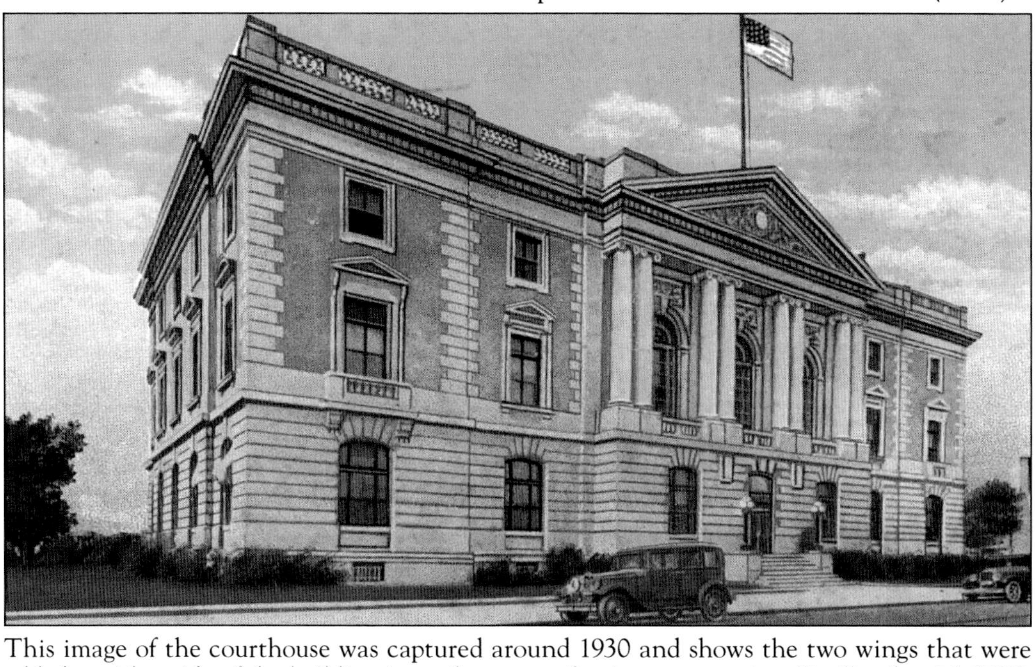

This image of the courthouse was captured around 1930 and shows the two wings that were added to either side of the building just a few years after its construction. On October 25, 2009, the District Court celebrated the building's centennial with a ceremony featuring a reading of the names of all the chief judges who have served in the building over the last 100 years. (SIUE)

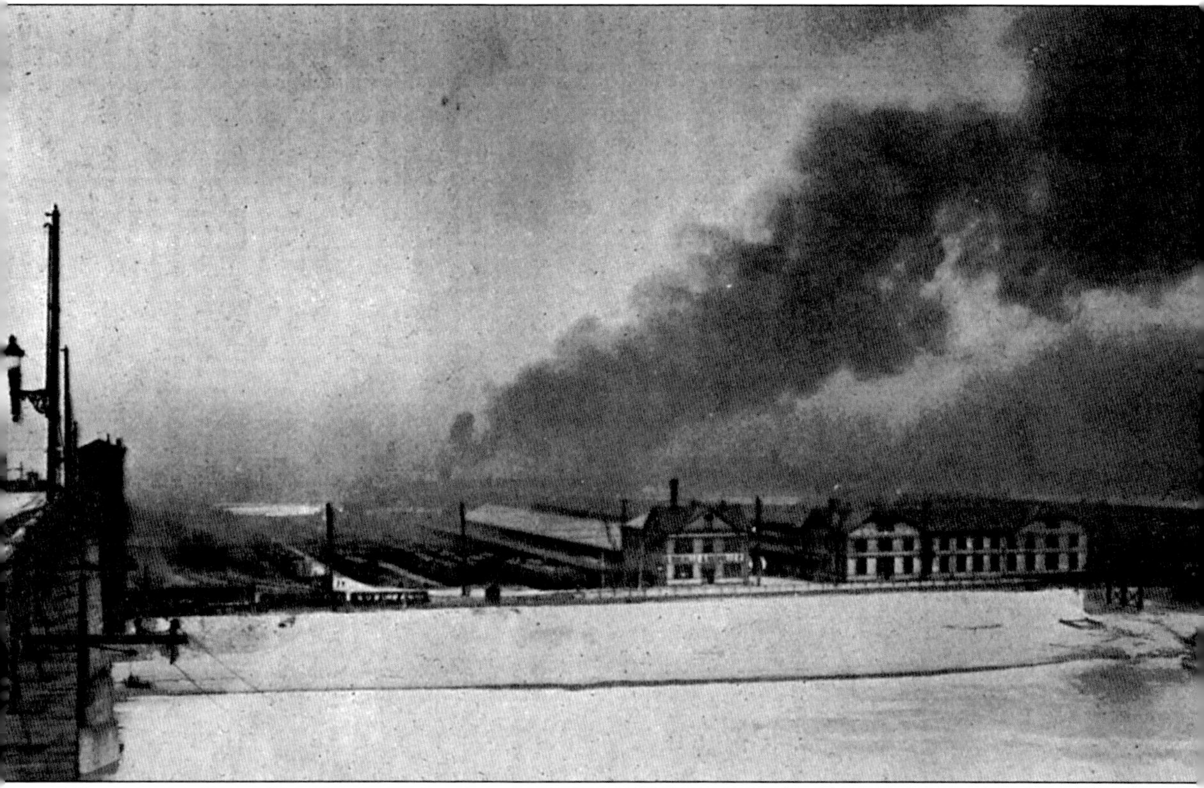

The darkest day in East St. Louis history was July 2, 1917. Hostility had been on the rise for some time in the city, and racial tensions had been rising too. The deaths of two police officers in a black neighborhood under questionable circumstances set off the bloody chain of events. Frustrated workers gathered at the Labor Temple on the 300 block of Collinsville Avenue. Inflammatory speeches were delivered, and calls were made for mob action to avenge the officers' deaths. This photograph of the riot's smoke was taken from the Missouri end of the Eads Bridge. Many buildings were burned. There are very few photographs of the actual riot because both rioters and officials confiscated cameras and destroyed the images. (SIUE)

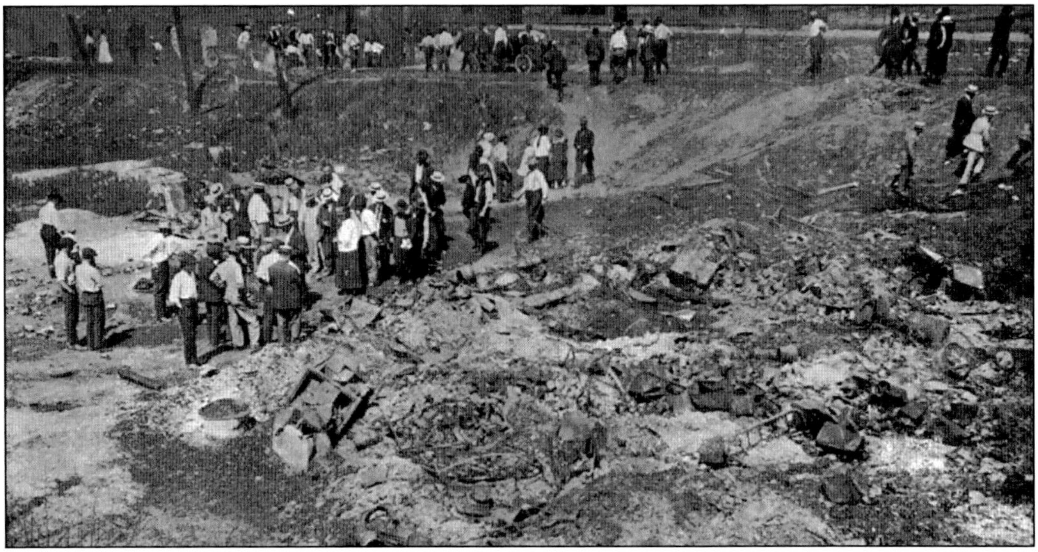

At Broadway Avenue, the mob began to grab black passers-by and beat them. Fires were set to drive African Americans from their homes, and they were shot while fleeing the flames. Bodies were hung from lamp posts. Men and women joined in the violence. The police were powerless to respond. The Illinois State Guard eventually got the mob under control. When the city raised the streets out of the floodplain starting in the 1880s, it did not raise the adjoining lots. These pits became centers of violence, as they frequently housed debris. Here, volunteers search for human remains. (SIUE)

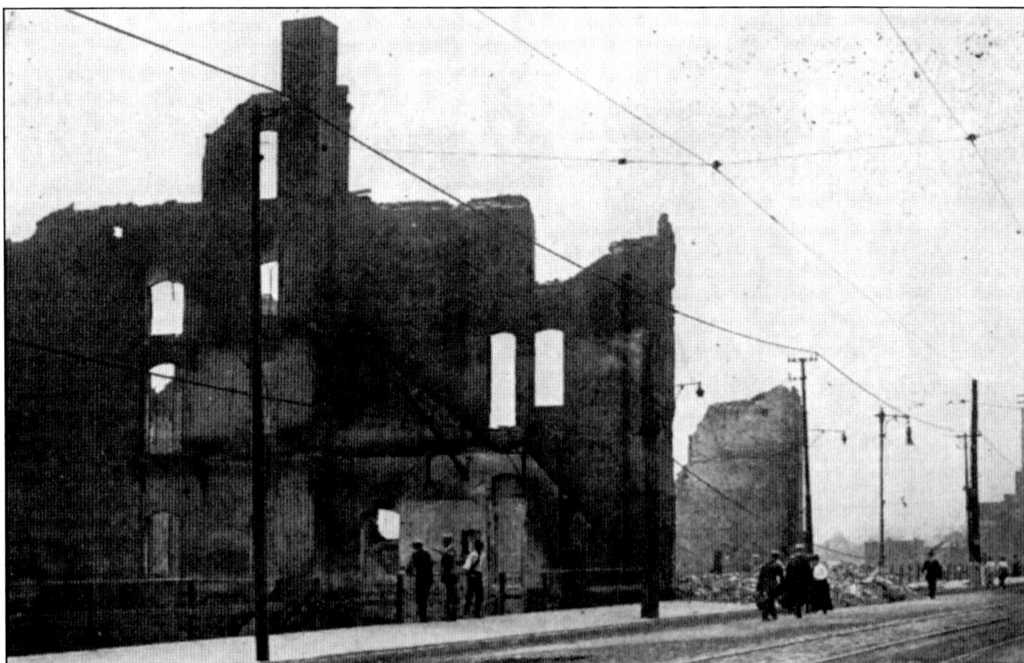

Whole sections of the city were in ruins. Many people remained in hiding—fearing a reprisal of the violence. The official death toll was 39 African Americans and nine Caucasians. The Broadway Opera House, shown here, stood near the site of the old Holiday Inn next to the Broadview Hotel. It was burned when blacks sought shelter in the building. (SIUE)

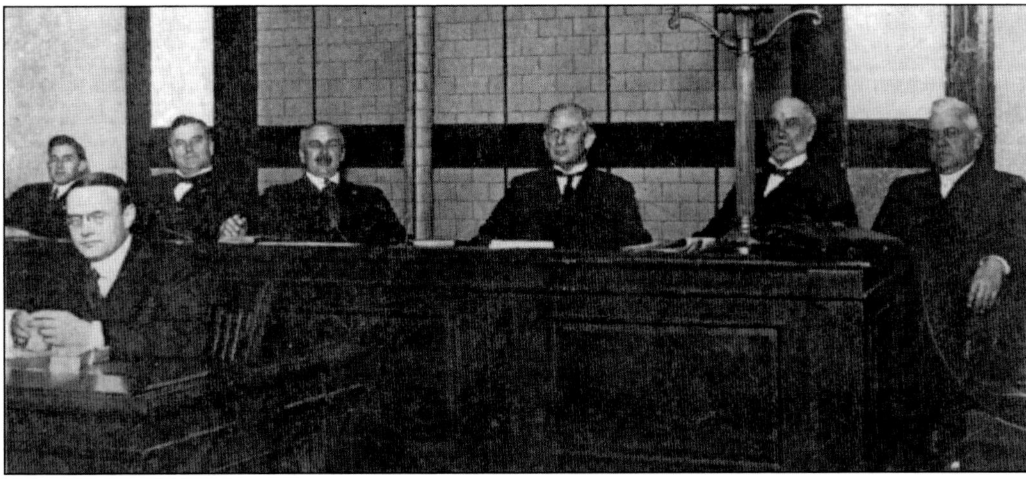

Congress investigated the uprising in the autumn of 1917, citing the riot's interference with interstate commerce. It issued a scathing report in 1918, which said, "East St. Louis is wallowed in a mire of lawlessness and unshamed corruption." Here, members of Congress meet in the city hall council chambers. (SIUE)

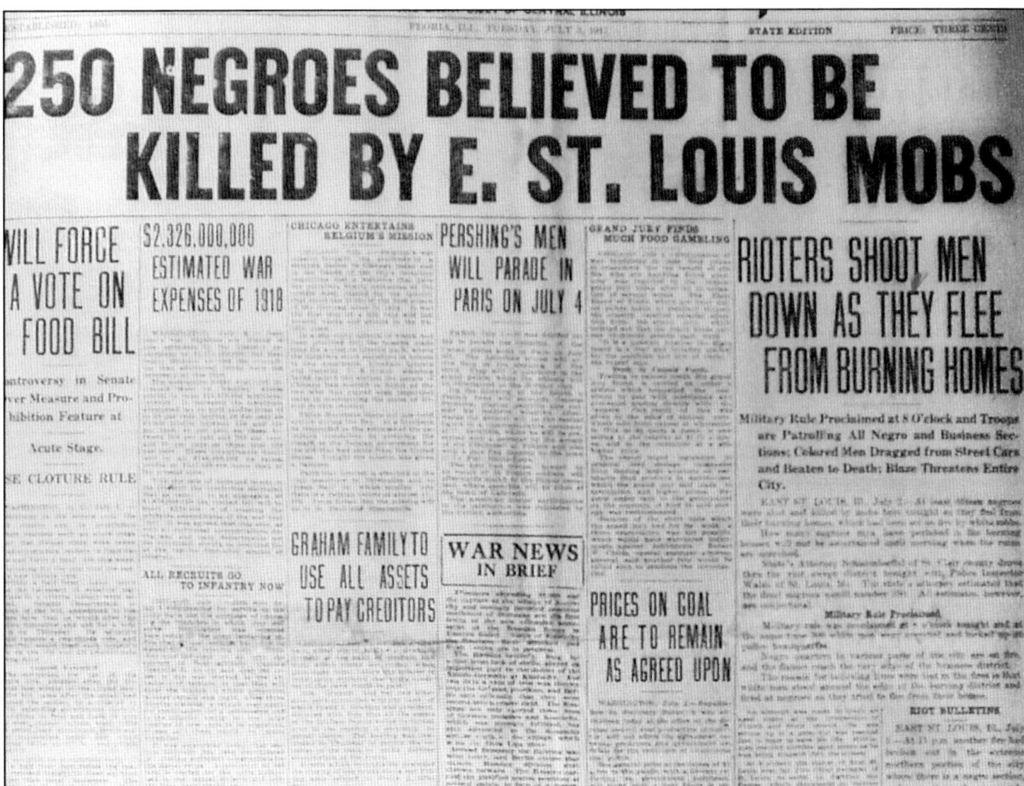

STATE EDITION

250 NEGROES BELIEVED TO BE KILLED BY E. ST. LOUIS MOBS

VILL FORCE A VOTE ON FOOD BILL

ntroversy in Senate ver Measure and Prohibition Feature at Acute Stage.

SE CLOTURE RULE

$2,326,000,000 ESTIMATED WAR EXPENSES OF 1918

ALL RECRUITS GO TO INFANTRY NOW

CHICAGO ENTERTAINS BELGIUM'S MISSION

GRAHAM FAMILY TO USE ALL ASSETS TO PAY CREDITORS

PERSHING'S MEN WILL PARADE IN PARIS ON JULY 4

WAR NEWS IN BRIEF

GRAND JURY FINDS MUCH FOOD GAMBLING

PRICES ON COAL ARE TO REMAIN AS AGREED UPON

RIOTERS SHOOT MEN DOWN AS THEY FLEE FROM BURNING HOMES

Military Rule Proclaimed at 8 O'clock and Troops are Patrolling All Negro and Business Sections; Colored Men Dragged from Street Cars and Beaten to Death; Blaze Threatens Entire City.

Military Rule Proclaimed

RIOT BULLETINS

This dramatic headline from Peoria, Illinois, proclaims a much higher death toll than what was actually believed. The official death toll was 48, which is likely too low. This paper describes the method used by the rioters—burning the buildings that housed African Americans and shooting them as they fled. Only the Los Angeles Riot of 1992 was bloodier, with an official count of 51. This was likely the bloodiest race riot in American history. It is a wound that never really healed. (SIUE)

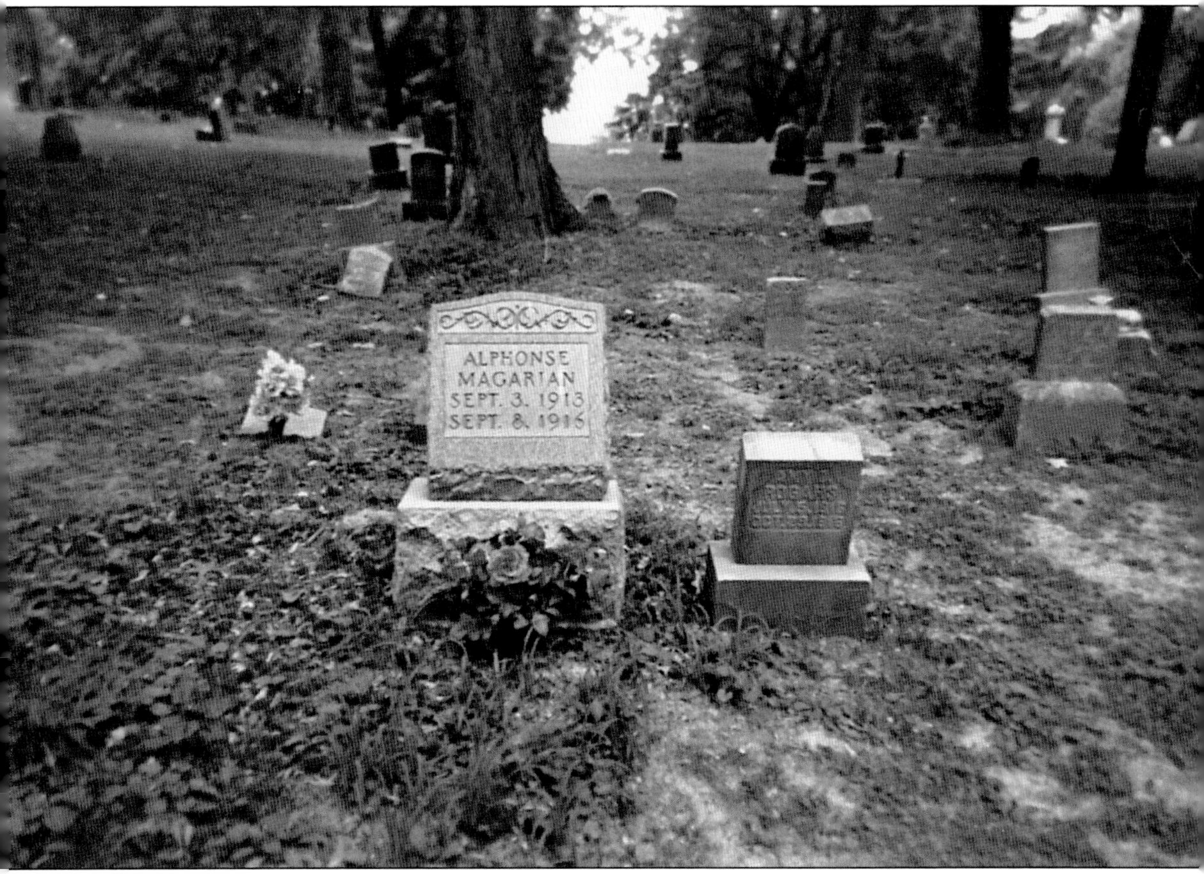

Seen here is the grave of Alphonse Magarian at Mount Hope Cemetery in Belleville. The poor child was an innocent victim of the violence that preceded the riot. His father, an Armenian baker, demanded repeatedly that a brothel operating next door be closed. Police felt pressured to act, raided the brothel, and closed it. Little Alphonse was kidnapped shortly thereafter. His decapitated body was left as a warning to anyone who would dare interfere with the vice of East St. Louis. This culture of violence was fertile ground for the race riot that would come months later. (AT)

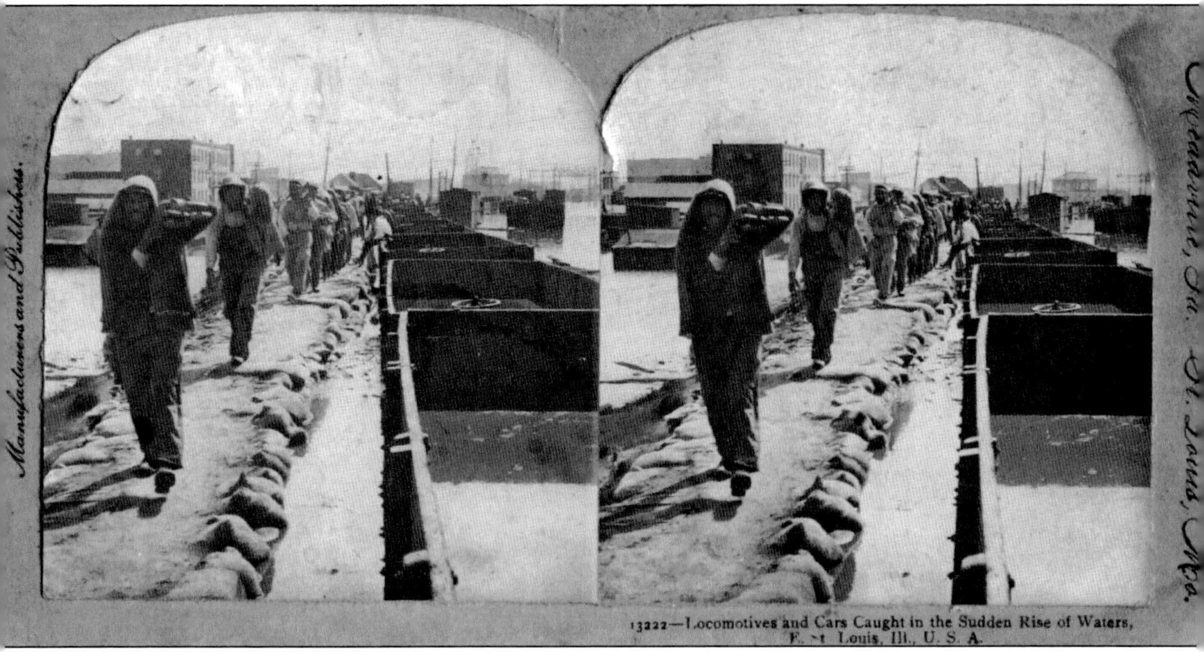

In June 1903, the city was stricken by natural disaster. Water levels on the Mississippi River had been rising 12 to 16 inches daily. Near midnight on June 9, floodwater breached the embankment provided by the Illinois Central Railroad tracks. Water rushed into the second and third wards of the city, inundating buildings with water three to twelve feet deep. The water continued to rise until it crested on June 11 at 40 feet above flood stage. In this old stereo card, workers carry sandbags along a temporary dike built beside a railroad embankment. Note the floodwater sitting in the railcars. (SIUE)

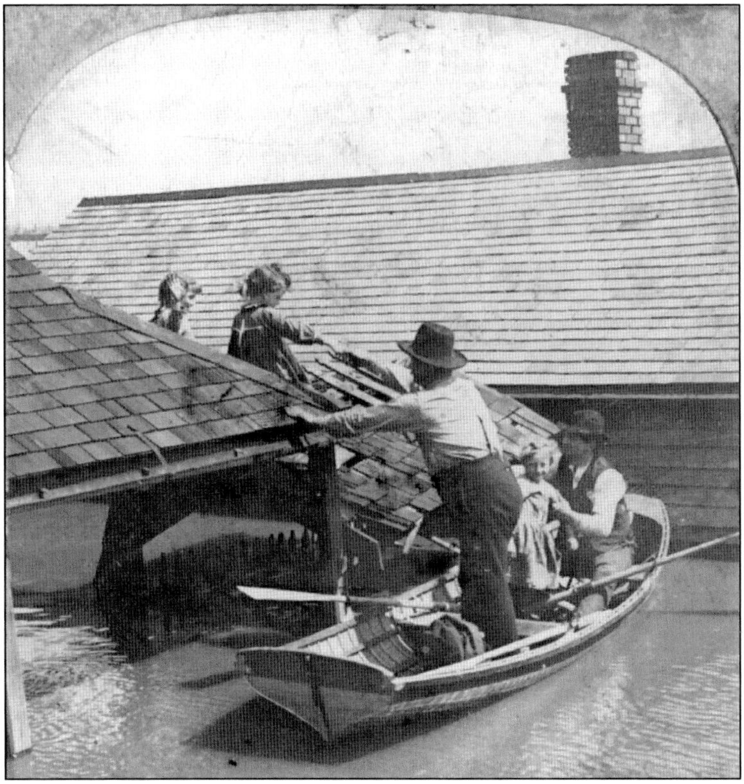

This picture shows how a city located on the floodplain of the Mississippi River is subject to the whims of Mother Nature. The city spent about a million dollars in 1890 to raise much of the downtown area by 8 to 10 feet. The raised portions of the city remained dry during this flood, but low-lying areas were devastated. Approximately 40 people drowned in the floodwaters. (SIUE)

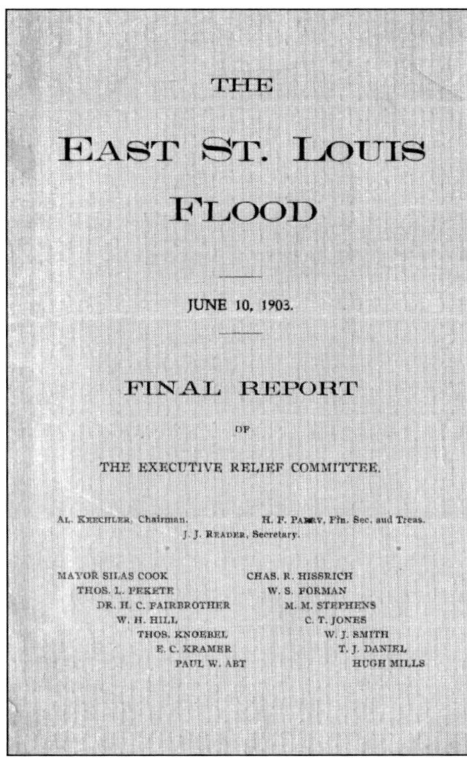

THE

EAST ST. LOUIS FLOOD

JUNE 10, 1903.

FINAL REPORT

OF

THE EXECUTIVE RELIEF COMMITTEE.

AL. KRECHLER, Chairman. H. F. PARRY, Fin. Sec. and Treas.

J. J. READER, Secretary.

MAYOR SILAS COOK
THOS. L. FEKETE
DR. H. C. FAIRBROTHER
W. H. HILL
THOS. KNOEBEL
E. C. KRAMER
PAUL W. ABT

CHAS. R. HISSRICH
W. S. FORMAN
M. M. STEPHENS
C. T. JONES
W. J. SMITH
T. J. DANIEL
HUGH MILLS

A relief committee was created and included many prominent citizens, among them Mayor Cook and his predecessor, former mayor M.M. Stephens. The committee set up two relief centers: Camp Washington for Caucasians and Camp Lincoln for African Americans. This image shows the committee's final report. (SIUE)

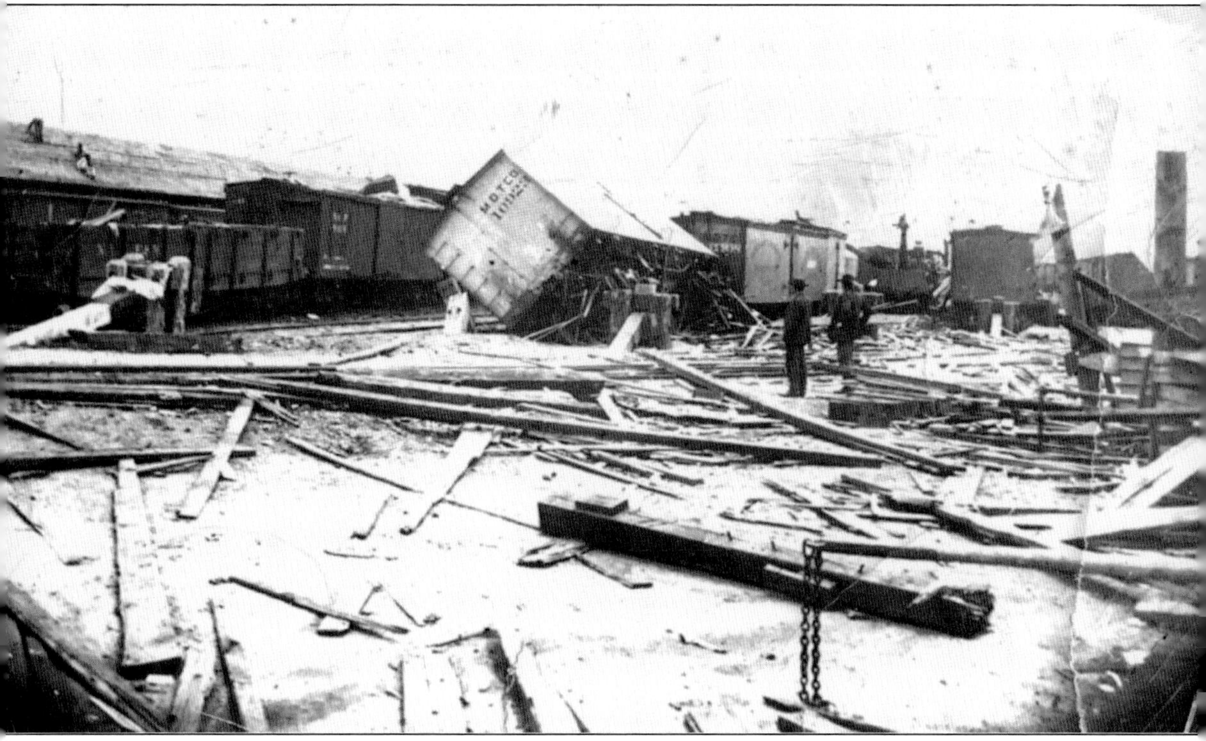

On May 27, 1896, a violent tornado formed over South St. Louis and moved eastward. It left a swath of destruction in its path, starting near Lafayette Park in St. Louis and crossing the Mississippi before striking East St. Louis starting at the Eads Bridge; it then cut through downtown and continued on to the National Stock Yards. Scientists today calculate that it was an F4 tornado—the most destructive type. The tornado crossed the Mississippi River at about 5:10 p.m. It pulled railroad cars from the tracks and scattered timber and ties everywhere, as seen here. (SIUE)

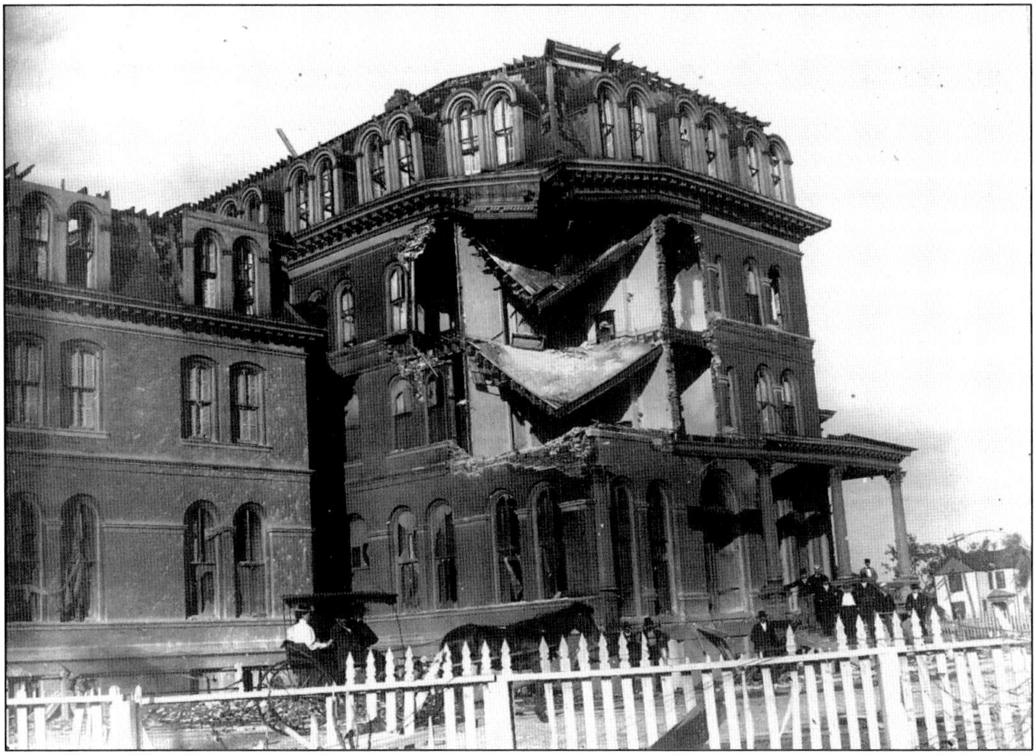

Near the end of the tornado's destructive path was the National Stock Yards. Seen above, the National Hotel lost a front corner and its roof. The building was repaired and eventually reopened. It was near the main entrance of the Stock Yards off St. Clair Avenue. Other businesses along St. Clair Avenue, such as the Benjamin Horn Cooperage, also sustained significant damage. (SIUE)

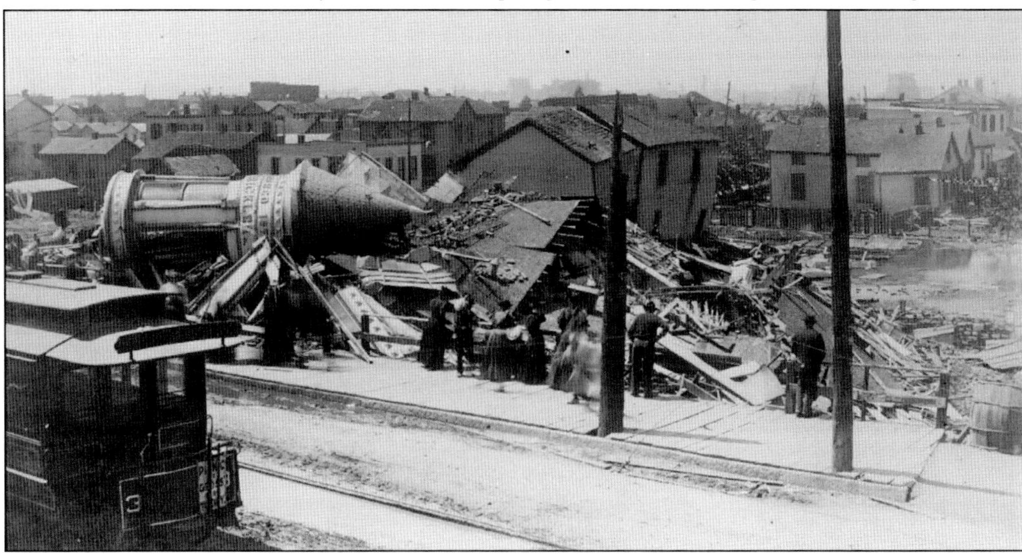

The Strickler Building lies in ruins. It stood at 301 Collinsville Avenue. Passers-by marveled at the destruction. The *New York Herald* proclaimed that the great cyclone "destroys East St. Louis." Typical of tornado damage, some houses are ripped to shreds, while neighboring houses appear untouched. (SIUE)

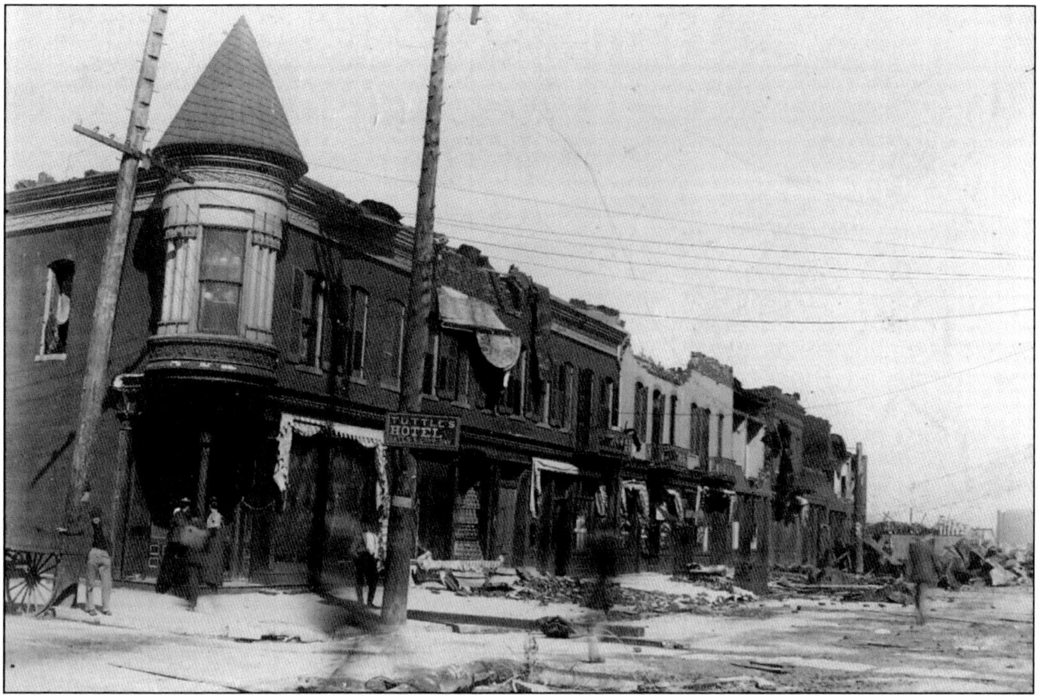

This is probably at or near the 200 block of Missouri Avenue. A makeshift hospital was set up at Tuttle's hotel at 201 Missouri Avenue. A curious story involved a man named Henry Collins. He was in a saloon when the cyclone hit. The roof collapsed, knocking him down and breaking his collarbone. Despite the tumult, he did not spill his drink—which he quickly consumed to relieve the pain in his shoulder. (SIUE)

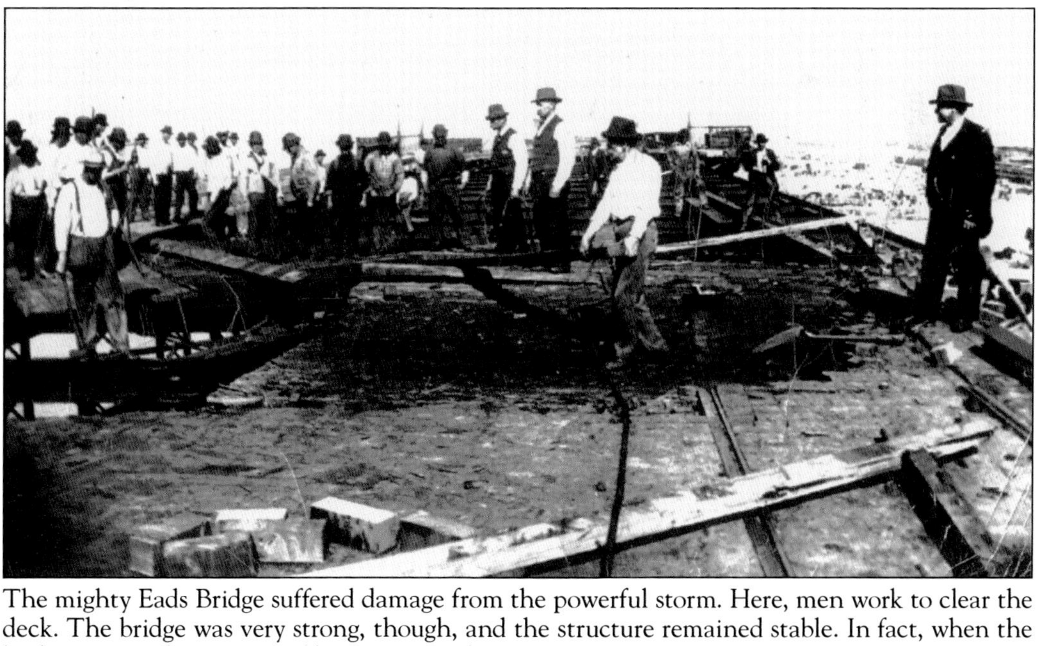

The mighty Eads Bridge suffered damage from the powerful storm. Here, men work to clear the deck. The bridge was very strong, though, and the structure remained stable. In fact, when the bridge reopened, it was tested by running 14 locomotive engines across it at one time—a testament to the bridge's sound design. (SIUE)

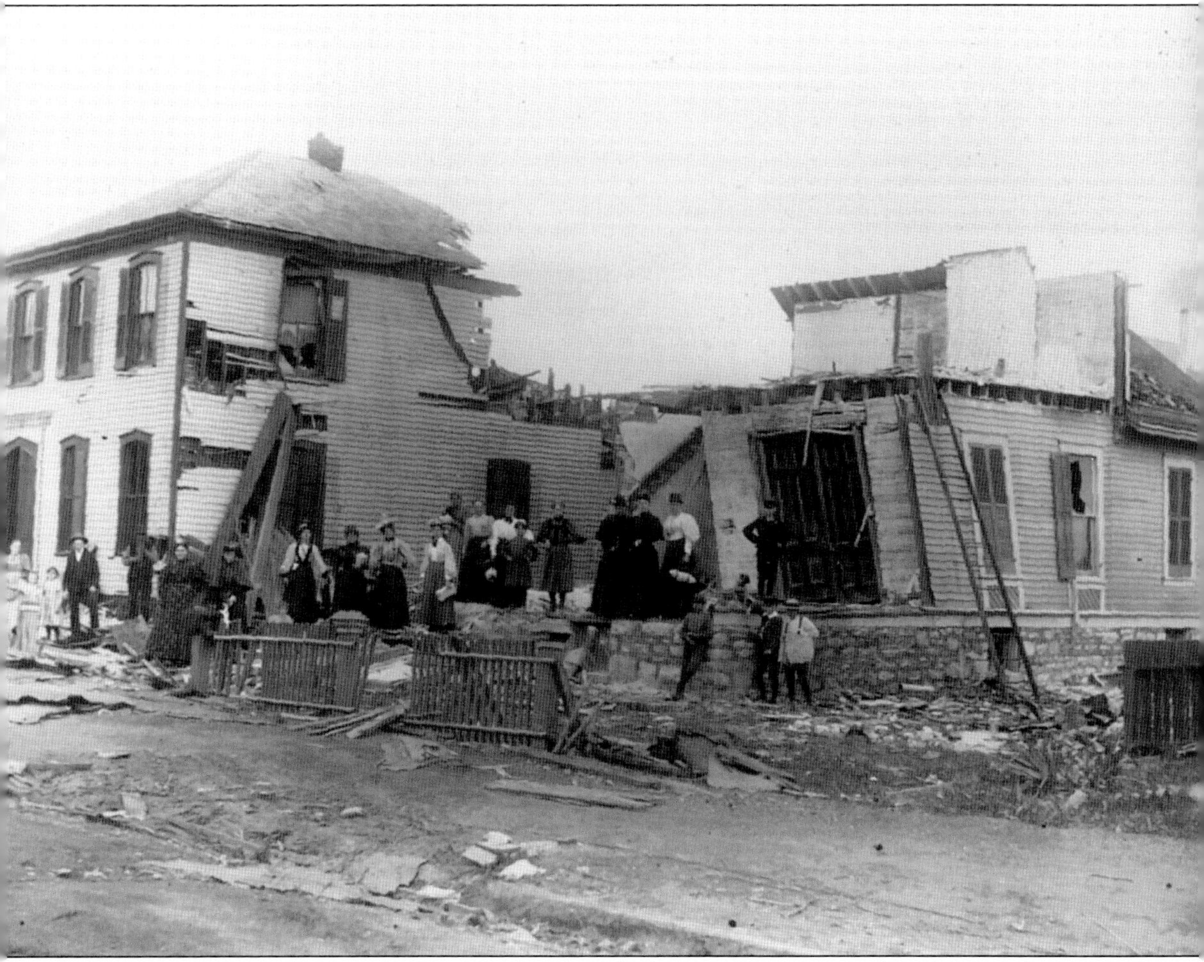

This is a curious photograph of people posing amid a destroyed home. Note that the tornado destroyed the front part of one house while also ravaging the back part of the home next door. Thieves took advantage of the destruction and began looting damaged homes. The militia was called in and announced that prowlers would be shot on sight. The city was described as "one huge mausoleum" by Julian Curzon, "covering no one knew how many dead." (SIUE)

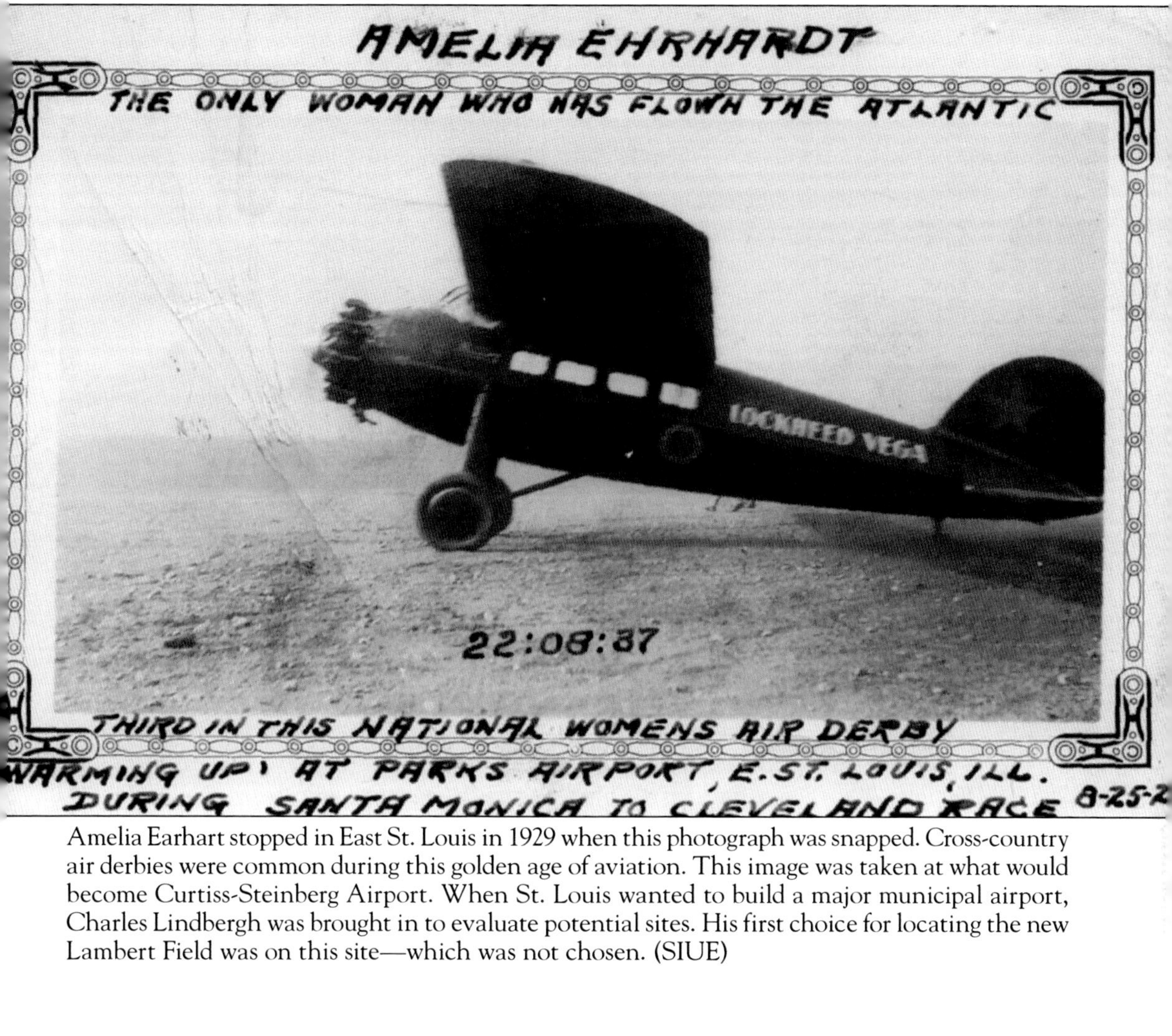

Amelia Earhart stopped in East St. Louis in 1929 when this photograph was snapped. Cross-country air derbies were common during this golden age of aviation. This image was taken at what would become Curtiss-Steinberg Airport. When St. Louis wanted to build a major municipal airport, Charles Lindbergh was brought in to evaluate potential sites. His first choice for locating the new Lambert Field was on this site—which was not chosen. (SIUE)

The Curtis-Steinberg Airport dedication in 1930 meant new airmail routes to serve East St. Louis. The postal cover is actually misspelled. It should read "Curtiss," as in the Curtiss Wright Aircraft Company of St. Louis. Oliver Parks took over operation of the airport in the 1930s. Today, it is the St. Louis-Downtown Airport, now in the city of Sauget, Illinois. (BN)

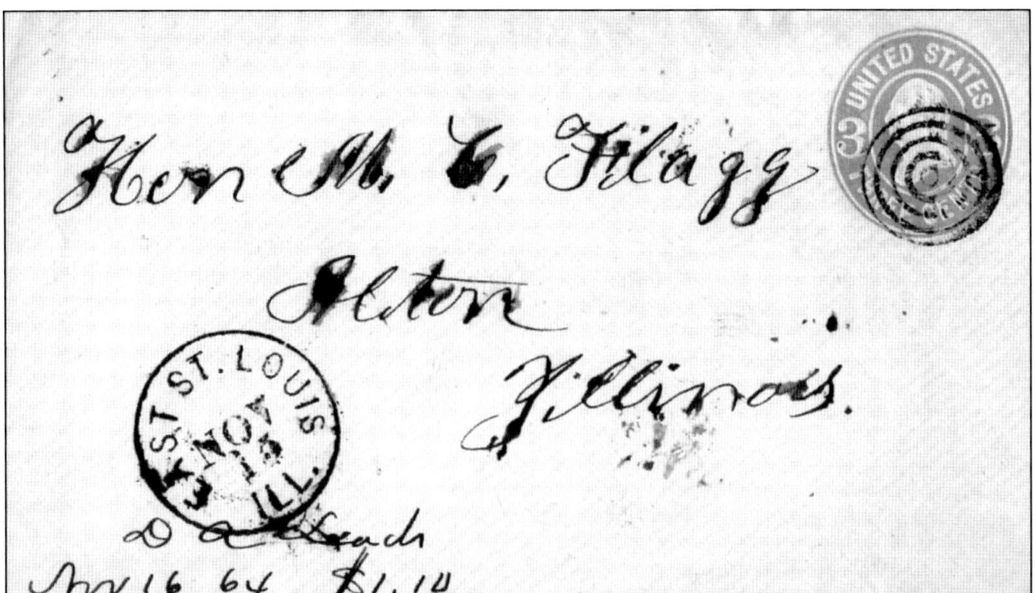

Above, a very rare postal cover shows an 1864 cancellation with "East St. Louis" as the post office—which had only been in existence for a few years at that time. (SIUE)

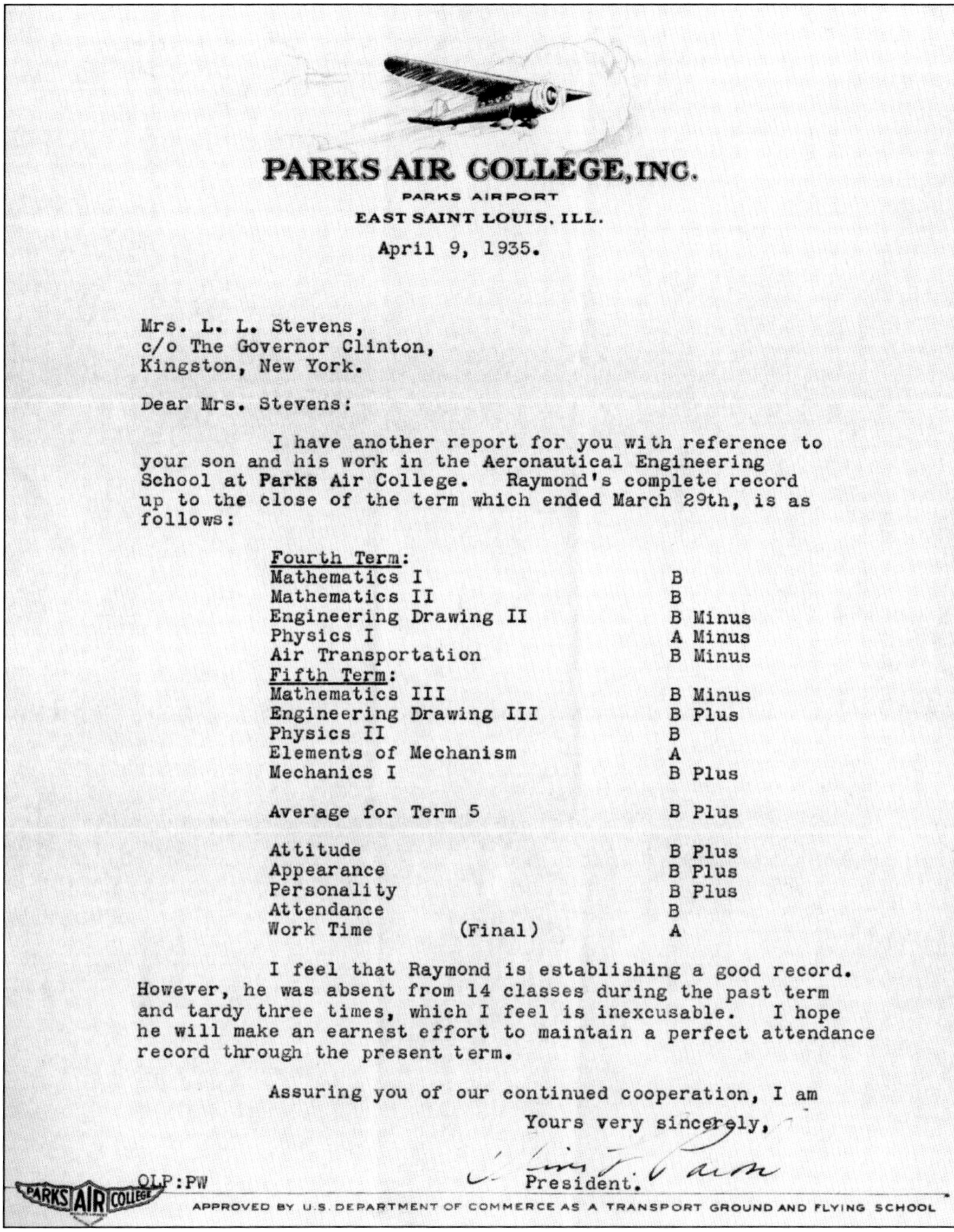

PARKS AIR COLLEGE, INC.
PARKS AIRPORT
EAST SAINT LOUIS, ILL.

April 9, 1935.

Mrs. L. L. Stevens,
c/o The Governor Clinton,
Kingston, New York.

Dear Mrs. Stevens:

I have another report for you with reference to your son and his work in the Aeronautical Engineering School at Parks Air College. Raymond's complete record up to the close of the term which ended March 29th, is as follows:

Fourth Term:	
Mathematics I	B
Mathematics II	B
Engineering Drawing II	B Minus
Physics I	A Minus
Air Transportation	B Minus
Fifth Term:	
Mathematics III	B Minus
Engineering Drawing III	B Plus
Physics II	B
Elements of Mechanism	A
Mechanics I	B Plus
Average for Term 5	B Plus
Attitude	B Plus
Appearance	B Plus
Personality	B Plus
Attendance	B
Work Time (Final)	A

I feel that Raymond is establishing a good record. However, he was absent from 14 classes during the past term and tardy three times, which I feel is inexcusable. I hope he will make an earnest effort to maintain a perfect attendance record through the present term.

Assuring you of our continued cooperation, I am

Yours very sincerely,

President.

OLP:PW

PARKS AIR COLLEGE

APPROVED BY U.S. DEPARTMENT OF COMMERCE AS A TRANSPORT GROUND AND FLYING SCHOOL

Oliver Parks, the Metro East aviation pioneer, signed this 1935 letter reporting on the progress of a student. The Parks Air College is now a unit of St. Louis University. Parks crashed his plane in 1927 near the St. Stanislaus Seminary in Florissant, Missouri. He felt indebted to the Jesuits for rescuing him. In 1946, he donated his Parks Air College to the Jesuit-operated St. Louis University. (SIUE)

In 1960, East St. Louis was named an All-America City by *Look* magazine. The following year, the city celebrated its centennial. Many remember these back-to-back celebratory events as the city's finest hour. The civic celebration was co-chaired by Mel Stonecipher and Robert Hackmann. The Centennial Planning Committee had a budget of $35,000, with various proceeds from the different events expected to offset many of the costs. (SIUE)

Three

Commerce and Industry

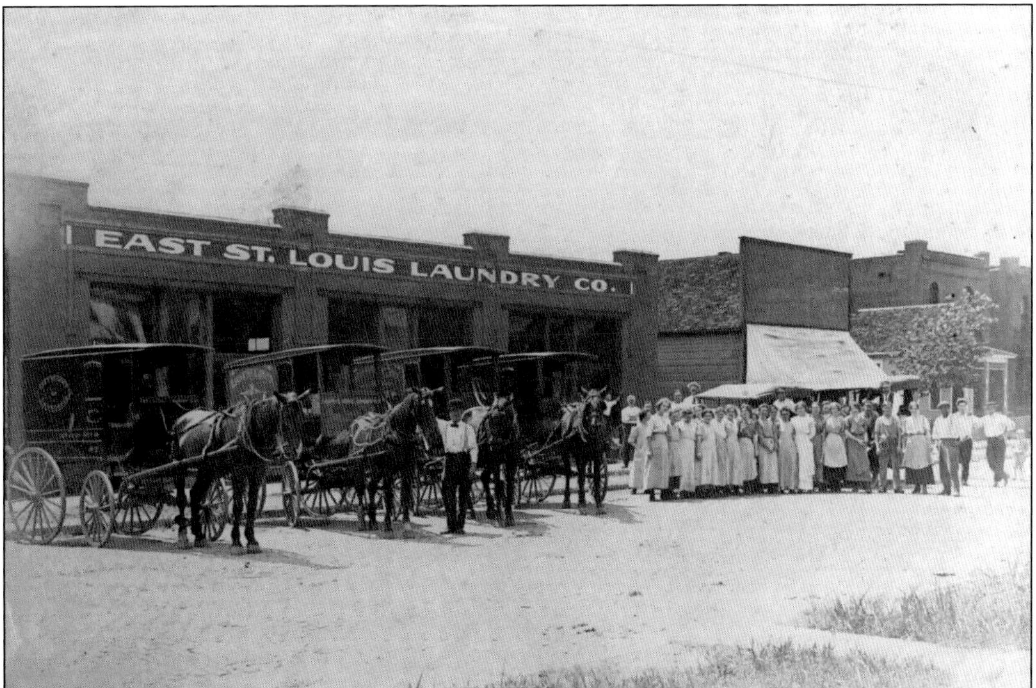

The East St. Louis Laundry Company, located at 1020 Gaty Avenue, advertised its "Clean Towel Service" to area hotels and restaurants. (SIUE)

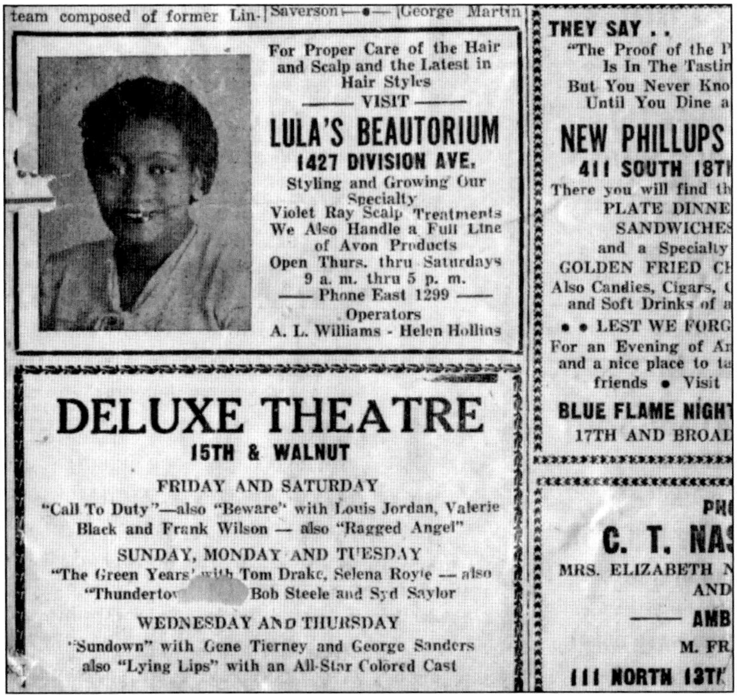
team composed of former Lin- | Saverson — • — | George Martin

For Proper Care of the Hair and Scalp and the Latest in Hair Styles
— VISIT —
LULA'S BEAUTORIUM
1427 DIVISION AVE.
Styling and Growing Our Specialty
Violet Ray Scalp Treatments
We Also Handle a Full Line of Avon Products
Open Thurs. thru Saturdays
9 a. m. thru 5 p. m.
— Phone East 1299 —
Operators
A. L. Williams - Helen Hollins

DELUXE THEATRE
15TH & WALNUT
FRIDAY AND SATURDAY
"Call To Duty"—also "Beware" with Louis Jordan, Valerie Black and Frank Wilson — also "Ragged Angel"
SUNDAY, MONDAY AND TUESDAY
"The Green Years" with Tom Drake, Selena Royle — also "Thunderto[illegible] Bob Steele and Syd Saylor
WEDNESDAY AND THURSDAY
"Sundown" with Gene Tierney and George Sanders also "Lying Lips" with an All-Star Colored Cast

THEY SAY . .
"The Proof of the P
Is In The Tastin
But You Never Kno
Until You Dine a
NEW PHILLUPS
411 SOUTH 18TH
There you will find th
PLATE DINNE
SANDWICHES
and a Specialty
GOLDEN FRIED CH
Also Candies, Cigars, C
and Soft Drinks of a
• • LEST WE FORG
For an Evening of A
and a nice place to t
friends • Visit
BLUE FLAME NIGHT
17TH AND BROAD

PH
C. T. NAS
MRS. ELIZABETH N
AND
— AMB
M. FR
111 NORTH 13TH

The Deluxe Theatre was located at 15th Street and Walnut Avenue, not far from Lincoln Park. Theaters were segregated in St. Louis and East St. Louis. The Deluxe served the African American community. This 1945 ad mentions the movie *Lying Lips* with "an All-Star Colored Cast." Katherine Dunham, who called East St. Louis home in the 1960s, was featured in several films for black audiences during the 1940s. (RP)

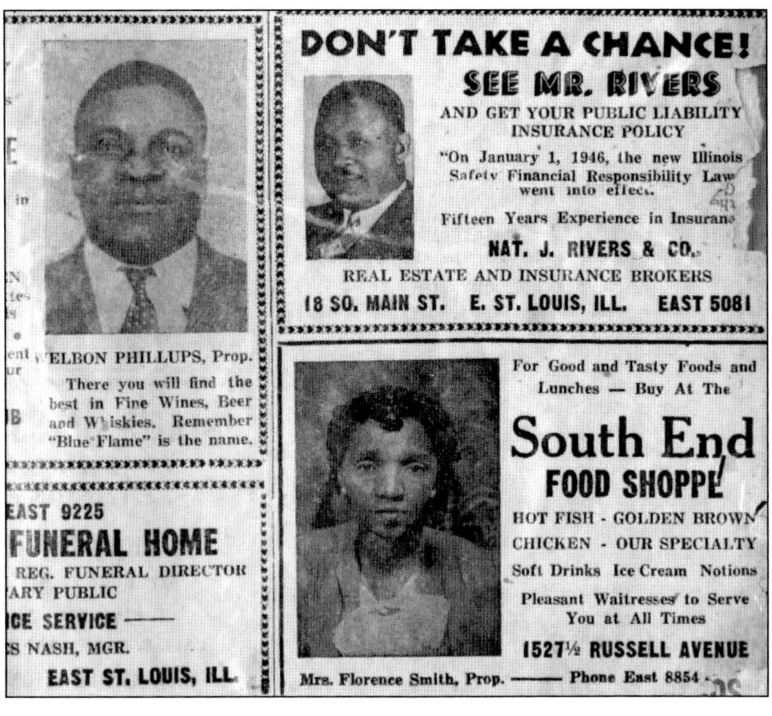
WELBON PHILLUPS, Prop.
There you will find the best in Fine Wines, Beer and Whiskies. Remember "Blue Flame" is the name.

EAST 9225
FUNERAL HOME
REG. FUNERAL DIRECTOR
ARY PUBLIC
ICE SERVICE —
S NASH, MGR.
EAST ST. LOUIS, ILL.

DON'T TAKE A CHANCE!
SEE MR. RIVERS
AND GET YOUR PUBLIC LIABILITY INSURANCE POLICY
"On January 1, 1946, the new Illinois Safety Financial Responsibility Law went into effect.
Fifteen Years Experience in Insurance
NAT. J. RIVERS & CO.
REAL ESTATE AND INSURANCE BROKERS
18 SO. MAIN ST. E. ST. LOUIS, ILL. EAST 5081

For Good and Tasty Foods and Lunches — Buy At The
South End
FOOD SHOPPE
HOT FISH - GOLDEN BROWN CHICKEN - OUR SPECIALTY
Soft Drinks Ice Cream Notions
Pleasant Waitresses to Serve You at All Times
1527½ RUSSELL AVENUE
Mrs. Florence Smith, Prop. — Phone East 8854

These 1945 ads from the *East St. Louis Citizen* highlight some of the businesses serving the South End neighborhood. (RP)

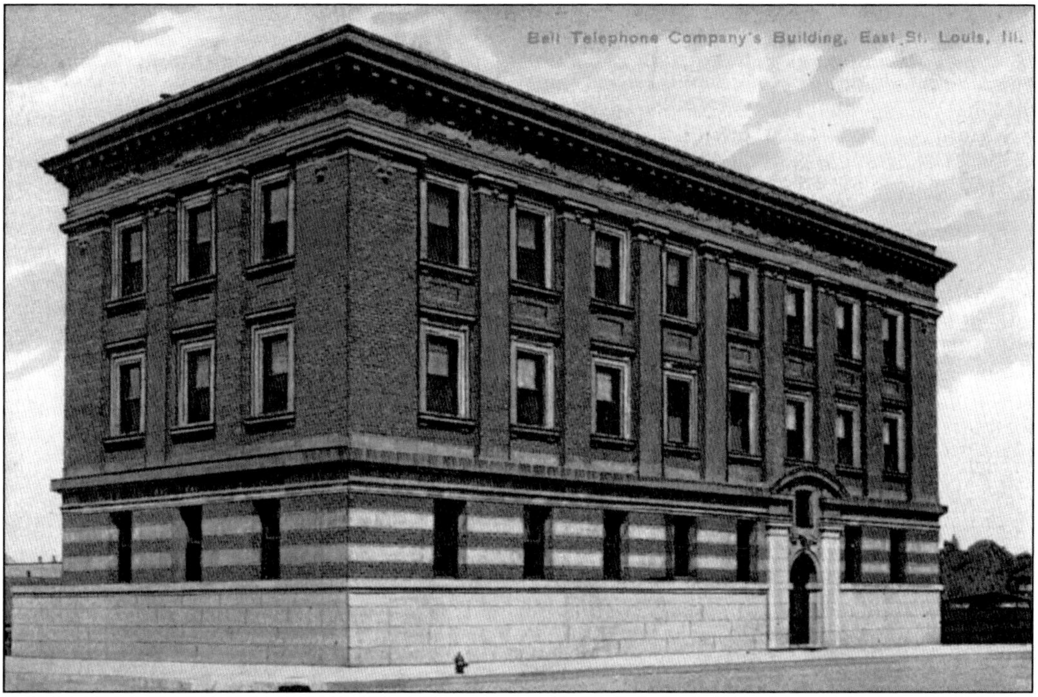

The Bell Telephone Building was located on the corner at 721 Missouri Avenue, across the street from the Federal Building. An addition on the west end was added after World War II. (HF)

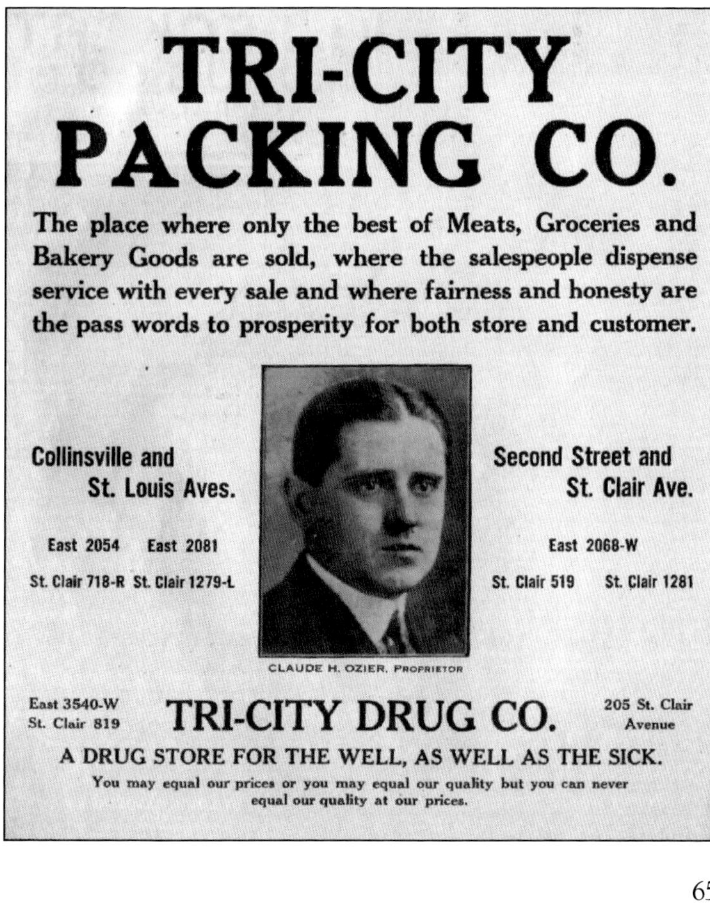

Claude Ozier's Tri-City Packing Company boasted two locations in this 1912 advertisement. There were many small grocers operating in East St. Louis in the early years. Several notable politicians were in the grocery business, including Mayor Maurice Joyce, Representative Frank Holten, and political boss Thomas Canavan. (SIUE)

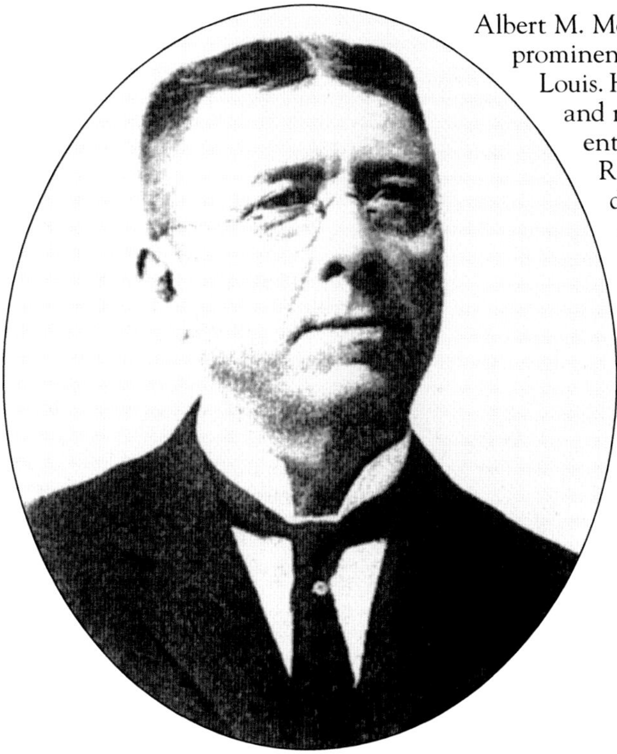

Albert M. Meints of 454 North Ninth Street was a prominent businessman and citizen in East St. Louis. He and his family were active in finance and real estate and owned several business enterprises, including the Royal Hotel. Real estate developers and financiers dominated the city's power base for many decades. (SIUE)

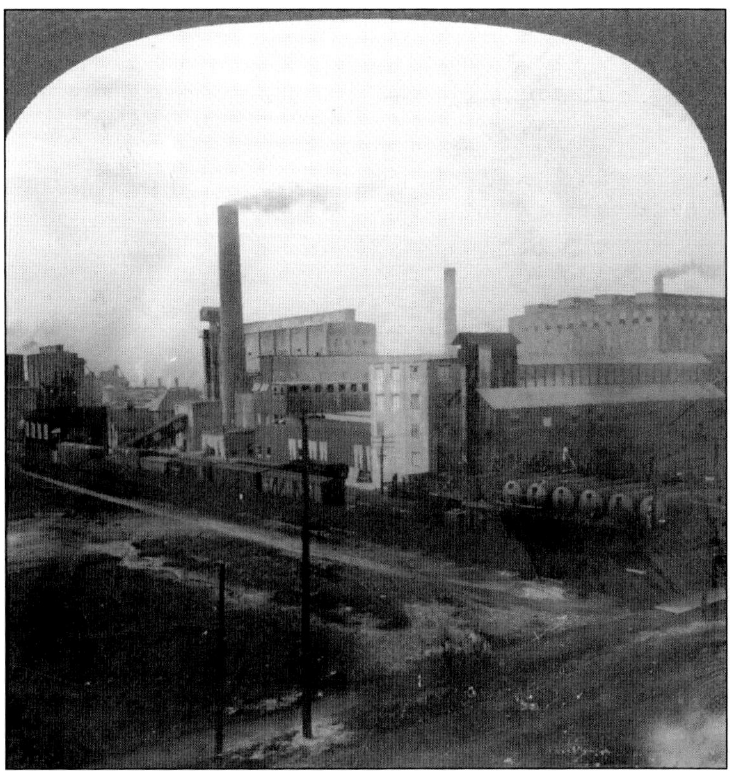

The Aluminum Ore Plant at 3300 Missouri Avenue began operations in 1902 as the Pittsburgh Reduction Company, processing bauxite. The name change to Aluminum Ore took place in 1910. The town around it incorporated in 1944. Its first name was Alcoa, but it was quickly changed to Alorton—which stood for "Aluminum Ore Town." The company brought the ore up from Arkansas in the *Sprague*, which was the largest boat operating on the Mississippi River in the 1920s. This plant became the largest processor of aluminum ore in the world. (SIUE)

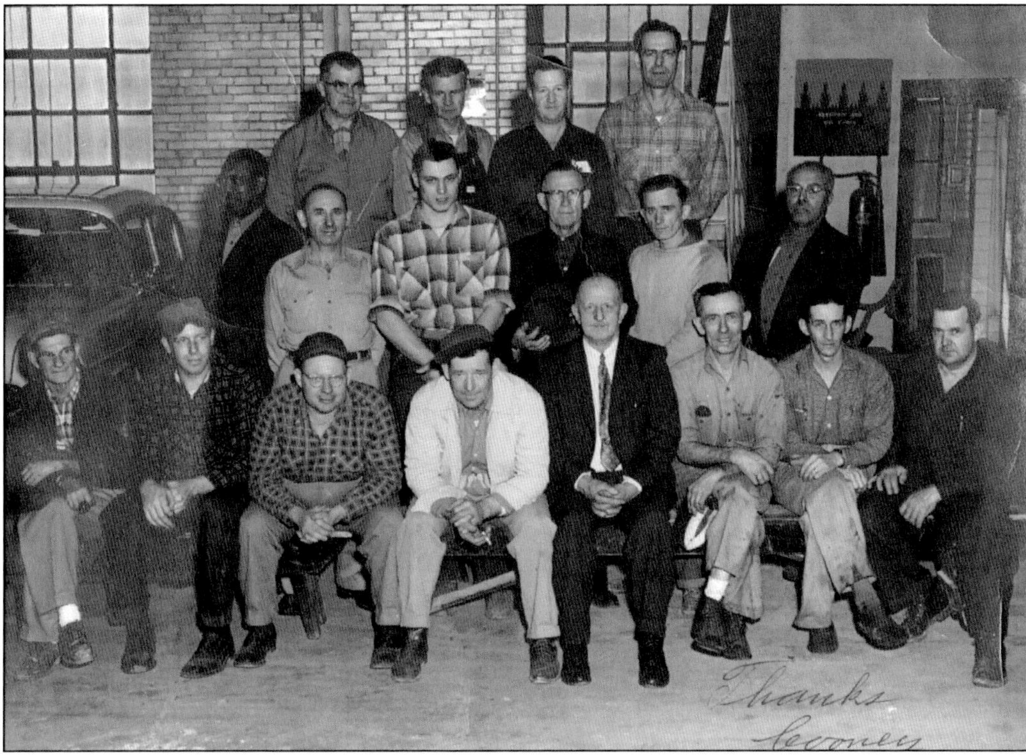

Seen above are workers at the Aluminum Ore plant during the 1950s. The plant site actually contained multiple operations—the refinery for ore and a manufacturing plant for aluminum cooking utensils. (SIUE)

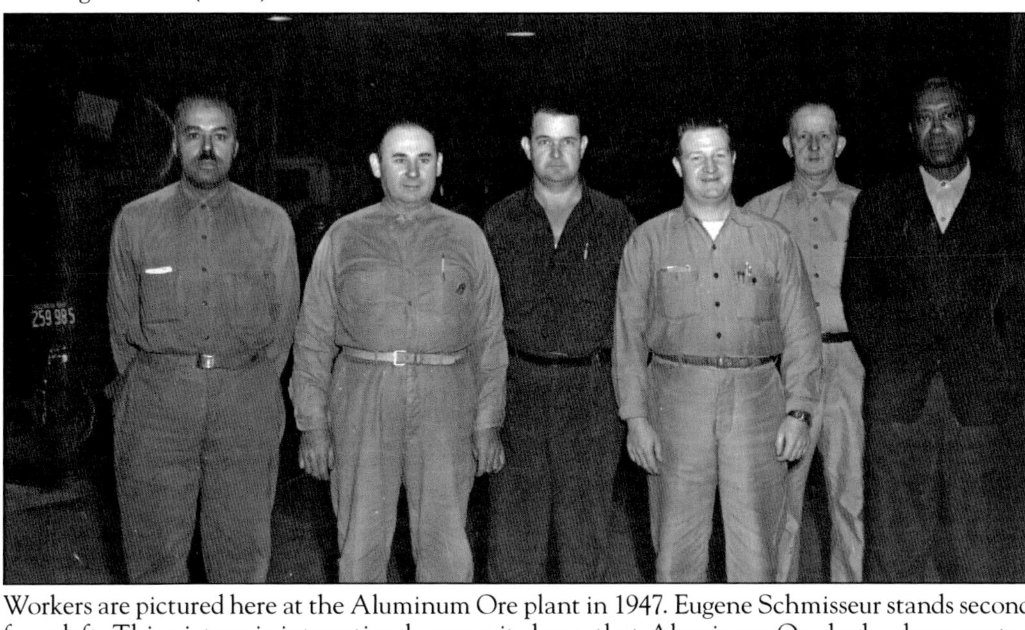

Workers are pictured here at the Aluminum Ore plant in 1947. Eugene Schmisseur stands second from left. This picture is interesting because it shows that Aluminum Ore had a desegregated workforce by this time. It was labor disputes at the Aluminum Ore Company that sparked the riot of 1917. (SIUE)

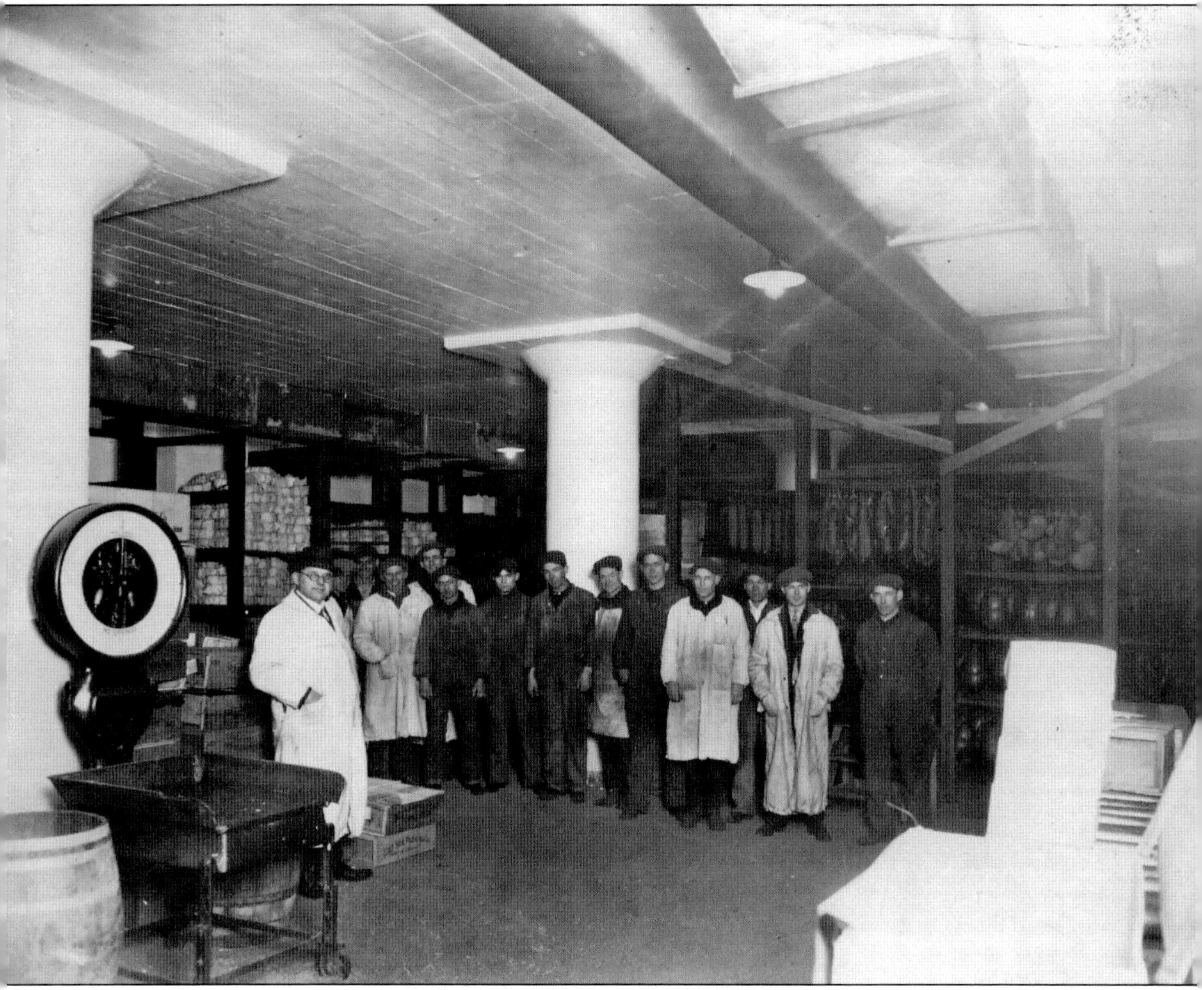

Above is a scene from the East Side Packing Company at 1250 Second Street. Note the ample supply of sausages, hams, and other meats on the shelves. Meat packing was the first major industry in East St. Louis, with the opening of the National Stock Yards in 1873. There were many secondary operators, such as East Side, that moved these products into people's homes. (SIUE)

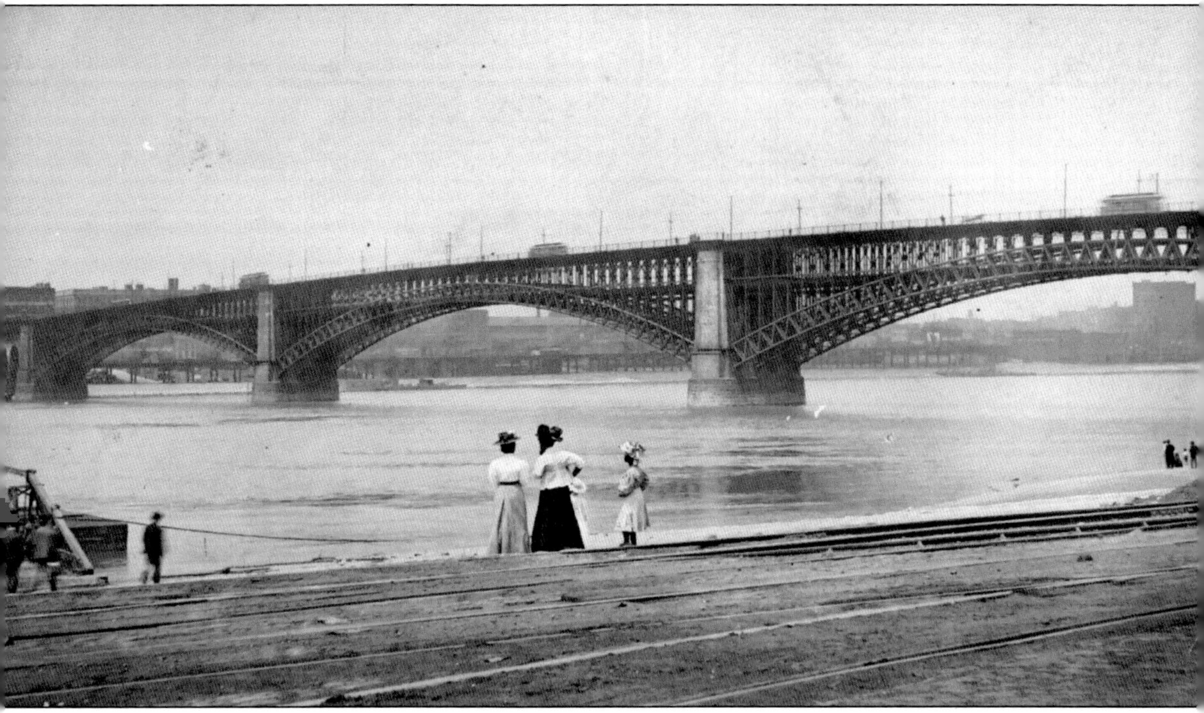

The historic Eads Bridge was completed in 1874. It was the first pedestrian/rail bridge to span the mighty Mississippi River. An engineering marvel, the bridge, designed by James B. Eads, was hailed as the Eighth Wonder of the Modern World. It became the first bridge depicted on a US postage stamp as a result of the 1898 Trans-Mississippi issue. Fourteen men died from the bends, also known as decompression sickness, while working on the piers in caissons at the bottom of the river. (SIUE)

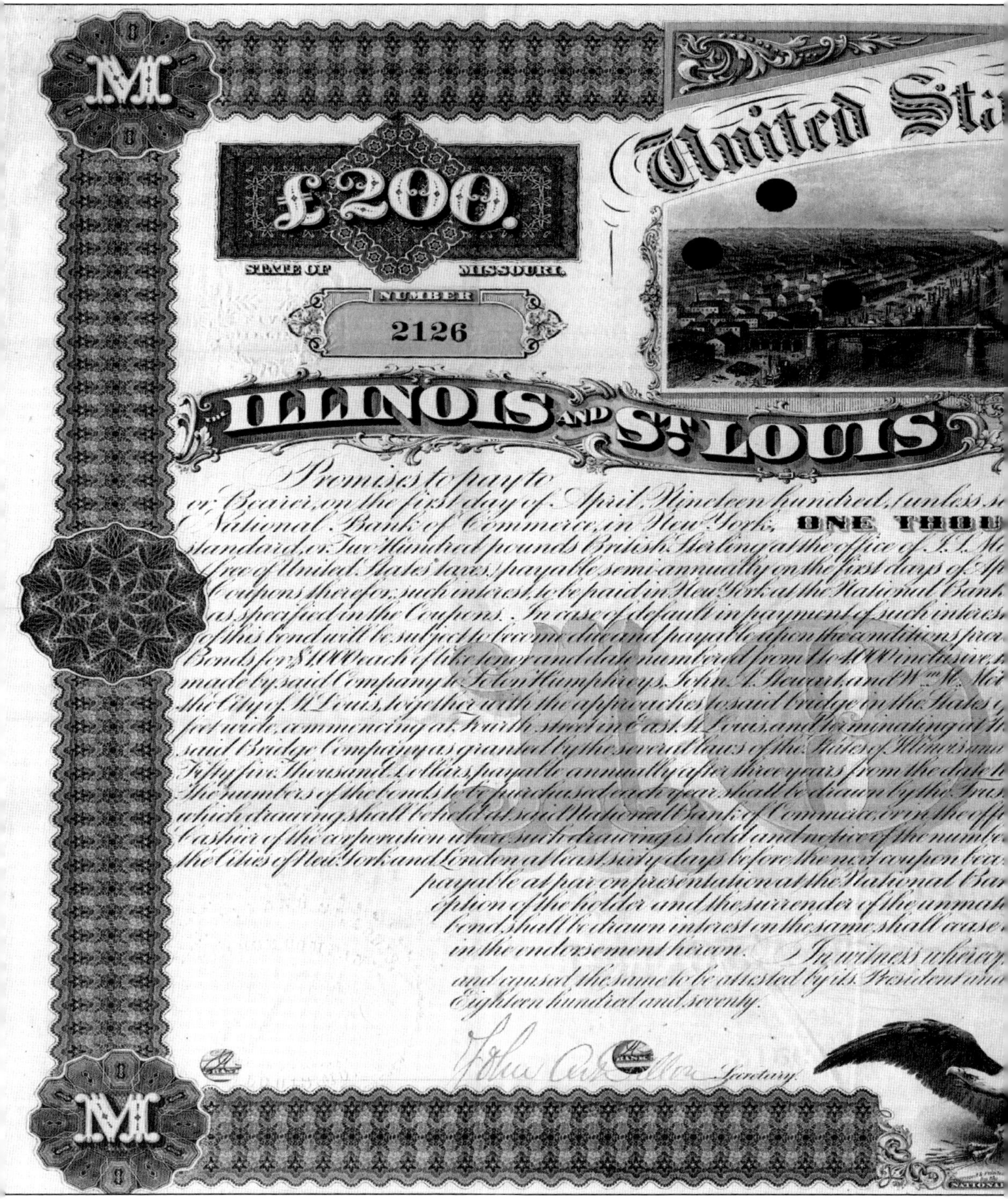

The company that actually built what is now the Eads Bridge was the Illinois and St. Louis Bridge Company. This bond, issued in both US dollars and British pounds, funded the construction. In the 19th century, private companies (particularly railroads) built most bridges. The owners of the new bridge defaulted on its bonds just over a year after the bridge's opening. It was auctioned and sold to

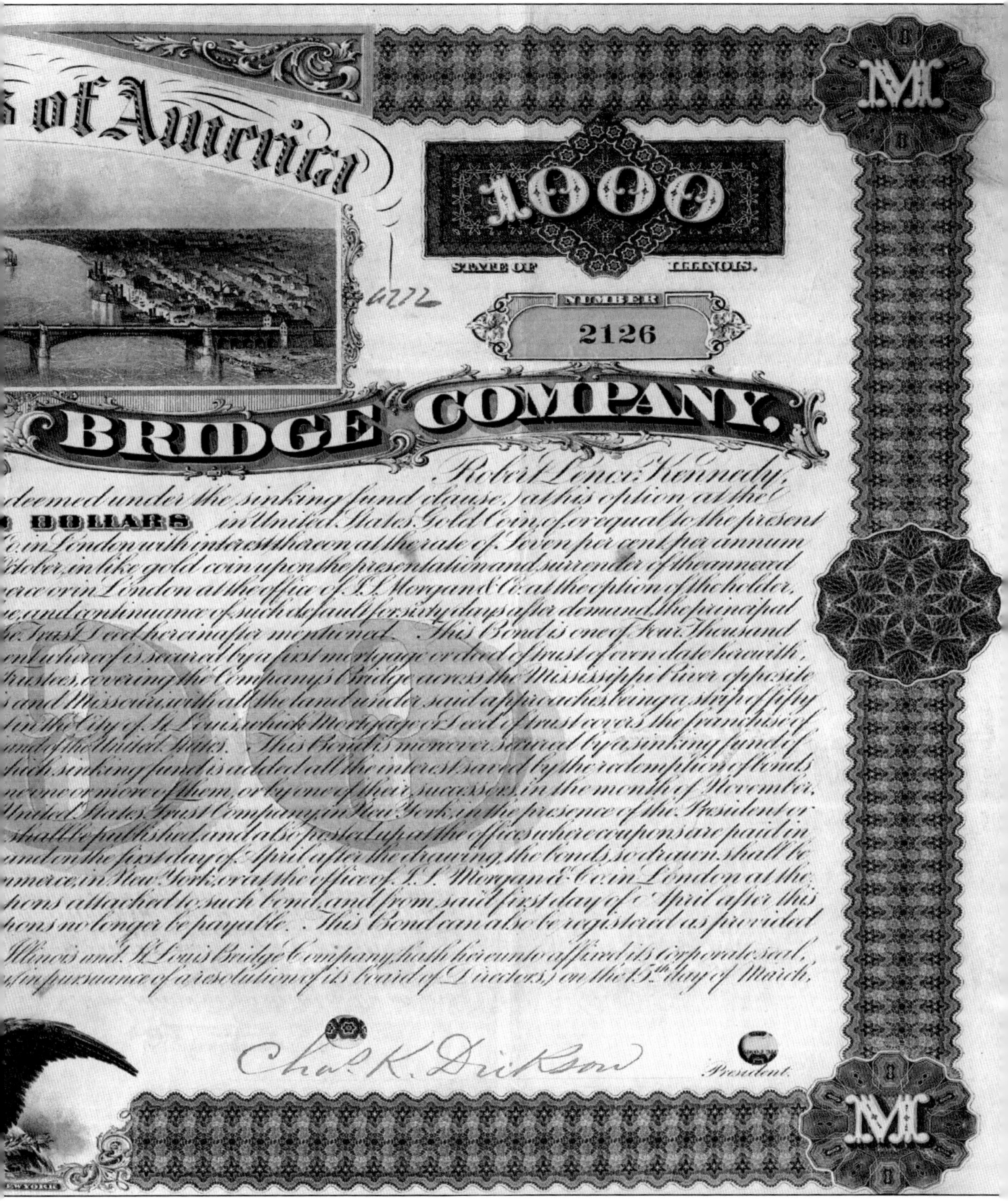

financier J.P. Morgan in 1875, who soon sold it again to railroad baron Jay Gould. After Gould's death, his railroad interests formed a new corporation here called the Terminal Railroad Association, which owned the bridge into the 1980s. (SIUE)

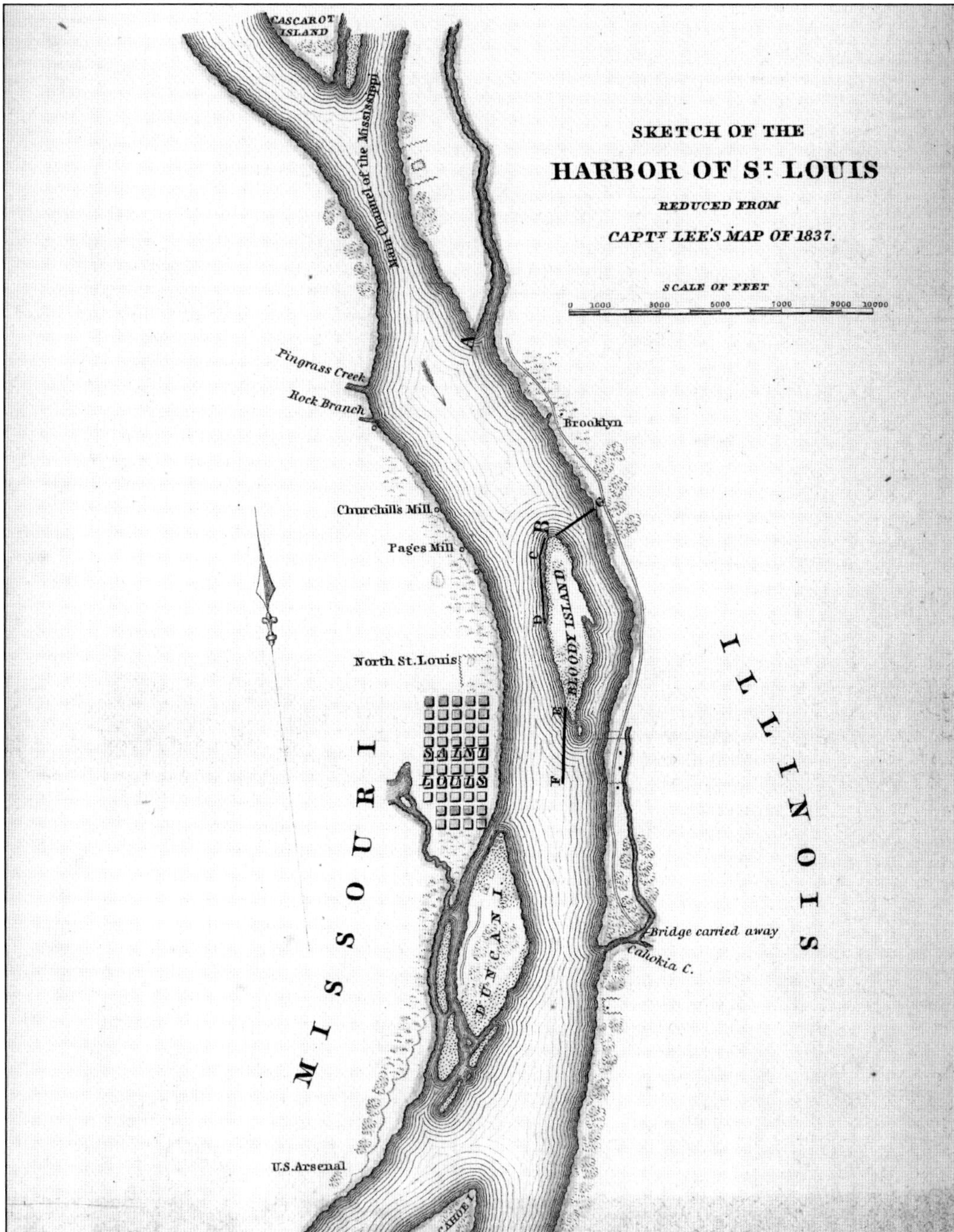

Bloody Island is featured prominently on this 1843 map. Future US senator from Missouri Thomas Hart Benton killed an opponent in a duel there in 1817, giving the place its famous moniker. As a lieutenant in the Army Corps of Engineers, Robert E. Lee was tasked with attaching the island to the East St. Louis shore in order to make the river channel deeper on the St. Louis side. The attached piece of land was subsequently home to many illicit activities and still retained the nickname "the island" even after it was part of the shoreline. Lee was promoted to captain for his success. (BN and SIUE.)

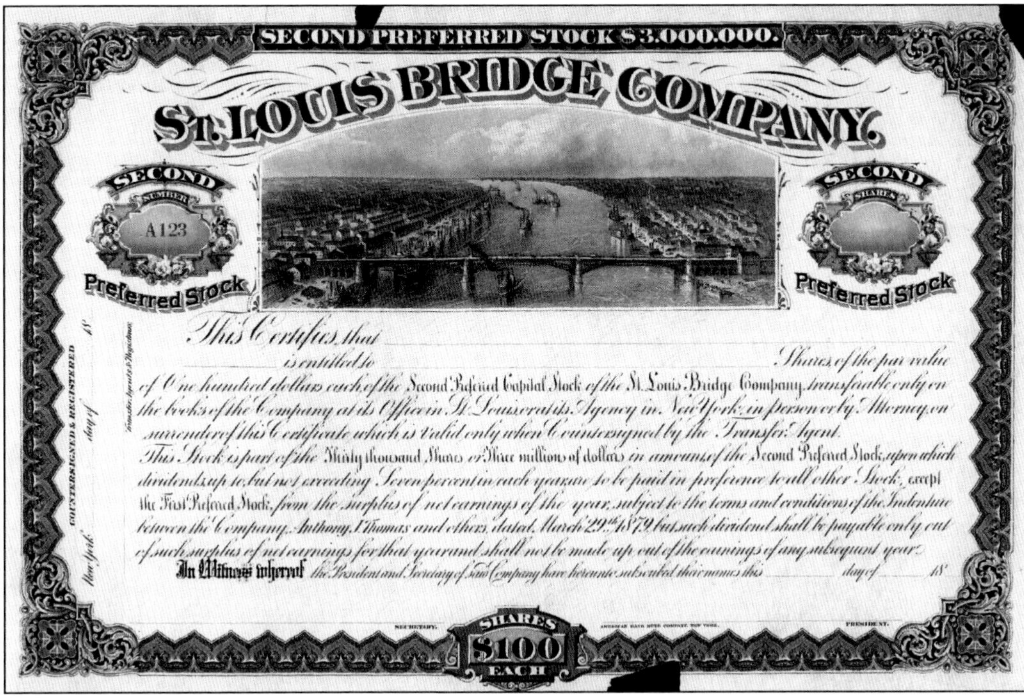

The Illinois and St. Louis Bridge Company defaulted on its loans just a year after opening the bridge. J.P. Morgan bought the bridge from bankruptcy and created the company for which this stock was issued, the St. Louis Bridge Company. (SIUE)

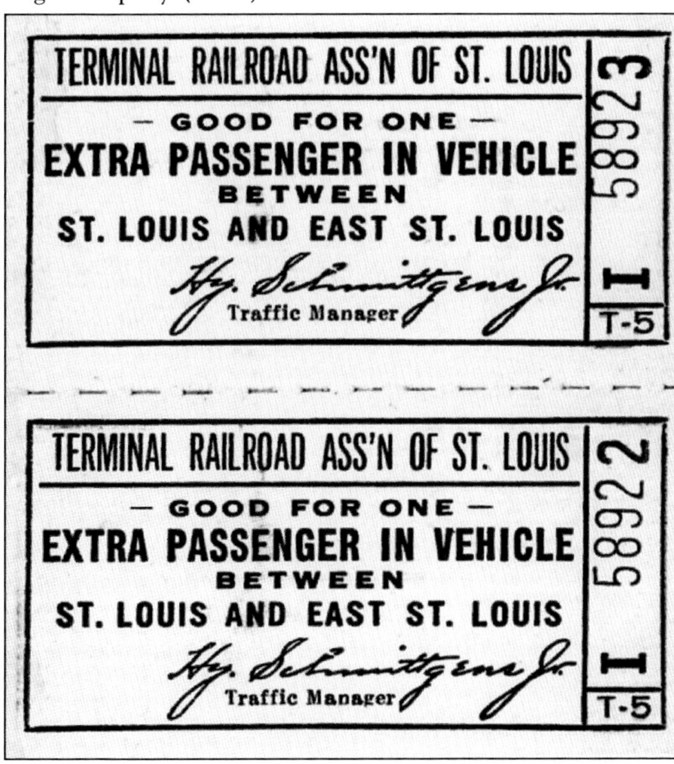

The Eads Bridge was a toll bridge for its first century, with a tollbooth near the St. Louis end on the upper deck. Those who used the bridge frequently bought blocks of tickets like these at a reduced rate. (BN)

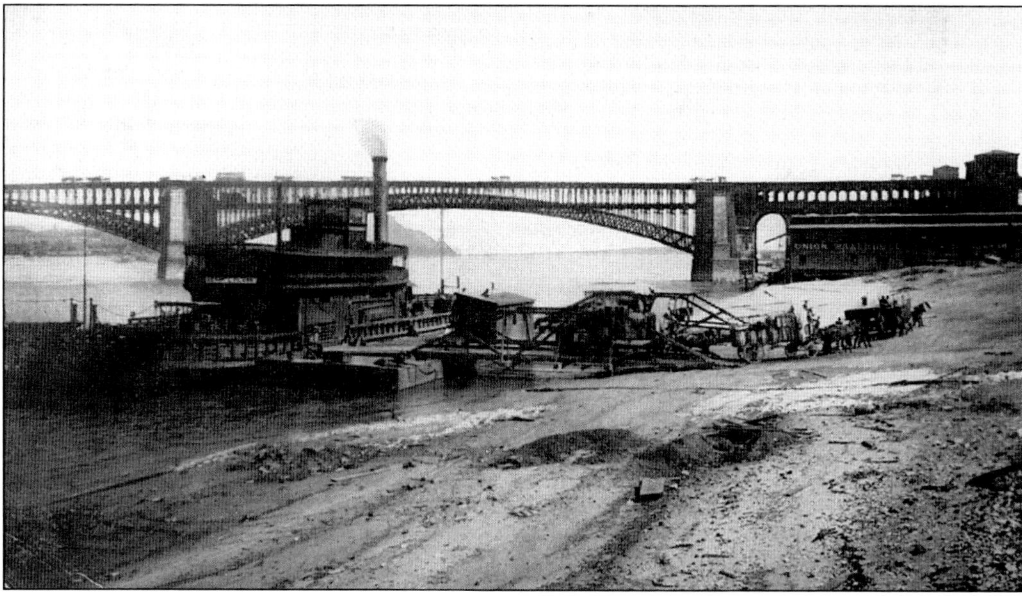

The Wiggins Ferry Company had a monopoly on ferry traffic at East St. Louis for nearly a century. It was the successor company to Piggott's Ferry, which had been created by James Piggott, a Revolutionary War officer and early settler of what is now East St. Louis. Piggott's great-great granddaughter was Hollywood actress Virginia Mayo. (SIUE)

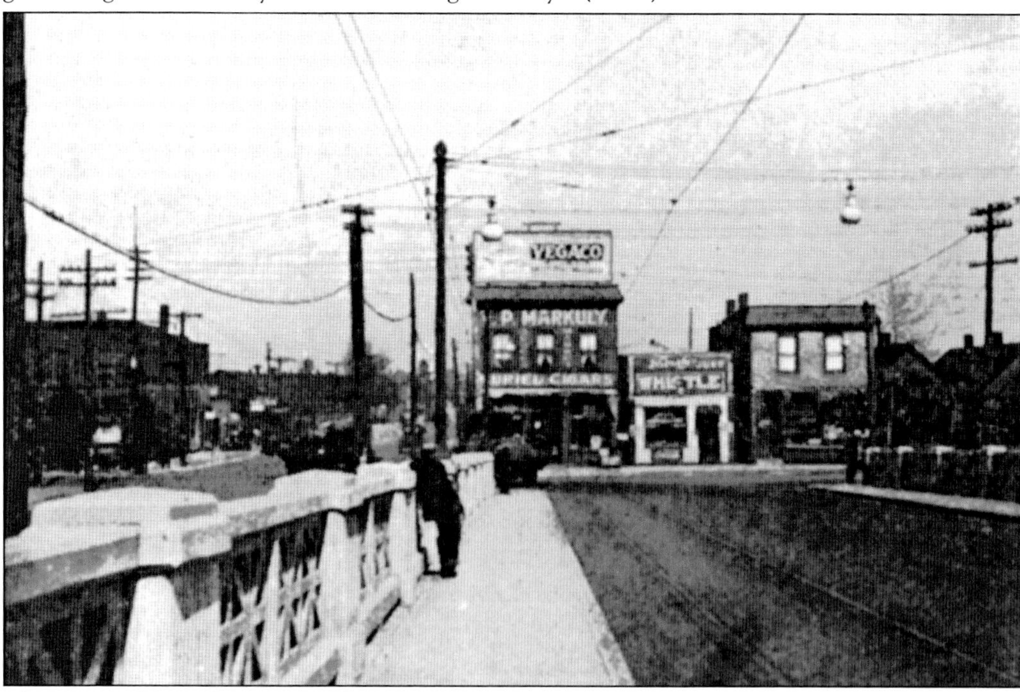

This image shows the Municipal Bridge connection to the South End neighborhood in East St. Louis about 1920. City planner Harland Bartholomew said this approach demonstrated weak land use for a major bridge approach. This was also called the "Free Bridge" because it was built with public money and did not charge a toll like the private bridges did. Today, it bears the name MacArthur Bridge and is owned by the Terminal Railroad Association. (SIUE)

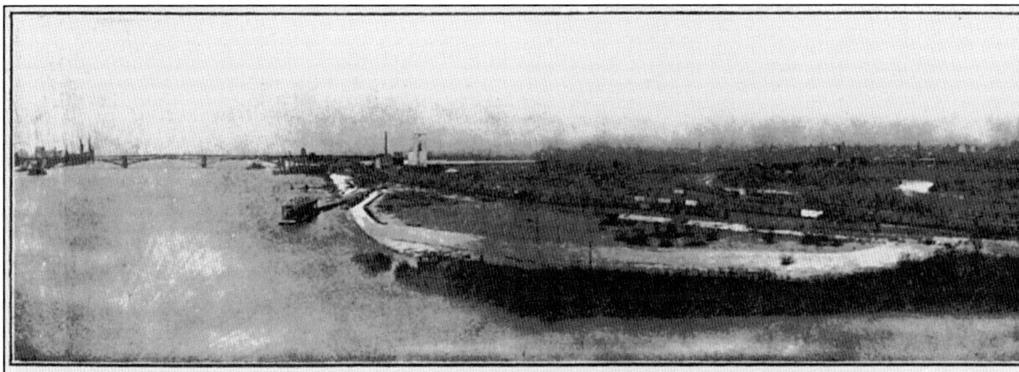

Panorama of the vast railroad properties along the Mississippi River front in East St. Louis. The Eads Bridge, spanning the Mississippi between St. Louis, Missouri, and East St. Louis, Illinois is shown in the background.

This interesting panoramic image was taken from Harland Bartholomew's 1920 city planning report on East St. Louis for the War Civics Committee. He used the picture to demonstrate how the railroads dominate the East St. Louis riverfront. (SIUE)

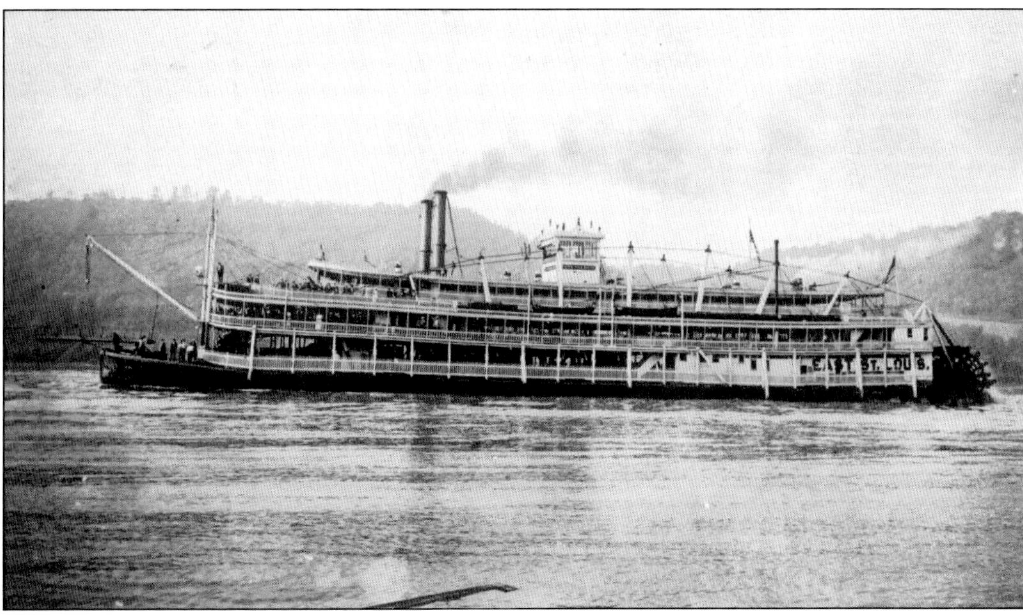

Majestic palace steamboats cruised the Mississippi River for decades, with Mark Twain being the river's most famous pilot. One of those fancy steamers was the *East St. Louis*, shown here about 1920. The boat was built in 1896 as the *Virginia* and went through several names over its years of service. The current riverboat *Natchez* is a replica of the old *East St. Louis*. (SIUE)

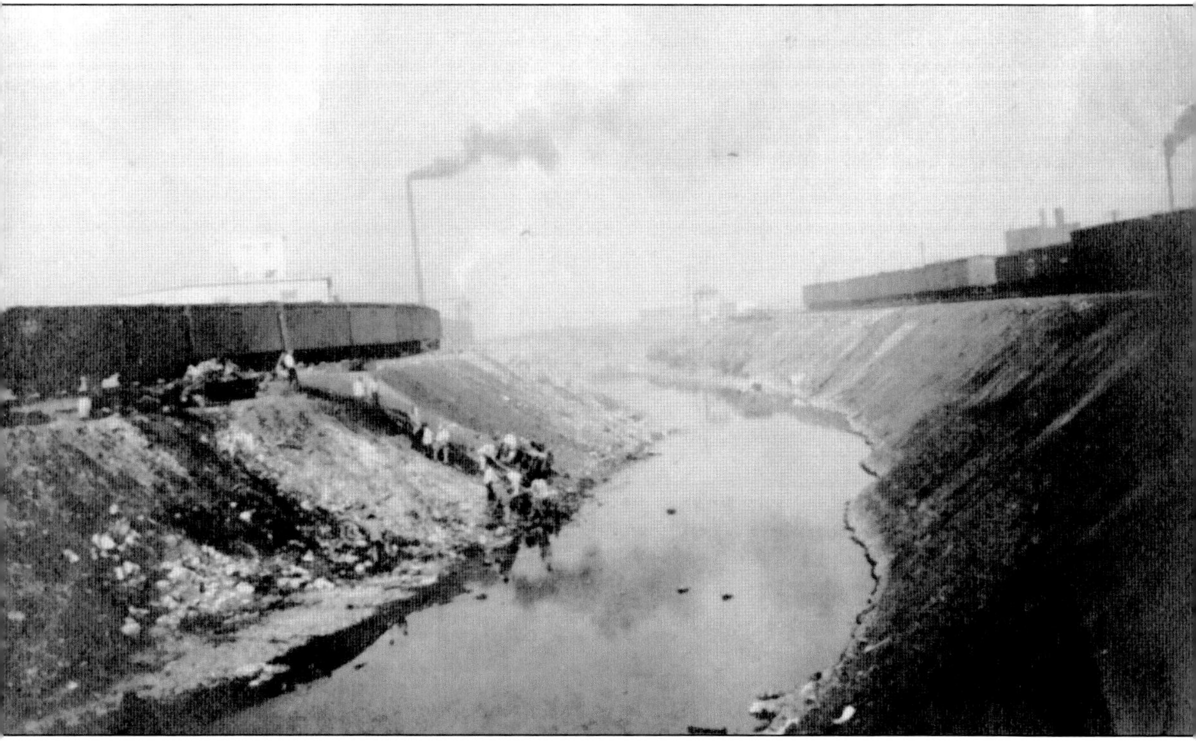

Cahokia Creek had its origins in Litchfield, Illinois, and snaked its way past West Edwardsville before it emptied into the Mississippi at Cahokia. This 1914 photograph shows the creek at East St. Louis lined by railroads and serving as a dumping stream. Note the smokestack belching in the background. The pestiferous creek wound its way near the East St. Louis business district, but during the 1930s, it was rechanneled so that it now empties into the river north of the old stockyards. (SIUE)

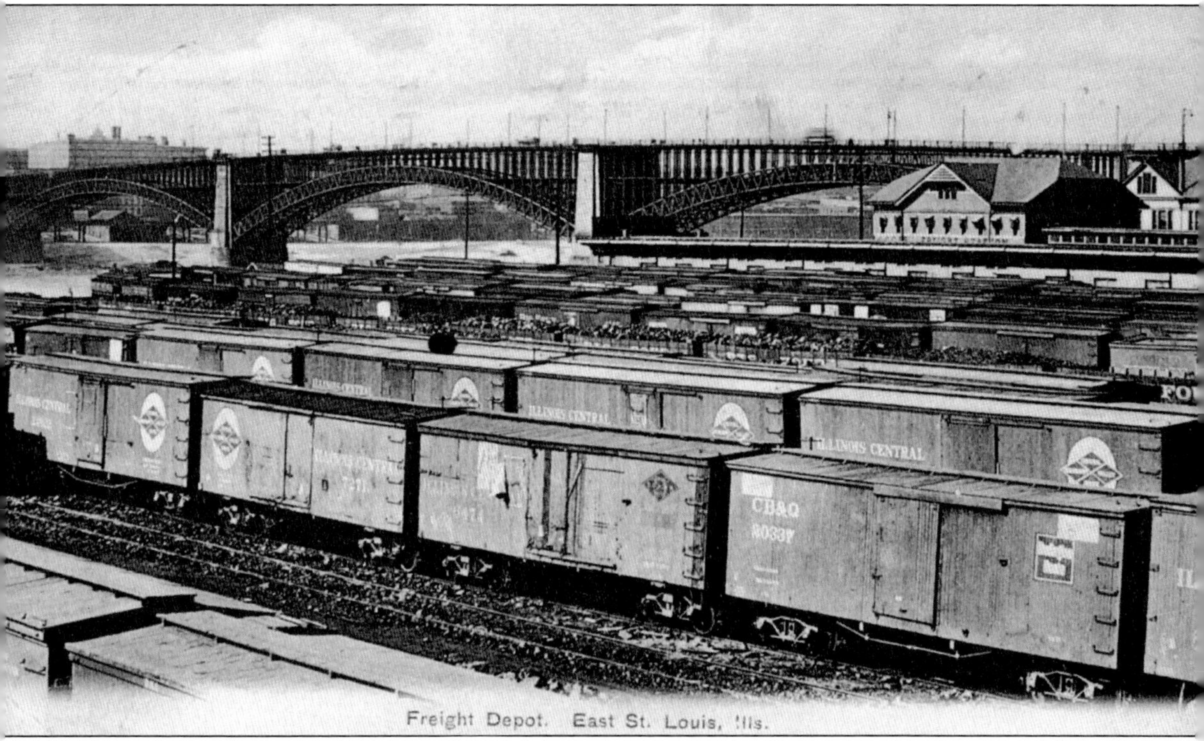

Twenty-seven railroads converged on East St. Louis, and many of them built humping yards, warehouses, offices, roundhouses and repair shops along the riverfront on what was known as the Island area. The site shown is now occupied by the casino. (SIUE)

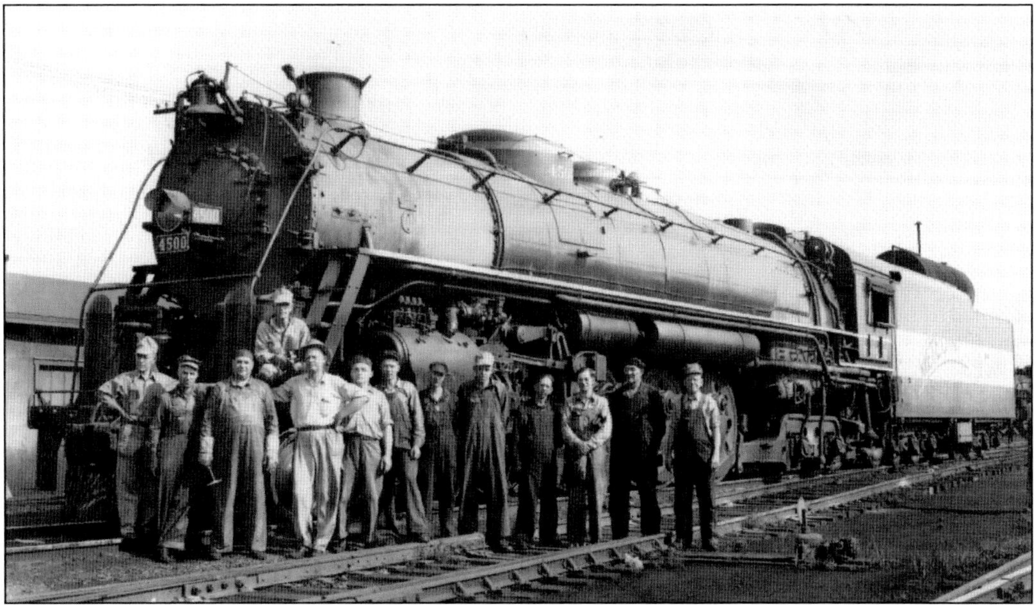

Railroad repair facilities were located throughout East St. Louis and the surrounding area. These men worked for the Frisco Railroad. (SIUE)

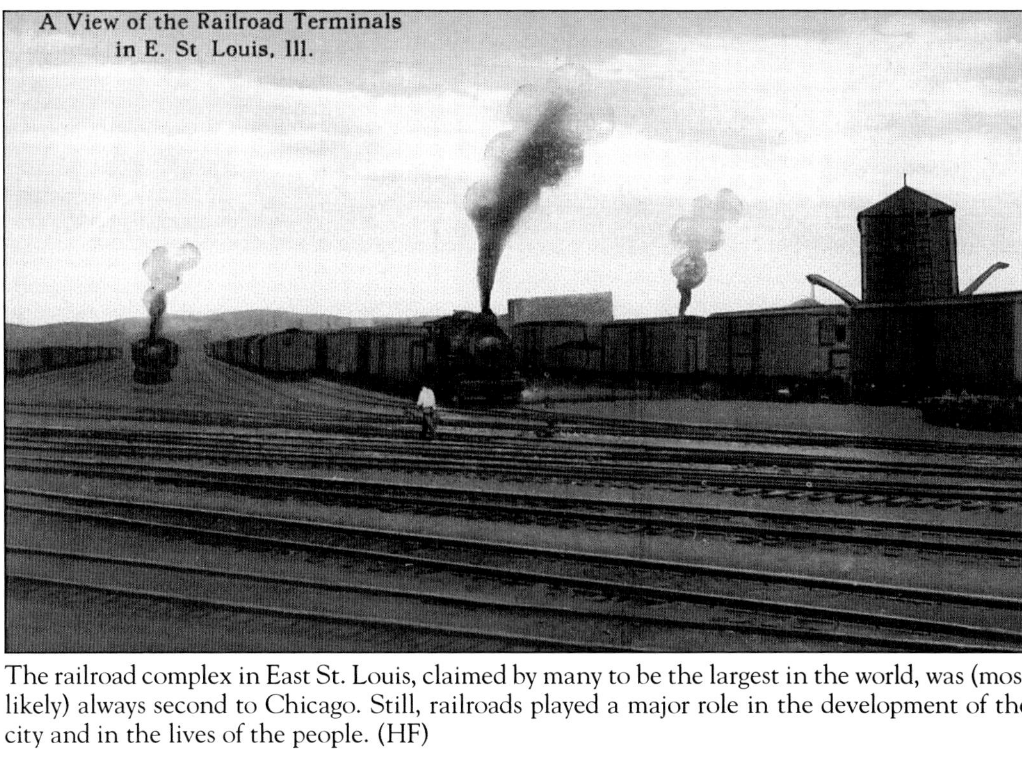

The railroad complex in East St. Louis, claimed by many to be the largest in the world, was (most likely) always second to Chicago. Still, railroads played a major role in the development of the city and in the lives of the people. (HF)

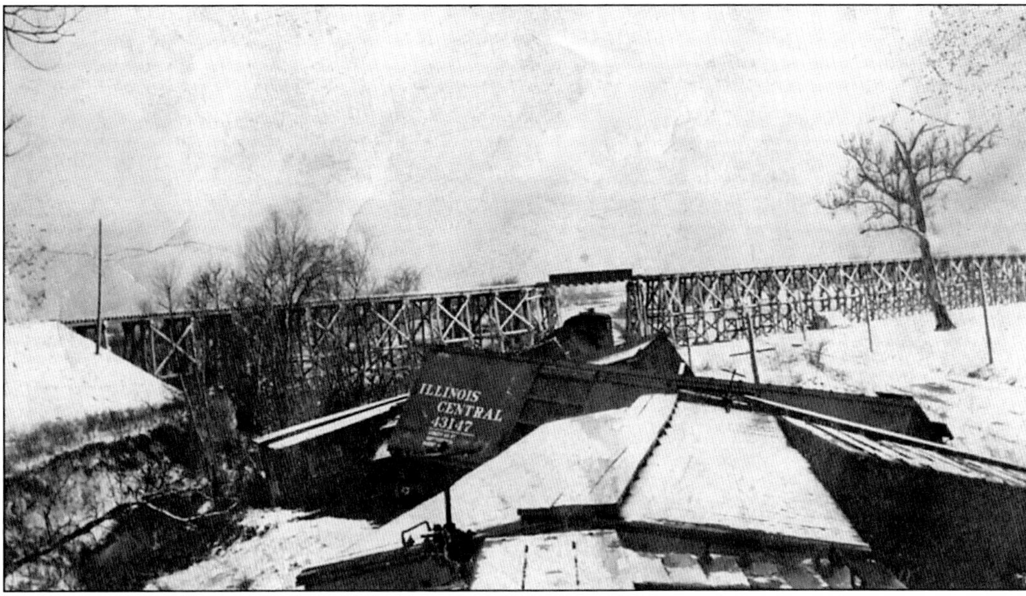

Just as cars have accidents on interstate highways, trains occasionally had mishaps. Here, cars from the Illinois Central crashed in 1917. (SIUE)

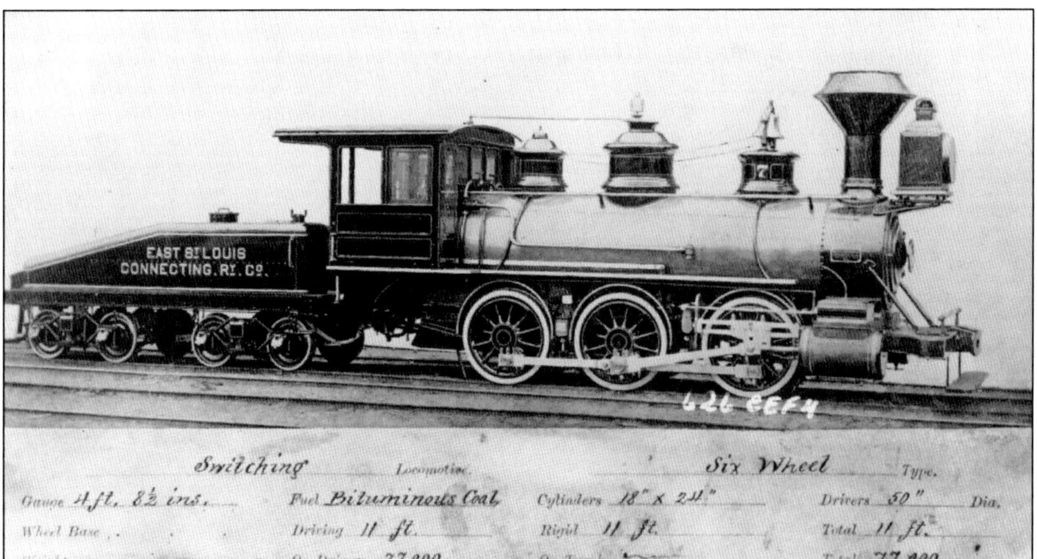

This is a manufacturer's illustration of a new engine built by the Schenectady Locomotive Works in New York for the East St. Louis Connecting Railway. It documents what the engine looks like as well as the specifications to which it was built. (SIUE)

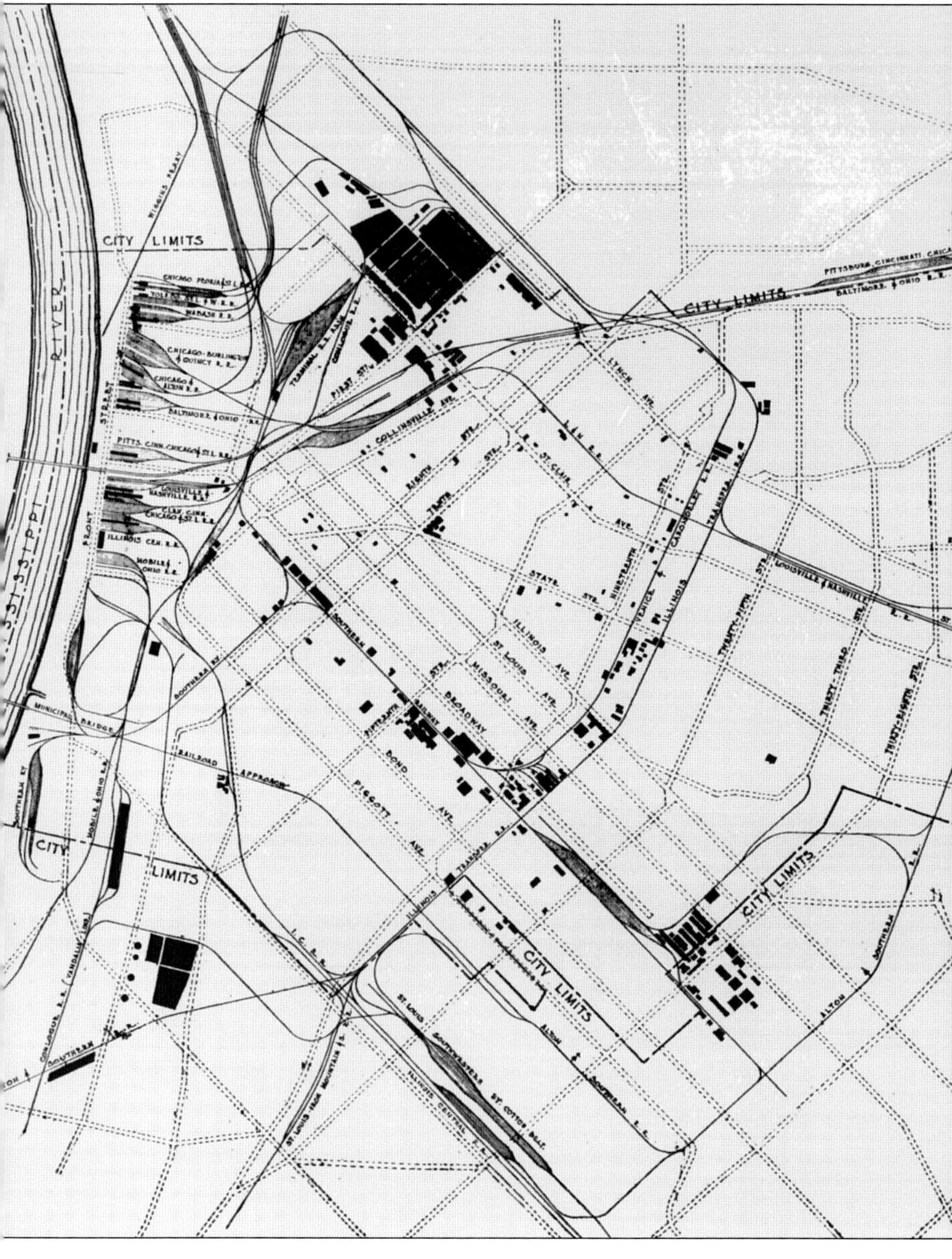
CITY LIMITS
RIVER
FRONT STREET
CHICAGO-BURLINGTON & QUINCY R.R.
CHICAGO & ALTON R.R.
BALTIMORE & OHIO R.R.
WABASH R.R.
LOUISVILLE & NASHVILLE R.R.
ILLINOIS CEN. R.R.
MOBILE & OHIO R.R.
PITTSBURG, CINCINNATI, CHICAGO
BALTIMORE & OHIO R.R.
FIRST STR.
COLLINSVILLE AVE.
LYNCH AVE.
ST. CLAIR AVE.
EIGHTH STR.
TENTH STR.
STATE STR.
NINETEENTH STR.
ILLINOIS AVE.
ST LOUIS AVE.
MISSOURI AVE.
BROADWAY
FIFTEENTH STR.
BOND AVE.
PIGGOTT AVE.
TWENTY-FIFTH STR.
THIRTY-THIRD STR.
THIRTY-EIGHTH STR.
LOUISVILLE & NASHVILLE R.R.
MUNICIPAL BRIDGE
RAILROAD APPROACH
SOUTHERN RY.
I.C.R.R.
ALTON & SOUTHERN R.R.
ST. LOUIS SOUTHWESTERN ST. COTTON BELT
ILLINOIS CENTRAL R.R.

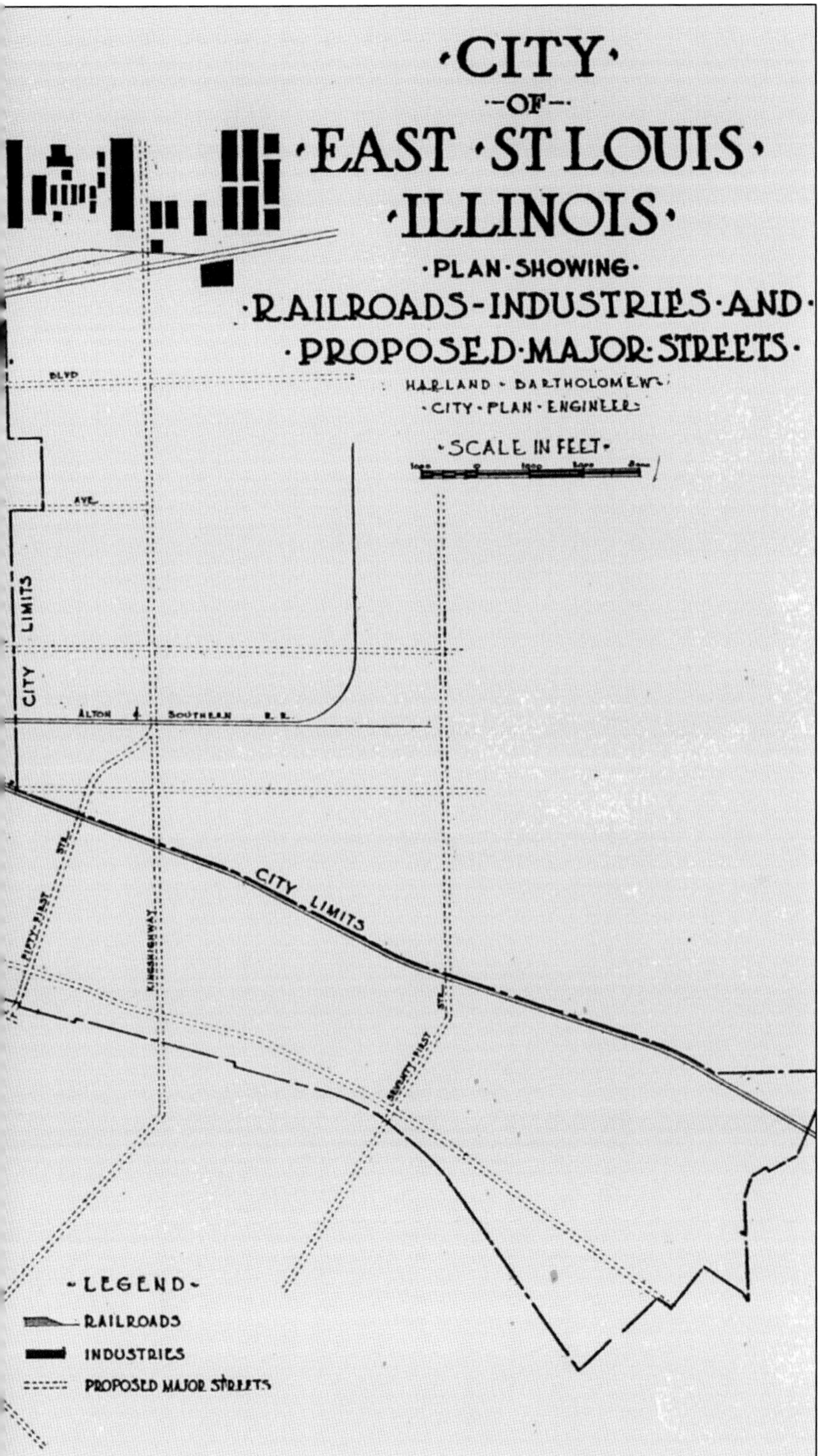

In 1920, Harland Bartholomew drew up this plan showing the existing railroads and the proposed street improvements to go along with them. This plan is striking because it illustrates the vast land holdings of the railroads in East St. Louis—particularly on the riverfront. (SIUE)

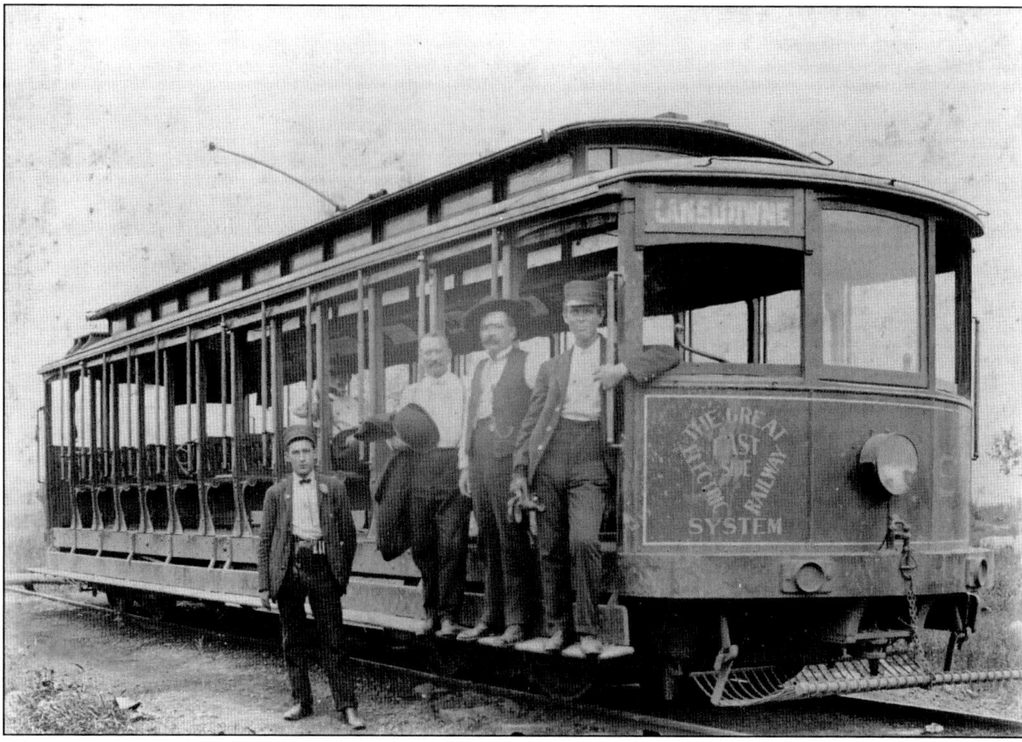

This streetcar of the East Side Electric Railway served the Lansdowne neighborhood. The photograph was taken around 1910. (SIUE)

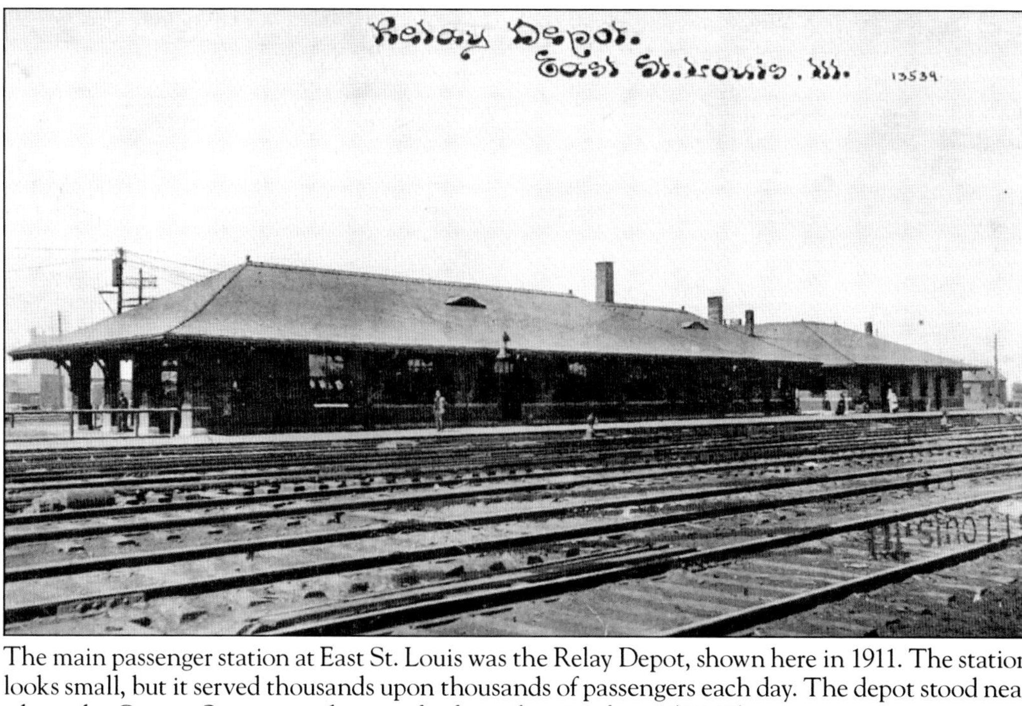

The main passenger station at East St. Louis was the Relay Depot, shown here in 1911. The station looks small, but it served thousands upon thousands of passengers each day. The depot stood near where the Casino Queen is today, not far from the riverfront. (SIUE)

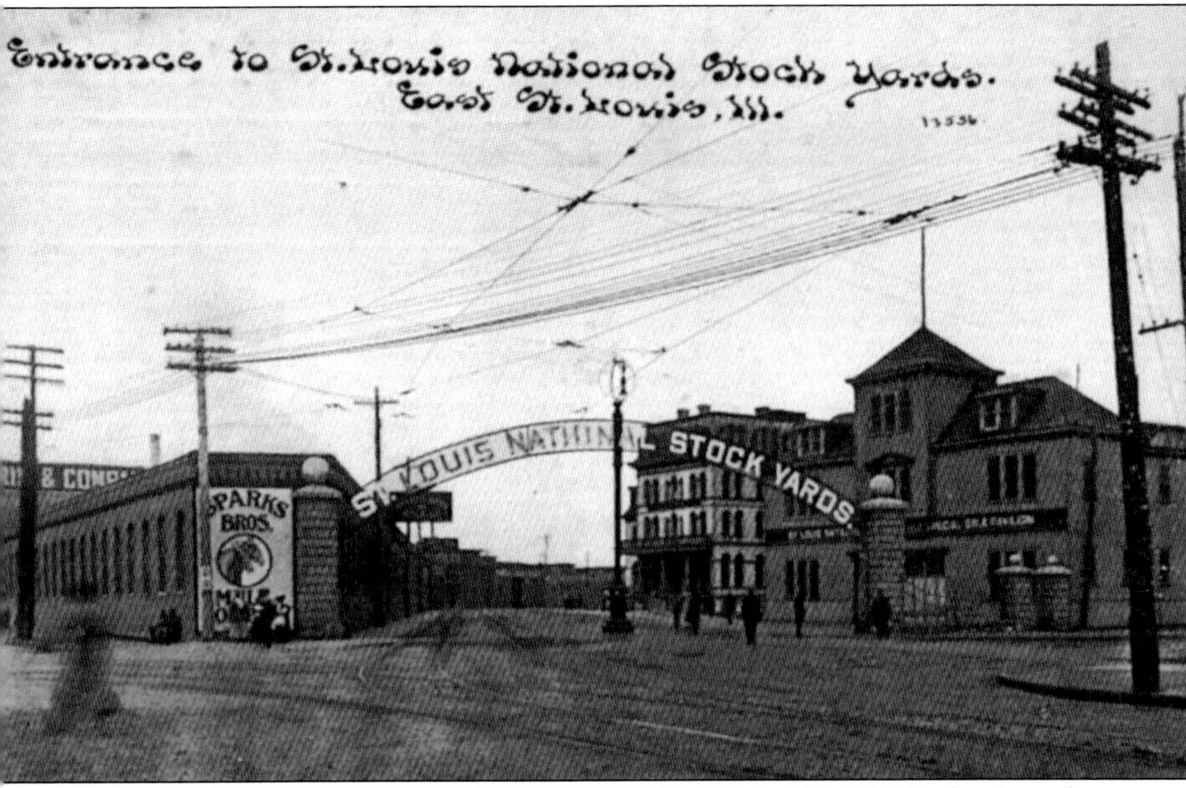

The National Stock Yards opened in 1873, just prior to the opening of the Eads Bridge. It was the first major industrial presence in East St. Louis outside of the railroads. When this photograph was taken in 1911, the entrance featured this grand gate. (SIUE)

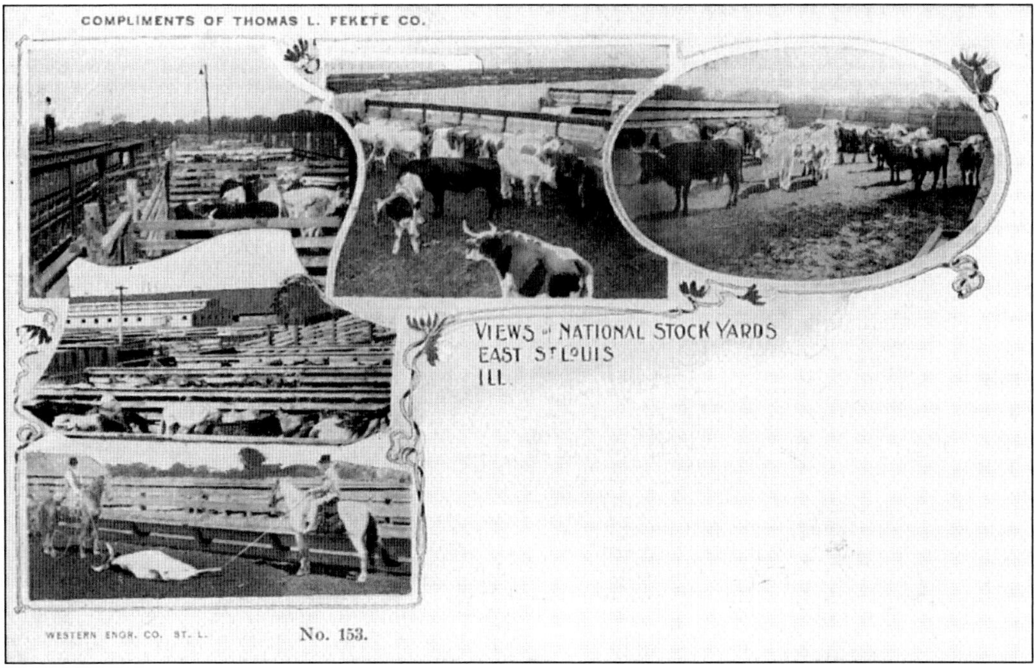

This private mailing card from around 1900 shows cowboys roping a bull in the lower left. The National Stock Yards was as close to a cowboy's lifestyle as one could find in East St. Louis. (SIUE)

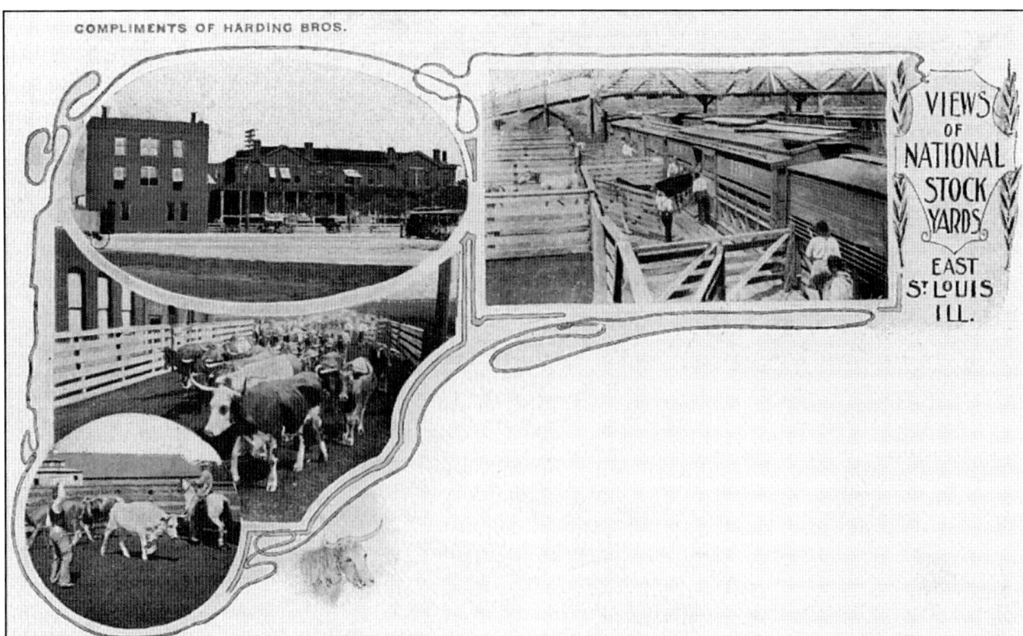

This private mailing card from about 1900 shows images of the National Stock Yards. This particular card has the unusual image of horses being unloaded from train cars in the upper right. (SIUE)

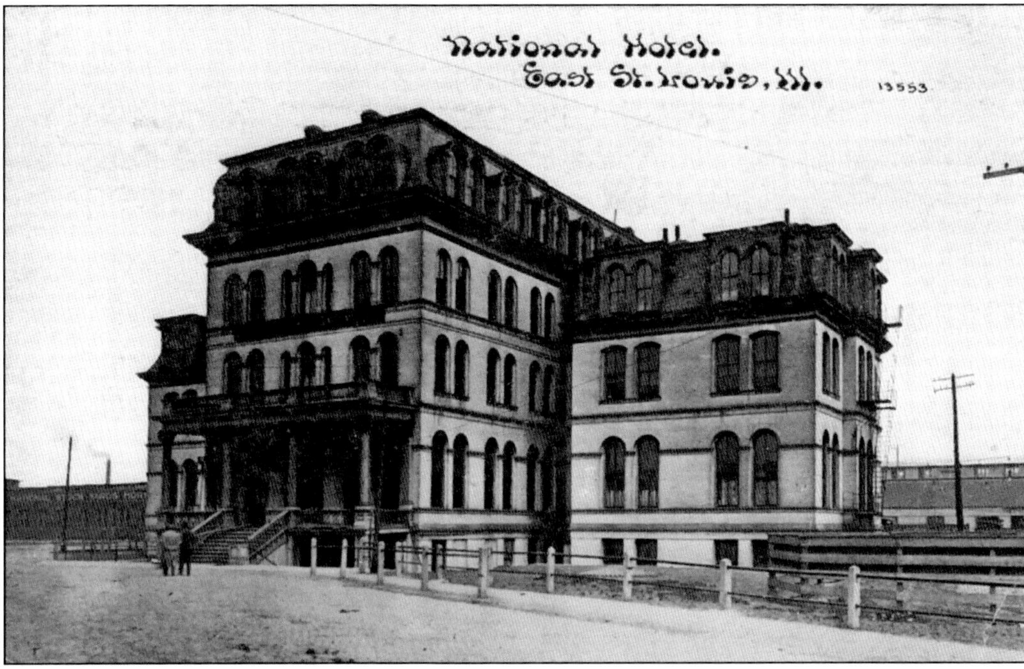

This 1911 photograph, taken from just inside the entrance gate, shows the National Hotel. As a condition of opening, the stockyards had to operate a first-class hotel. Supposedly, this hotel could rival any in Downtown St. Louis. It opened originally as Allerton House in 1873. (SIUE)

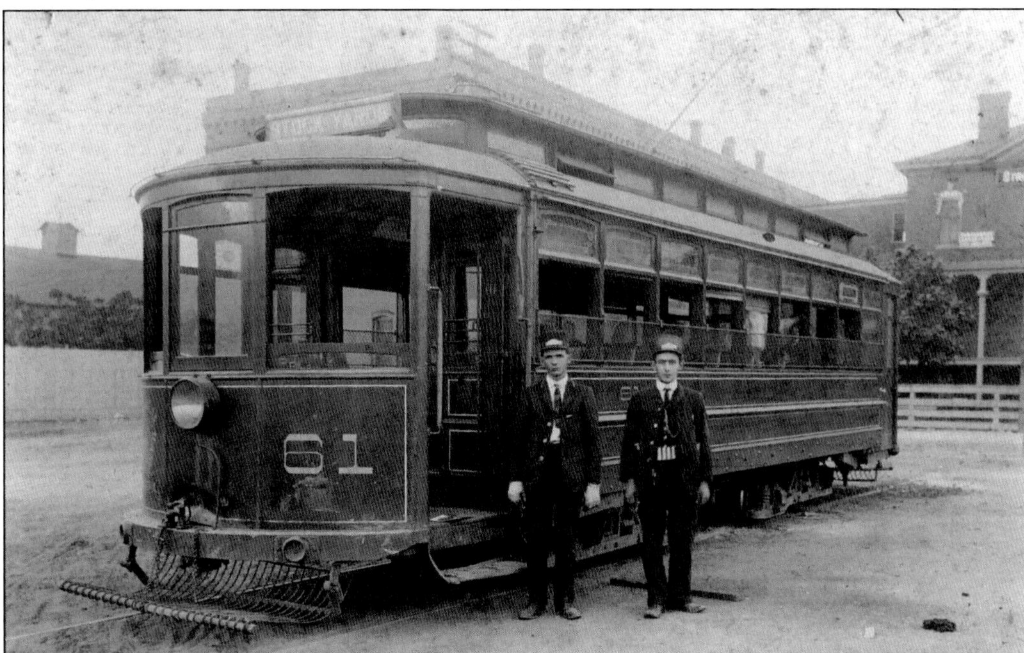

This streetcar served the National Stock Yards and made its turnaround at the Exchange Building. The old Exchange Building, barely seen in the background at right, is one of the few historic structures left at the National Stock Yards site. (SIUE)

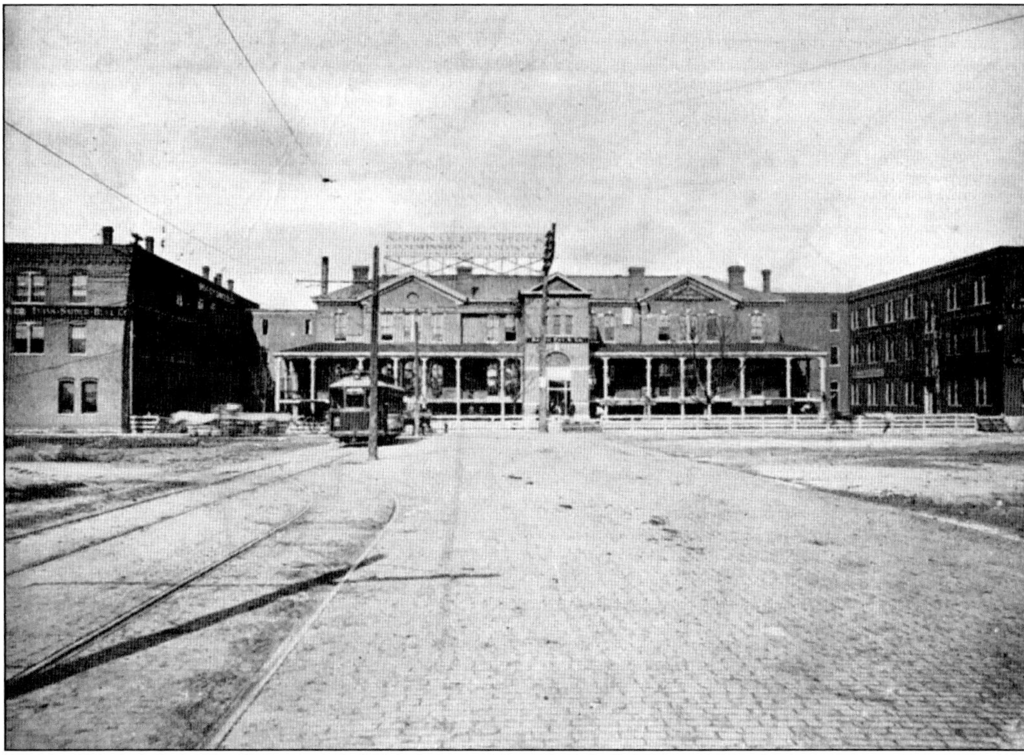

The Exchange Building at the stockyards was where the commission offices were located. Dozens of firms helped facilitate the sale of animals to the packinghouses and other buyers. (SIUE)

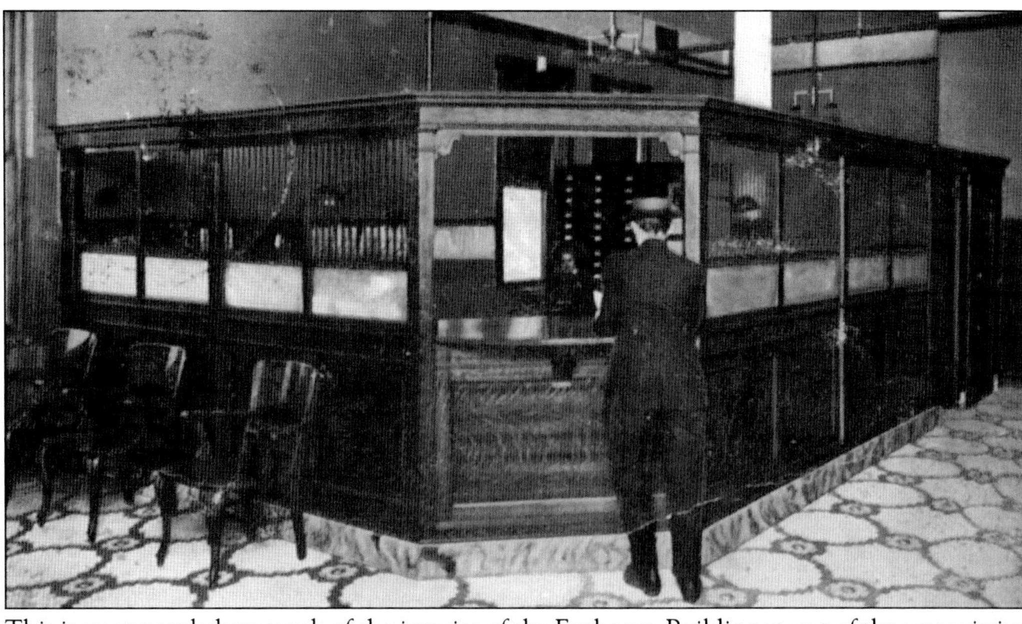

This is an unusual photograph of the interior of the Exchange Building at one of the commission offices. Not only did the stockyards require physical laborers for the plants, but also many administrative workers to process the paperwork associated with the animals. (BN)

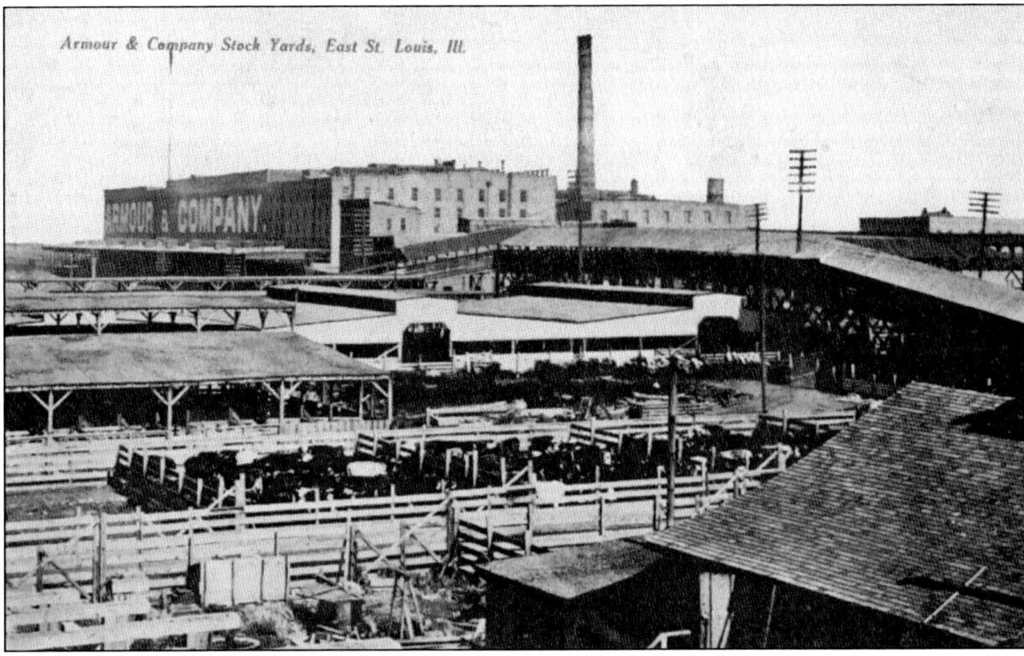

The Armour and Company plant, established in 1903, was located at the National Stock Yards. Other packing companies located there included Meyer (which evolved into Hunter), Swift, Crescent, Morris, Krey, Mayrose, East Side Packing, Royal, and Circle. (SIUE)

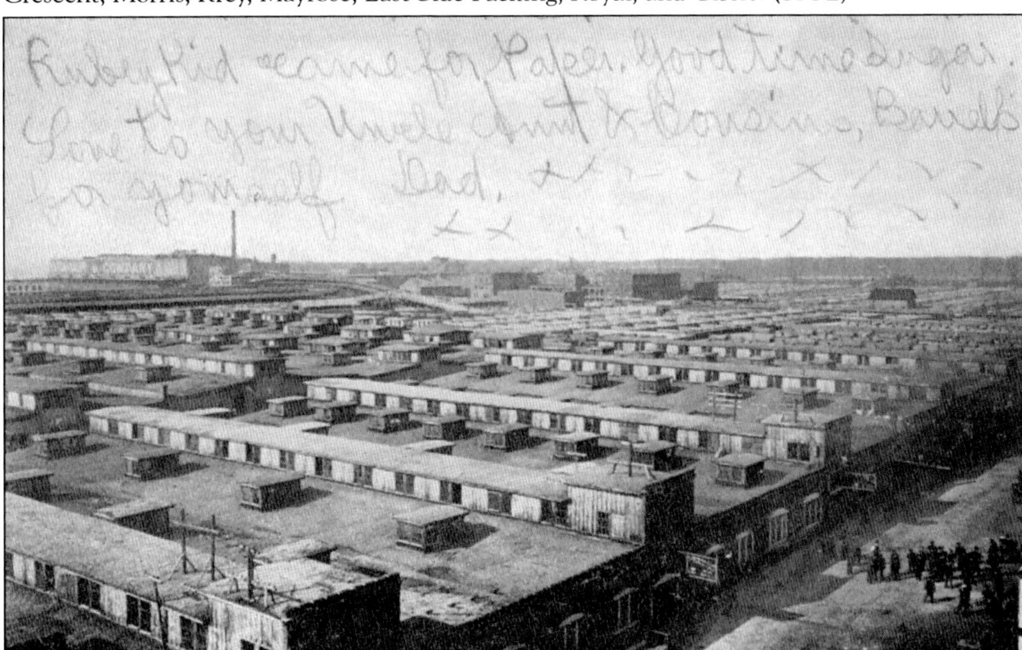

This image shows the extensive covered pens that made up the 600-acre site. The Armour plant is visible in the background. When the stockyards opened, 60 acres were covered with sheds and another 100 acres were covered with open pens. All of this construction has disappeared over the years. (SIUE)

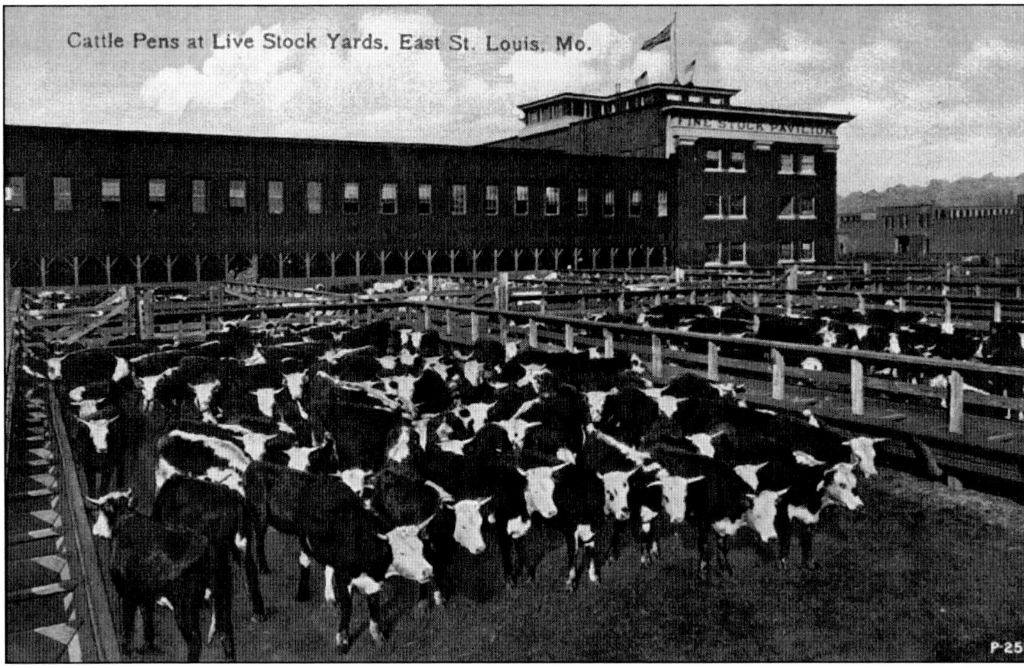

A herd of cattle await auction at the stockyards. By 1900, the National Stock Yards generated over $2 million annually. The stockyards had a planned capacity of 15,000 cattle, 10,000 sheep, and 20,000 hogs at one time. (SIUE)

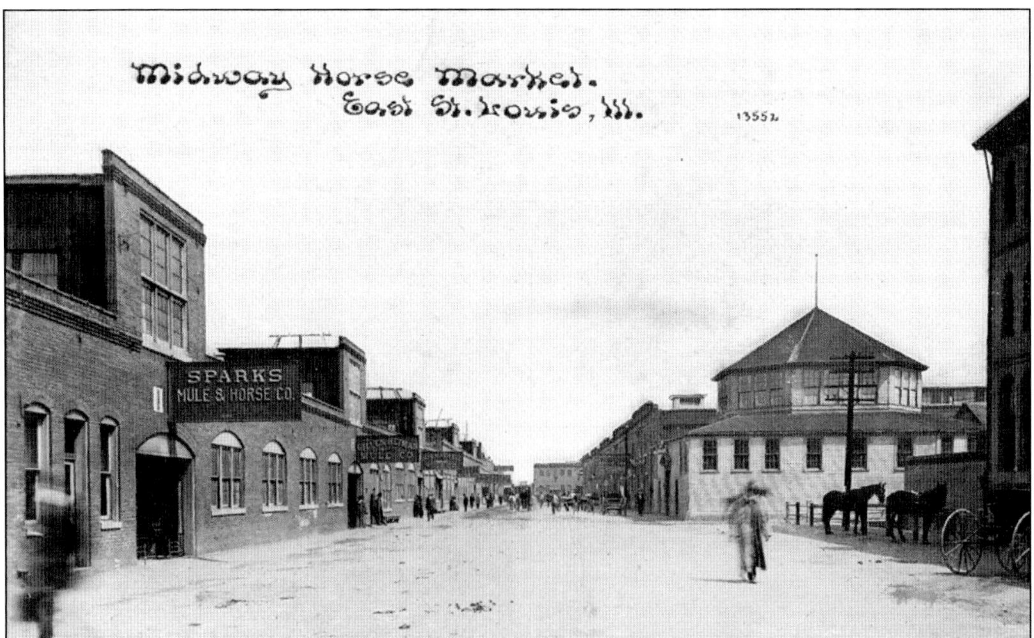

The Horse and Mule Market at the National Stock Yards was the largest in the world, larger even than Chicago's Union Stock Yards. The National Stock Yards represented about $1.5 million in construction when it was built. (SIUE)

Pens of horses await auction with the Armour plant in the background. Note that the pens have flat rails at the top. Other photographs show workers walking on top of these rails as they evaluated the animals. (SIUE)

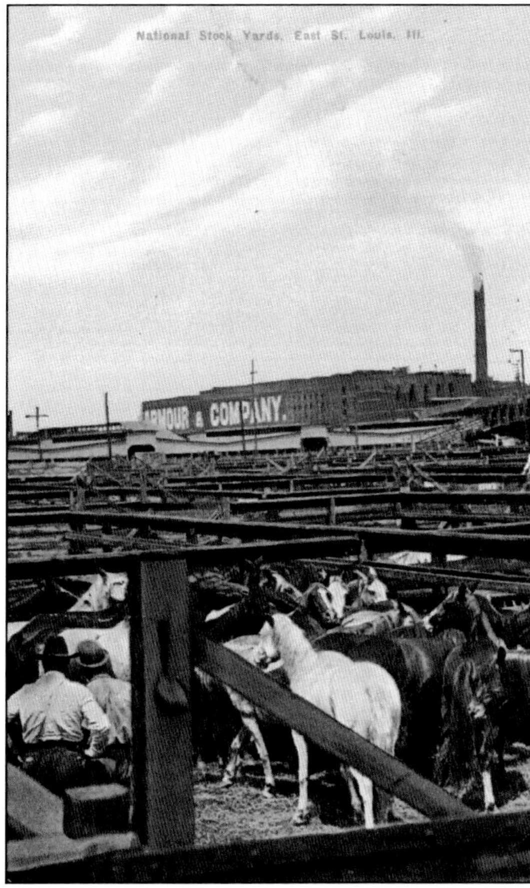

One of the reasons the Horse and Mule Market was so large is seen here. The US Army bought many of its horses and mules from the National Stock Yards. In the early 1900s, there was considerable military demand for animals. (SIUE)

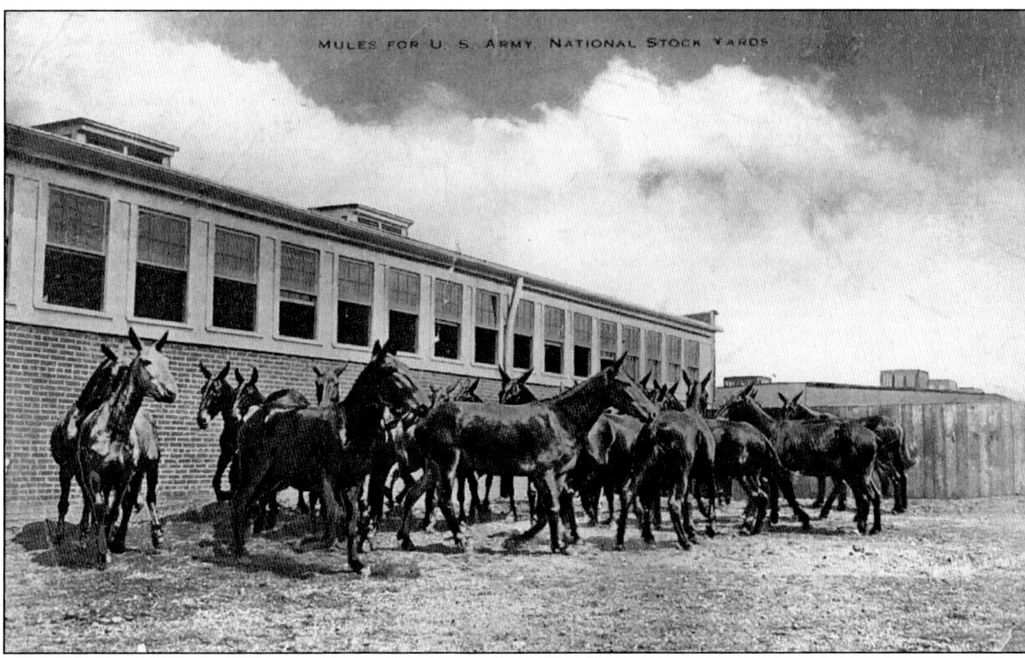

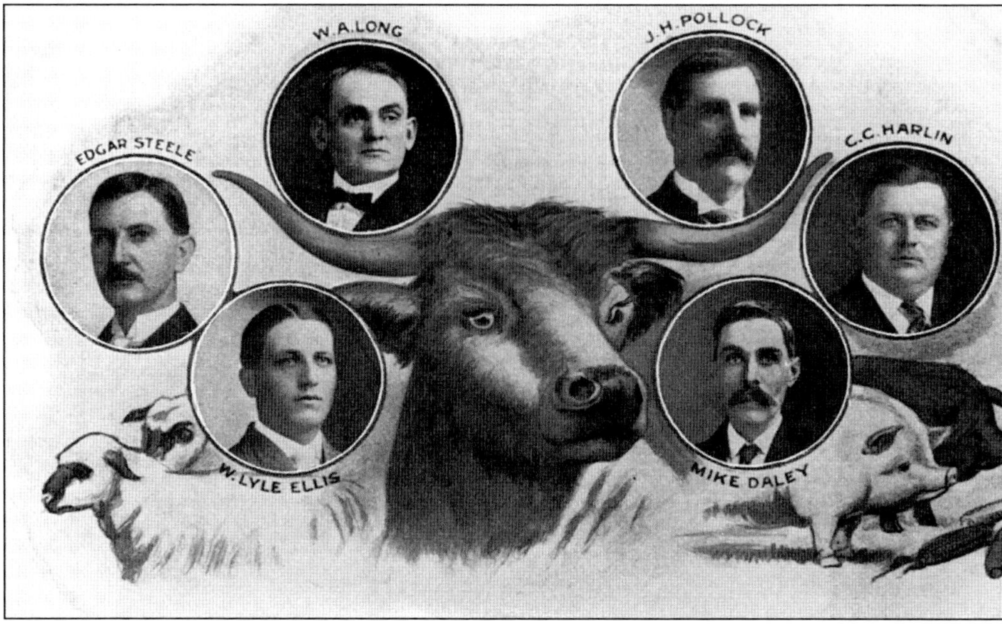

Seen above are commission agents for the Steele-Long-Pollock Company. They specialized in cattle, hogs, and sheep. Many commission firms operated out of the National Stock Yards. These were the agents who facilitated the sale of livestock from farmers to the packing houses. (SIUE)

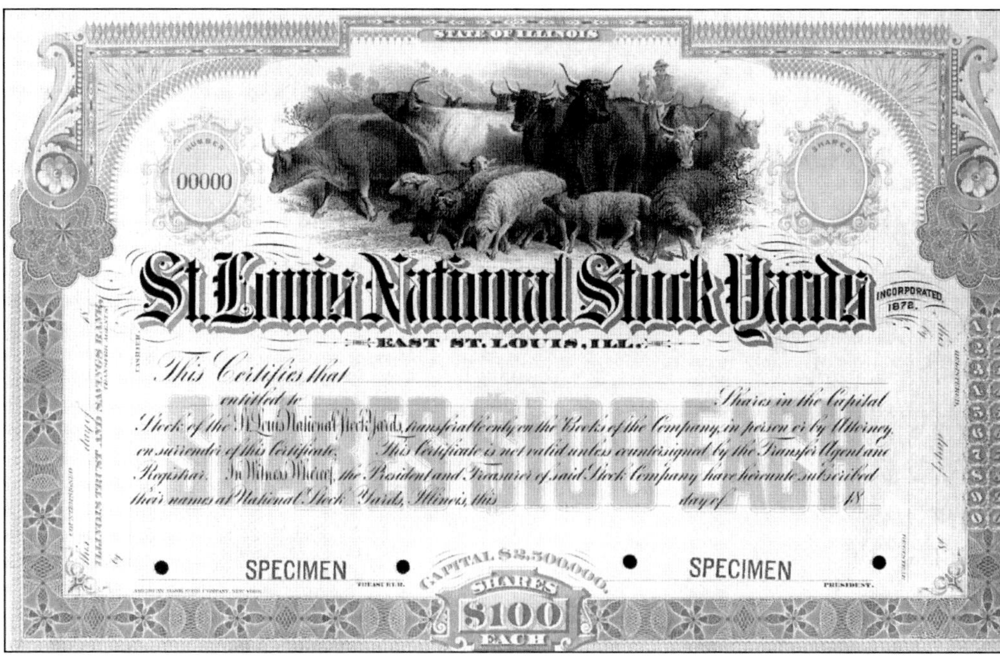

Seen here is a specimen stock certificate for the National Stock Yards. Cornelius Vanderbilt and his heirs were among the major investors. Other officers of the National Stock Yards included Wabash Railroad president Azariah Boody, Pennsylvania Railroad president I.N. McCullough, and executives from four other east coast railroads. John Bowman, founder of East St. Louis, was an executive of the company. (SIUE)

In this image from 1915 is an unidentified worker. In the early 1900s, the stockyards employed 1,200 workers and processed 50,000 animals each week. (RP)

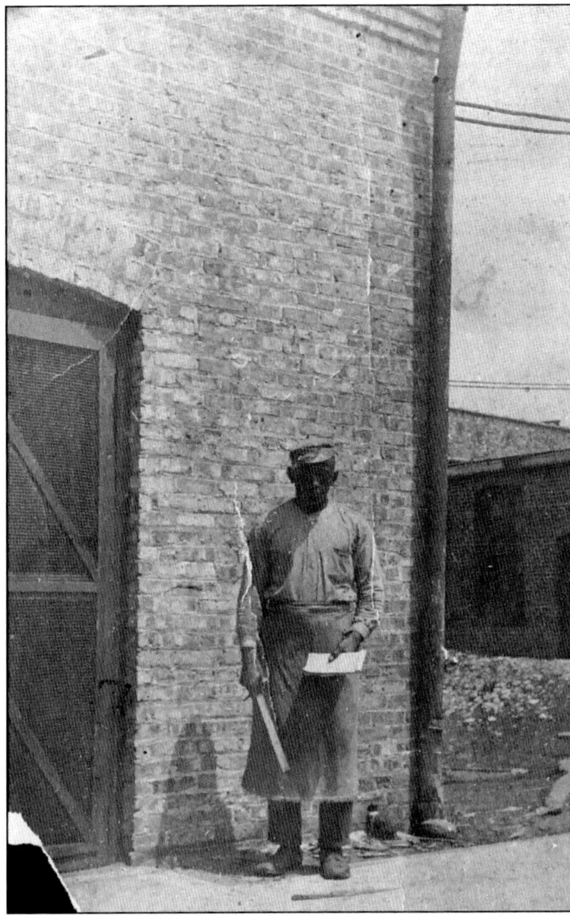

This 1914 photograph shows the road leading to the National Stock Yards. St. Clair Avenue here was nicknamed "Whiskey Chute" due to the many taverns that lined the road, hoping that farmworkers with cash in their pockets would stop for a drink before leaving town. (SIUE)

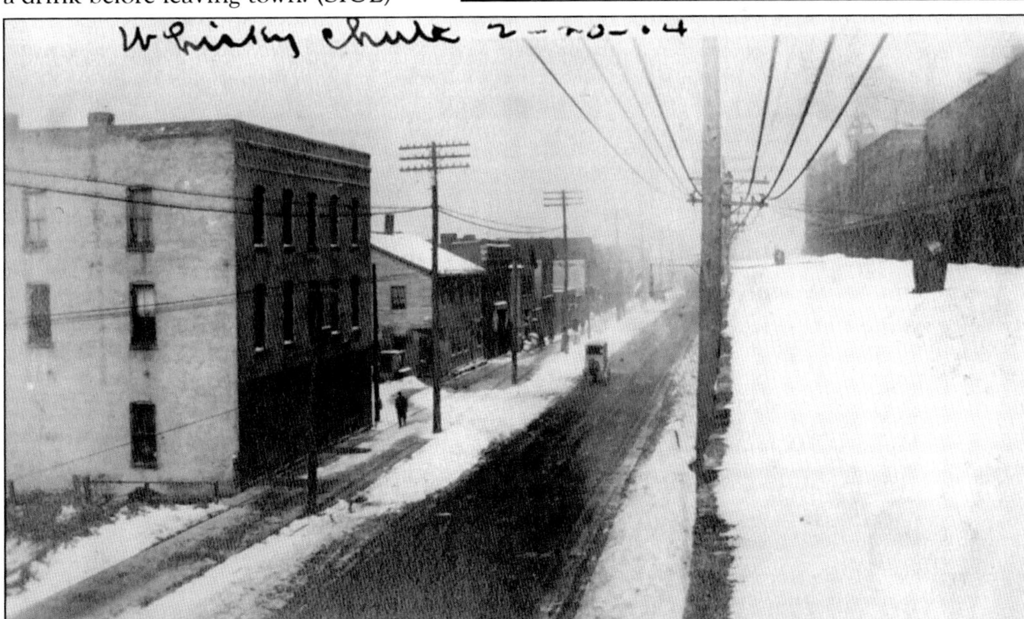

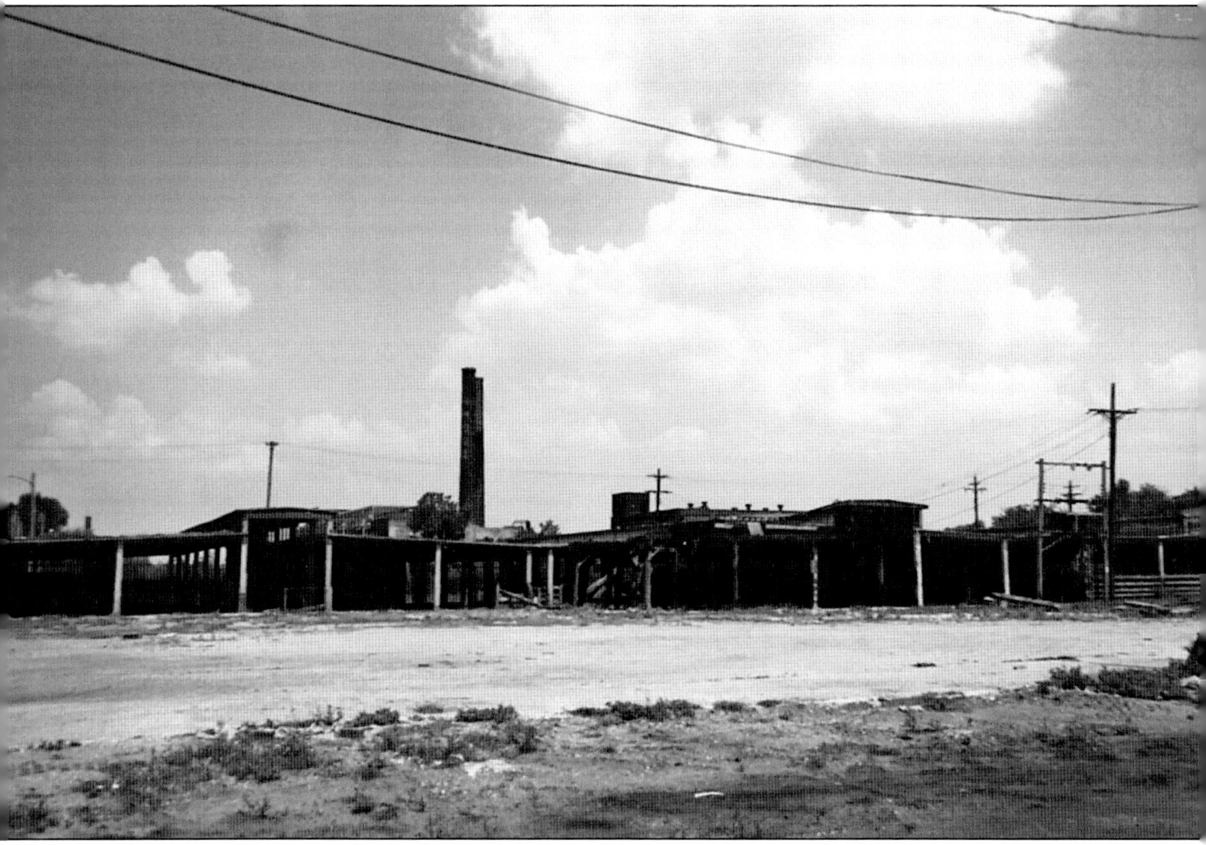

This image from 2000 shows the last of the covered animal pens and the long-abandoned Armour plant in the background. The pens are all demolished now, as are many other abandoned structures at the site, to make way for the new Interstate 70 bridge over the Mississippi. (AT)

Four

Government

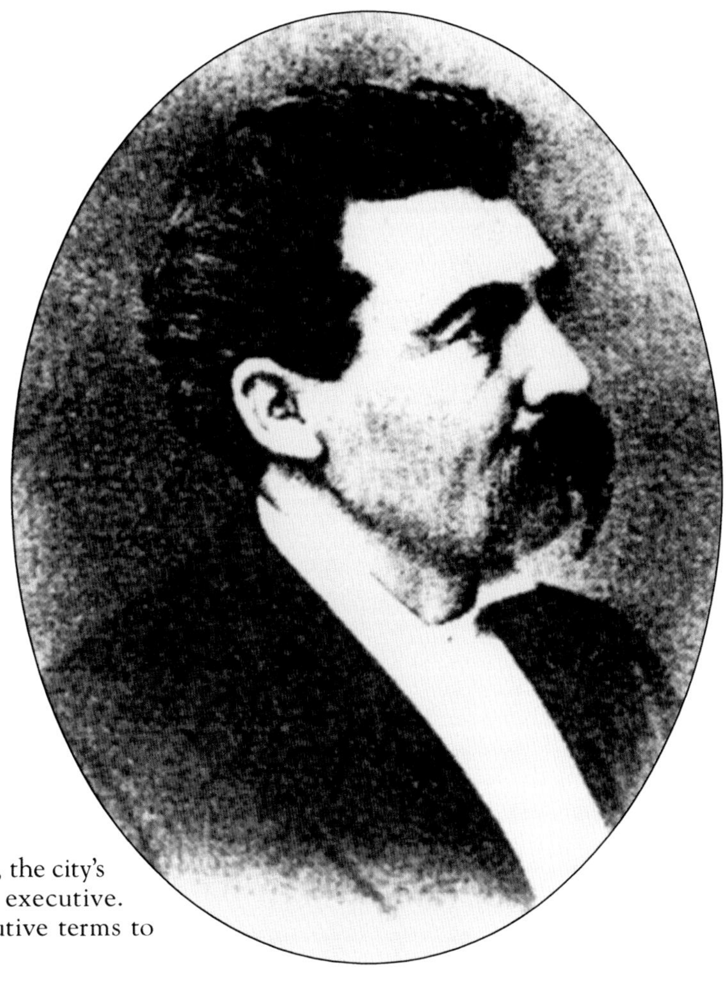

At right is John B. Bowman, the city's founder and first elected executive. He served five nonconsecutive terms to 1879. (SIUE)

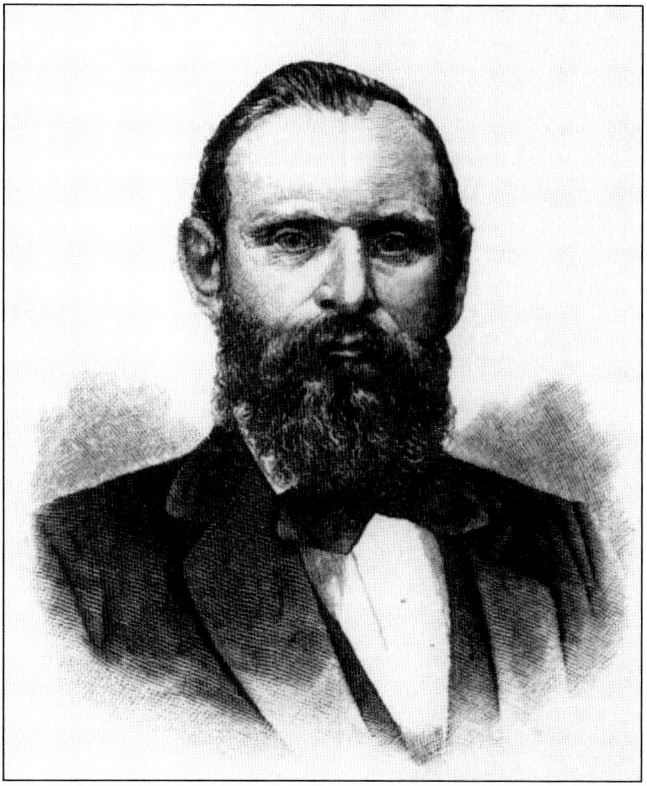

Ernest W. Wider was mayor of East St. Louis from 1877 to 1879, during the infamous dual-government crisis. In 1877, the city's founder, John Bowman, pushed through a new city charter at a special election. Questions were raised about the legality of the special election—and so the city operated with two governments for the next two years, one organized under the old charter and one under the new. The Illinois Supreme Court voided the new charter in 1879. Wider died in his sleep unexpectedly at age 46. This image is from 1881. (SIUE)

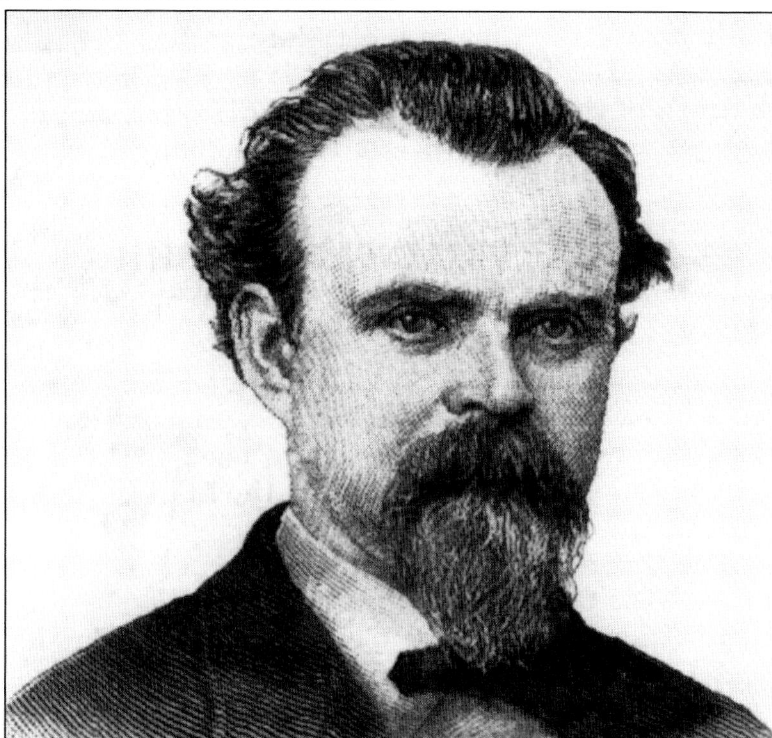

Maurice Joyce, right, was mayor from 1879 to 1881 and again from 1885 to 1887. His son was Maurice V. Joyce, who would run for mayor in 1909. (SIUE)

Malbern M. Stephens, protege of John Bowman, was the city's longest-serving mayor. He was elected in 1887 and reelected six times in the early part of his political career. He was a man of great integrity and the mayor who transformed East St. Louis into an industrial powerhouse. (SIUE)

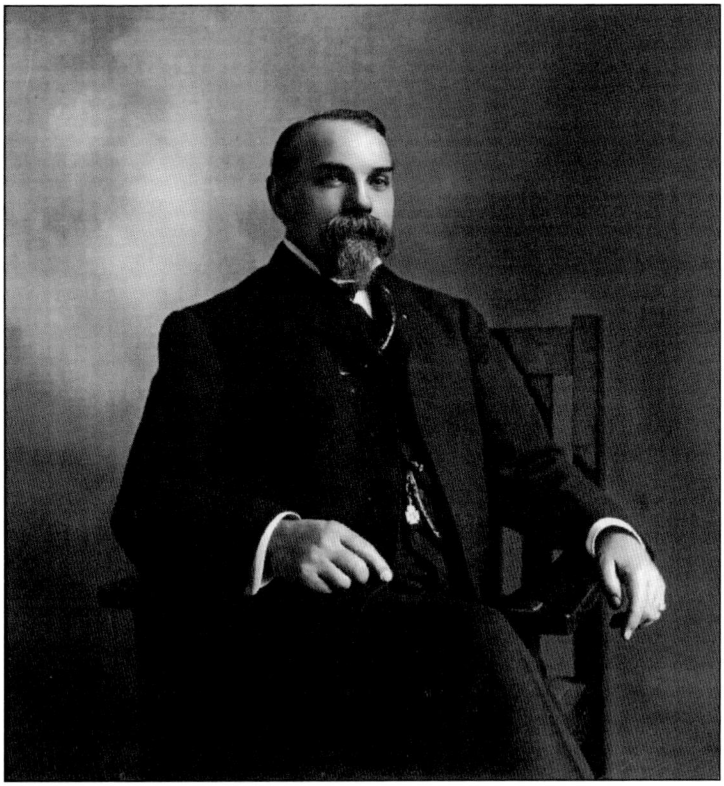

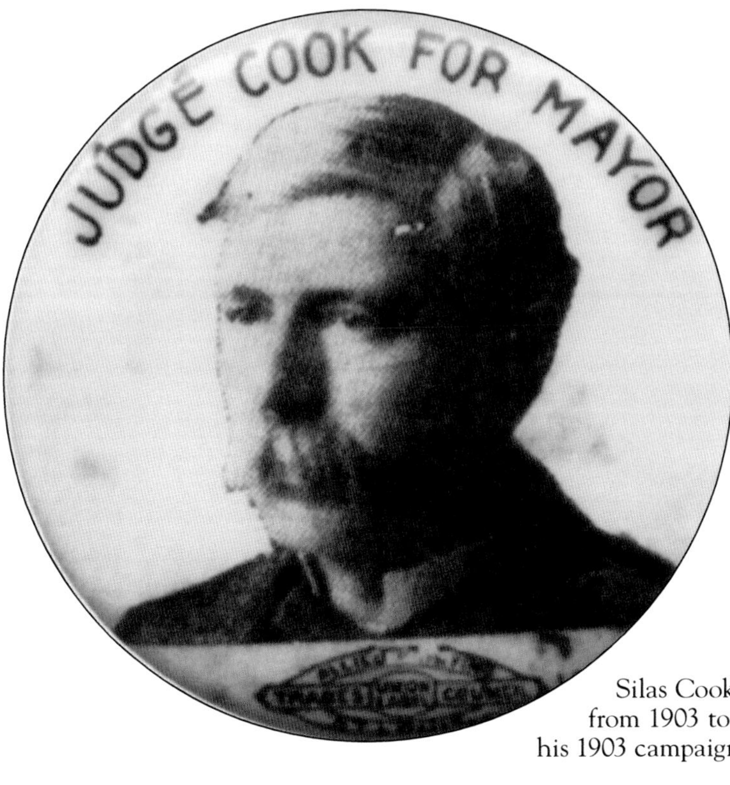

Silas Cook, a former city judge, served from 1903 to 1911. This button was from his 1903 campaign. (SIUE)

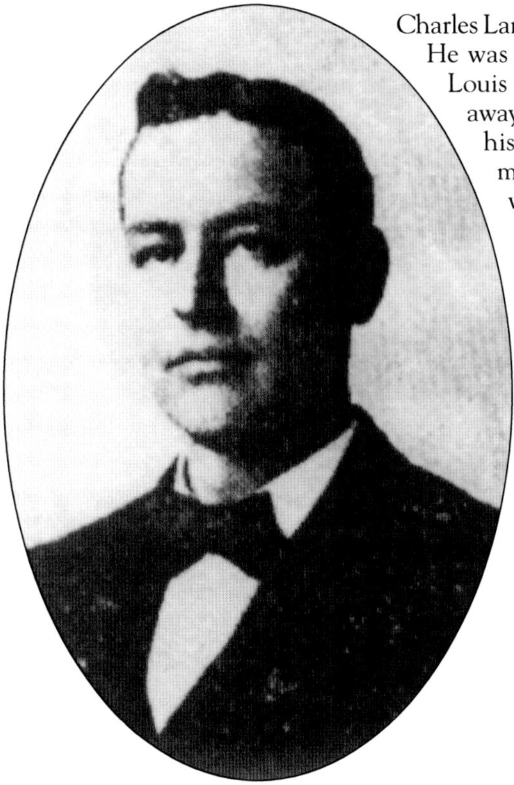

Charles Lambert served one term as mayor from 1911 to 1913. He was the Anheuser-Busch representative in East St. Louis and served as Mayor Cook's city clerk. He broke away from the Cook machine in 1909 and defeated his former boss in 1911. He is the only East St. Louis mayor to be put on trial for corruption. The jury would not convict him. (SIUE)

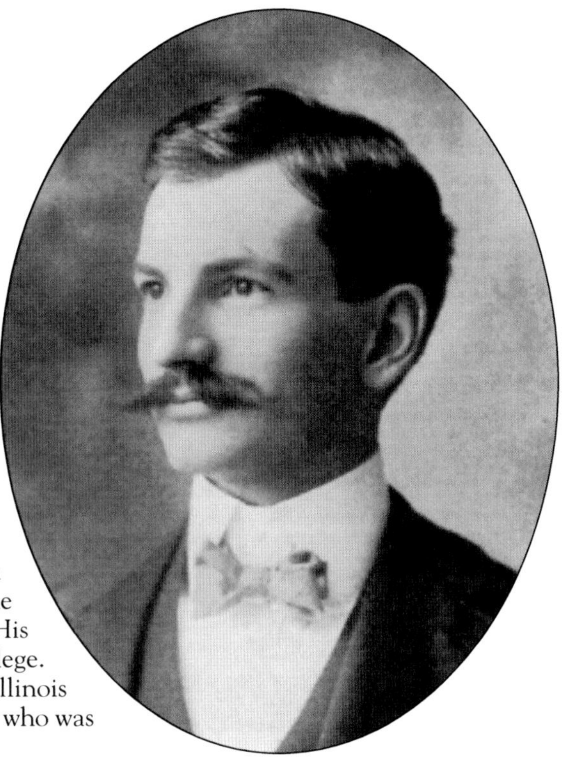

John Chamberlin served one term as mayor from 1913 to 1915. When he cooperated with investigators looking into city corruption, he lost political favor with the power brokers. His family was affiliated with McKendree College. He served on the school board and in the Illinois Legislature. He was a seemingly honest man who was surrounded by corrupt colleagues. (SIUE)

Fred Mollman was mayor from 1915 to 1919. The 1917 Race Riot occurred during his tenure. His family ran Mollman Harness Company on Missouri Avenue. (SIUE)

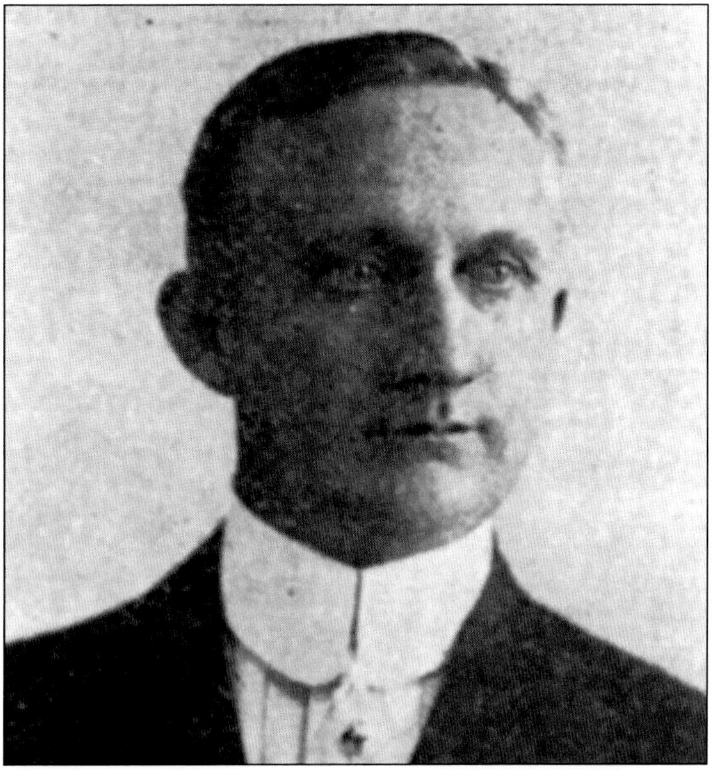

Malbern M. Stephens, seen here in about 1923, was called out of retirement in 1919 to bring peace to the city after the riot. He reluctantly served another eight years as mayor, and East St. Louis again enjoyed peace and prosperity under his tenure. He served a total 22 years in office. (SIUE)

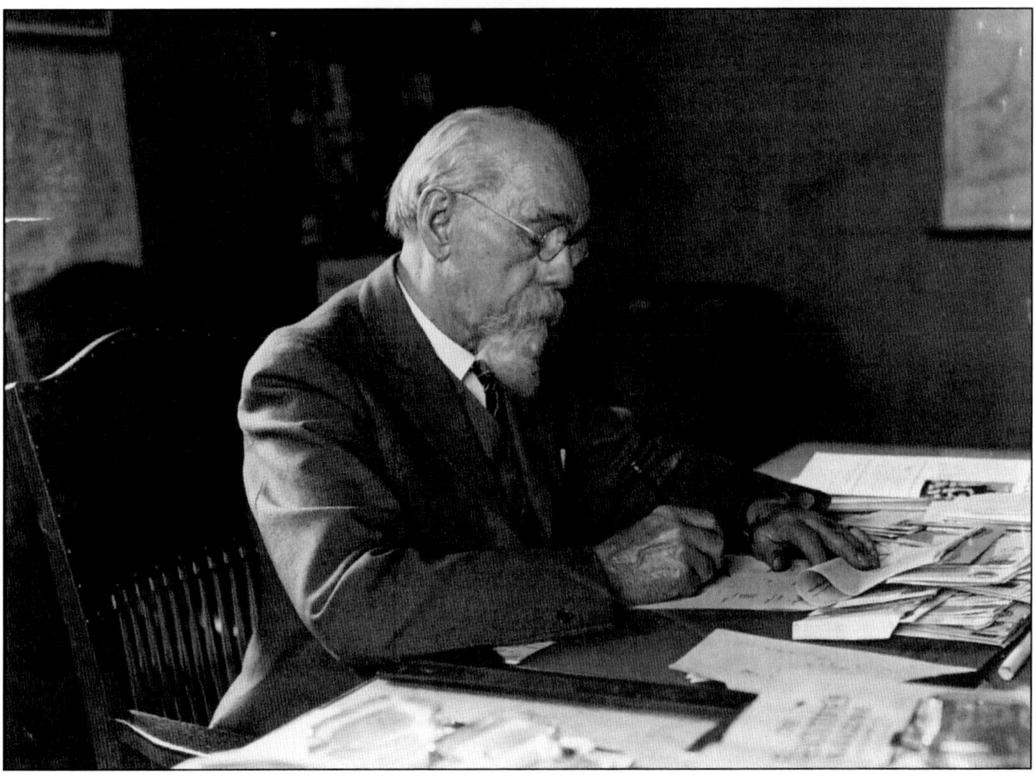

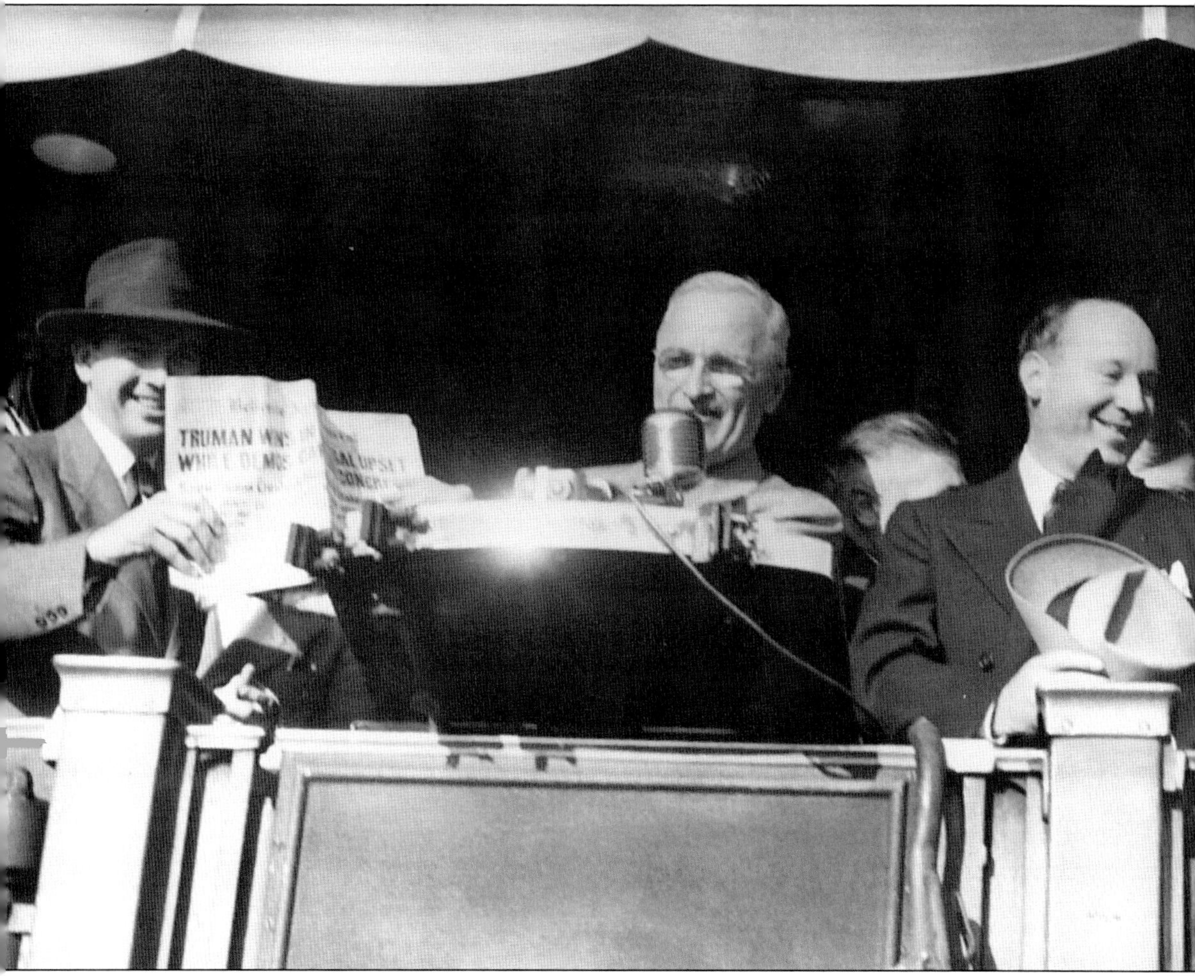

President Truman speaks in East St. Louis from the back of his railcar. Mayor John Connors is at left and Congressman Mel Price is at right. Many presidents spoke like this in East St. Louis since it frequently took a long time to do necessary engine switches before crossing the bridge into St. Louis. (BN)

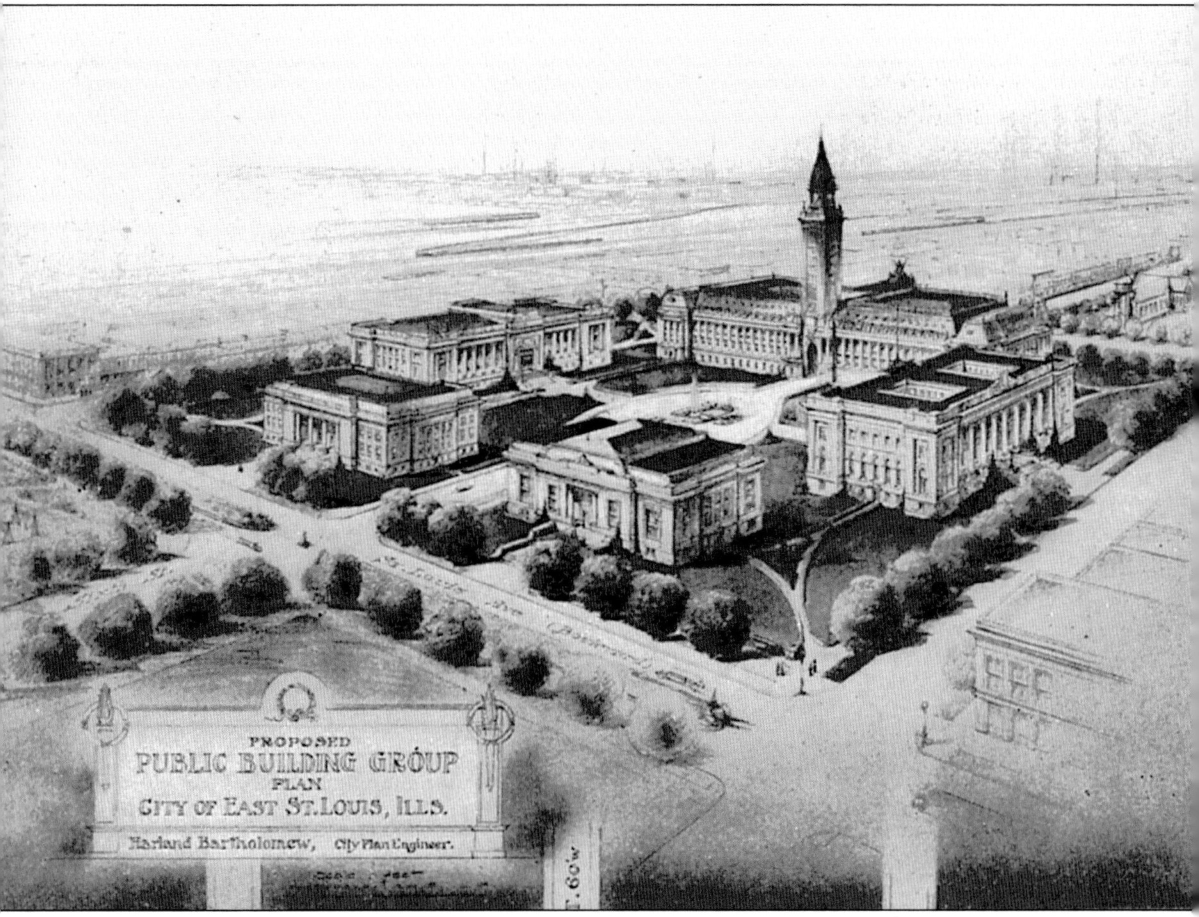

In 1920, city planner Harland Bartholomew designed a new city hall and public buildings group for East St. Louis to be located at Sixth Street and St. Louis Avenue. It was never built. Bartholomew was not impressed with the way East St. Louis was being developed. He wrote, "There has scarcely been any public action that can be pointed to as evidence of or regard for the development of a great metropolis." (SIUE)

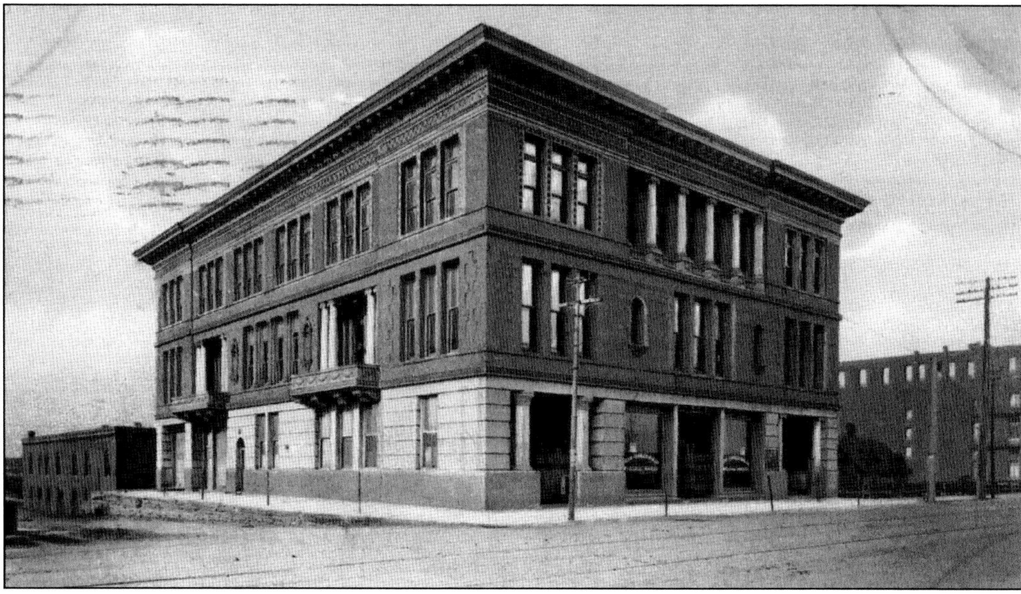

The Adele Building at Broadway Avenue and Main Street was built in 1892. The public library was housed on the third floor of this building. (HF)

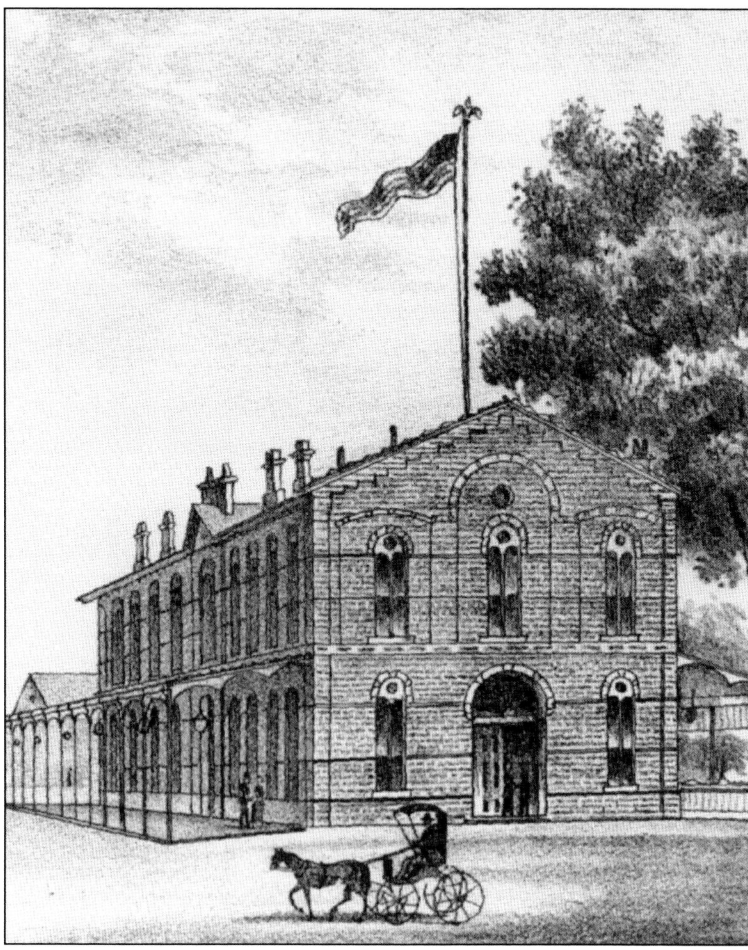

The Market House was built in 1869 and served as the East St. Louis City Hall in its earliest years. (SIUE)

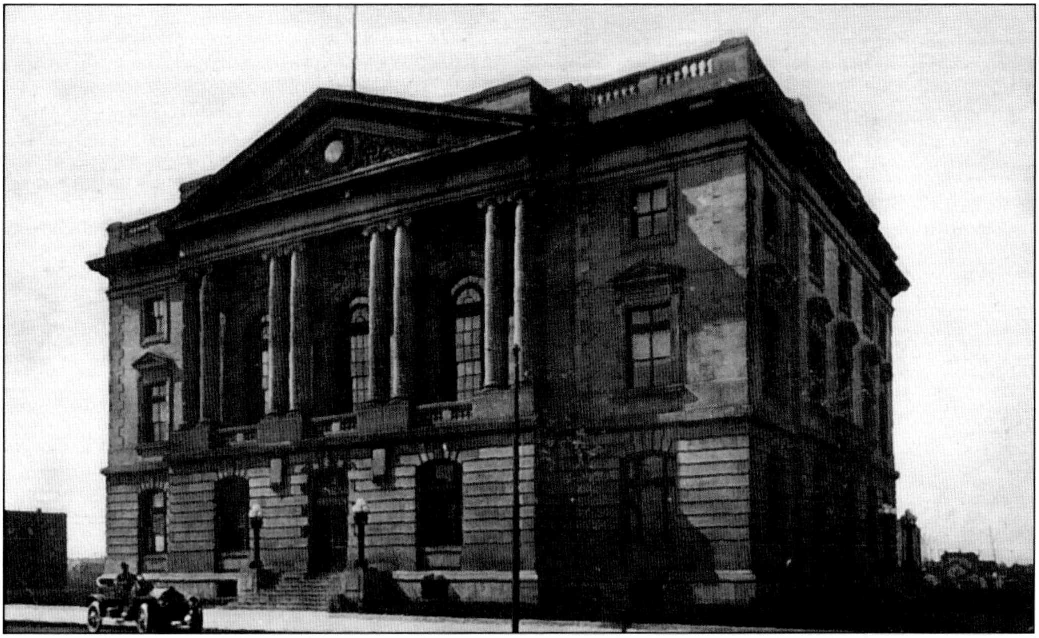

The federal courthouse, seen here about 1912, was dedicated by President Taft in 1909. (SIUE)

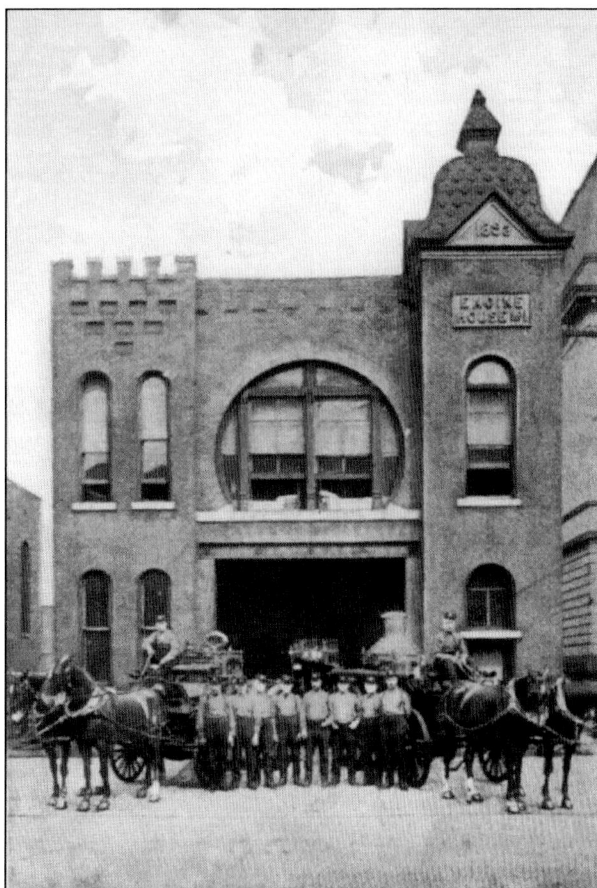

This image, captured sometime around 1910, shows the fire station that stood behind the East St. Louis City Hall. (SIUE)

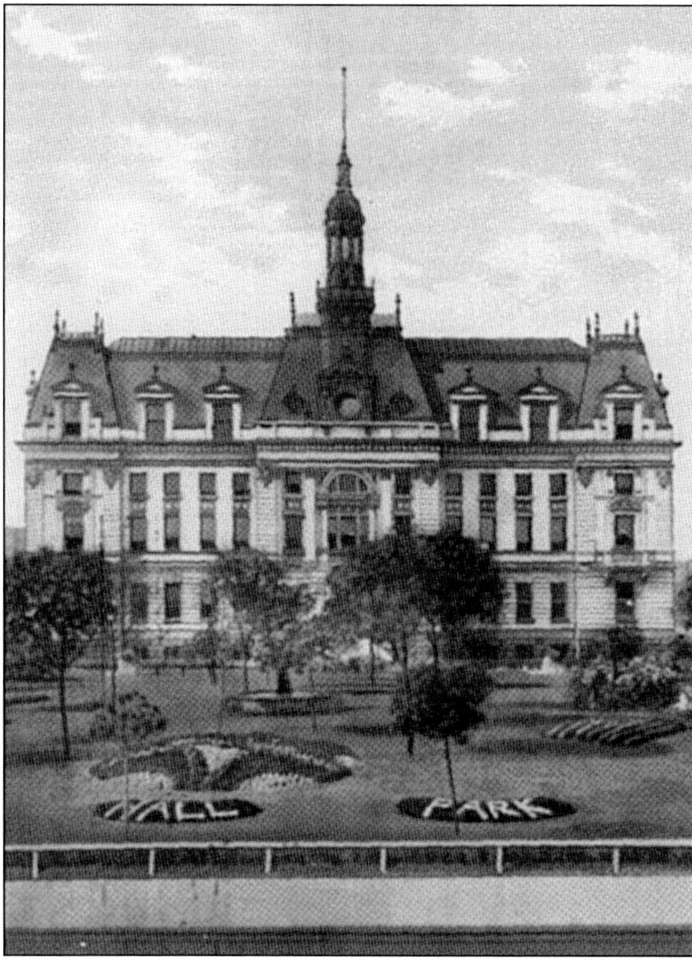

The impressive East St. Louis City Hall building was completed in 1900. It featured beautiful gardens in front. (SIUE)

This private mailing card from 1900 was a souvenir of the new city hall. It shows the building along with an image of Mayor M.M. Stephens. (SIUE)

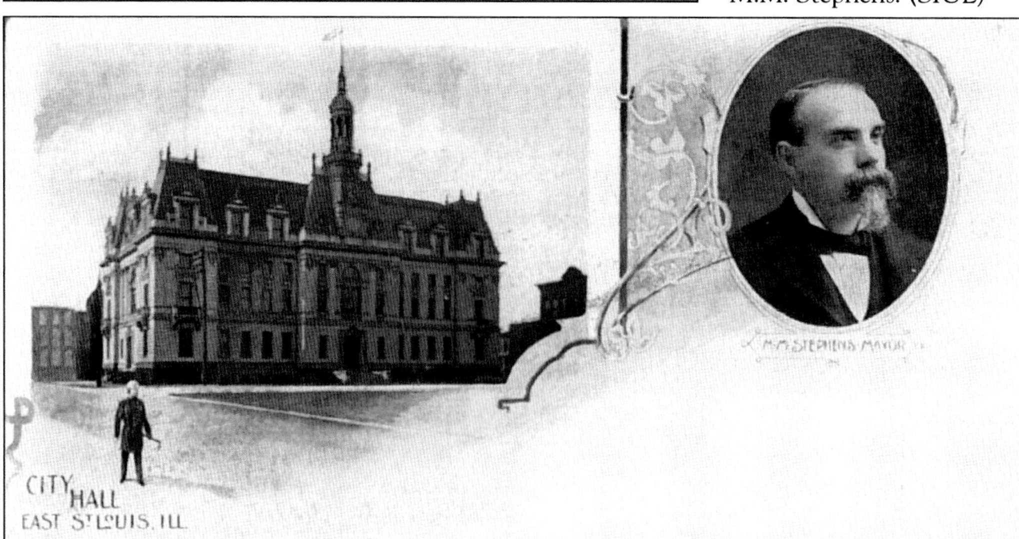

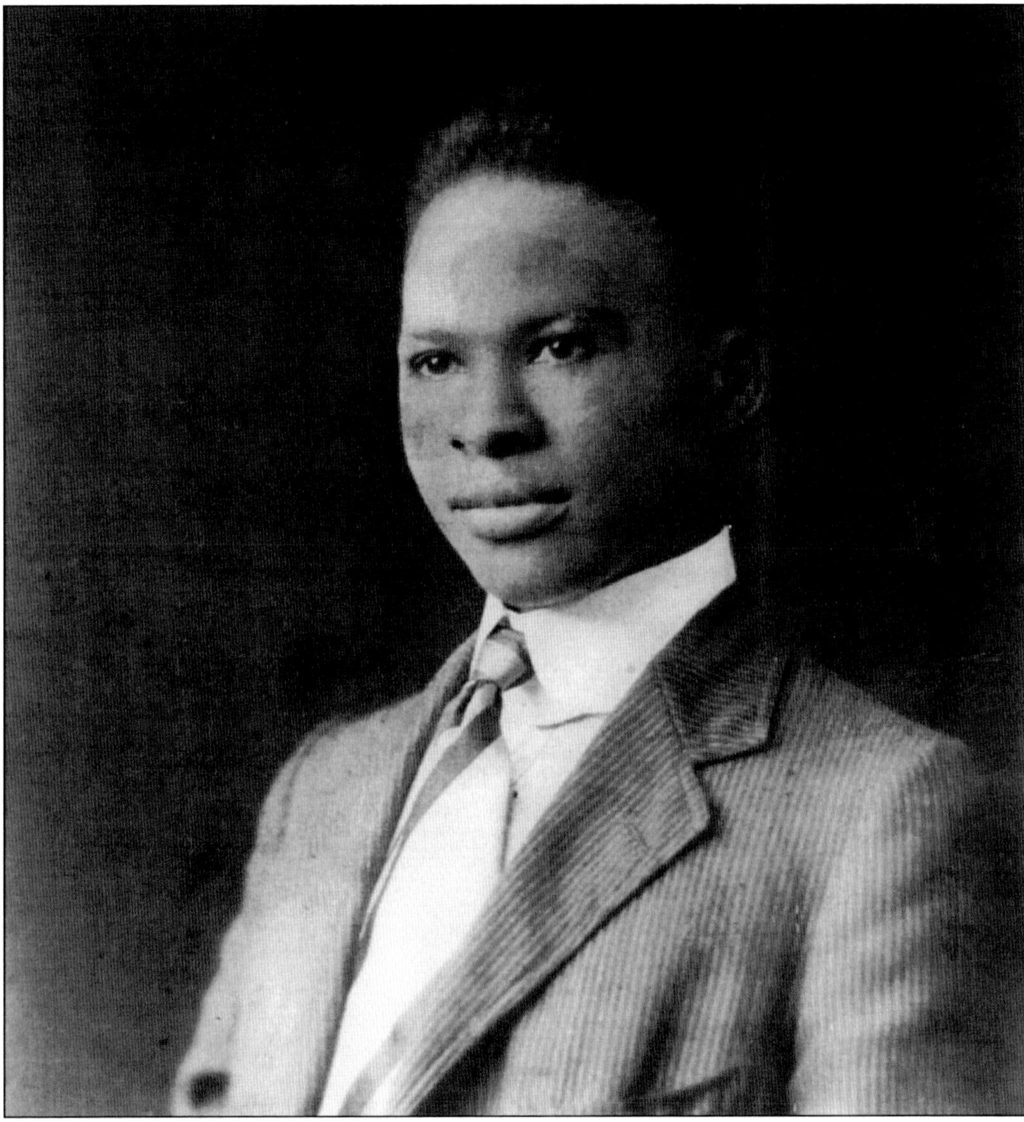

Horace Adams, civil rights leader, community activist, and founder of the Paramount Democratic Club, is seen here around the time of his untimely death in 1935. Adams was killed in an automobile accident. His family has been prominent in the leadership of the city and the school district. (Dr. Lillian Parks.)

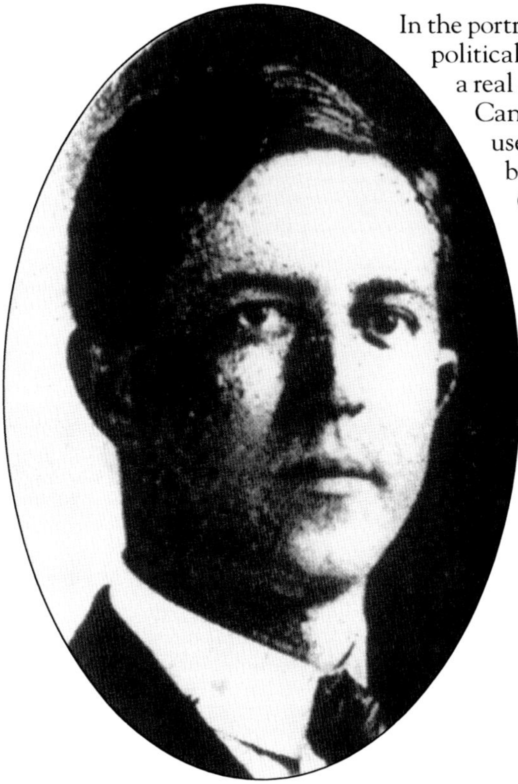

In the portrait at left is George Locke Tarlton, the undisputed political boss of East St. Louis during the 1910s. He was a real estate developer and business partner of Thomas Canavan. He served on the Levee District board and used it for his personal profit. He was the kingpin behind mayors Lambert (1911–1913), Chamberlin (1913–1915), and Mollman (1915–1919). (SIUE)

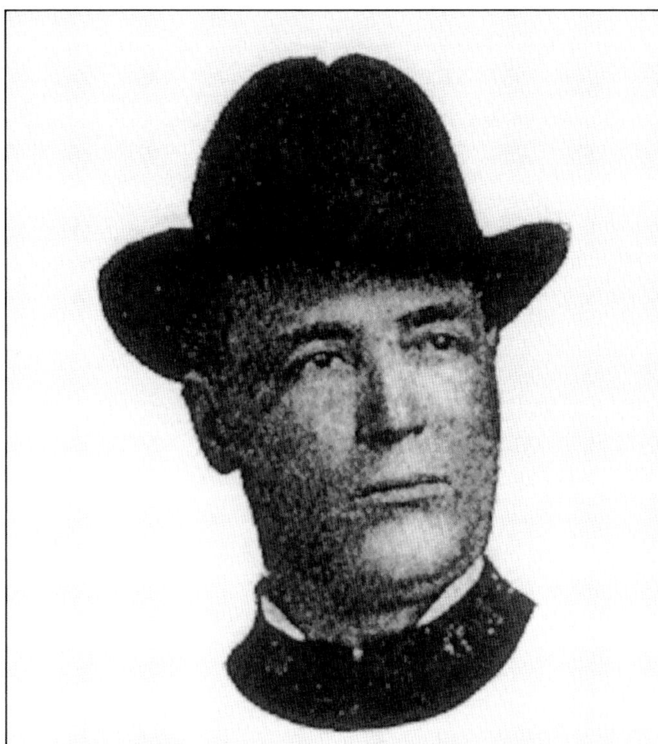

Seen here is George Purdy, chief of police under Mayor Silas Cook (1903–1911) and political boss. Purdy, a brick maker by trade, was notoriously corrupt. Laws were selectively enforced during his reign, and he was regularly lambasted in the newspaper. (SIUE)

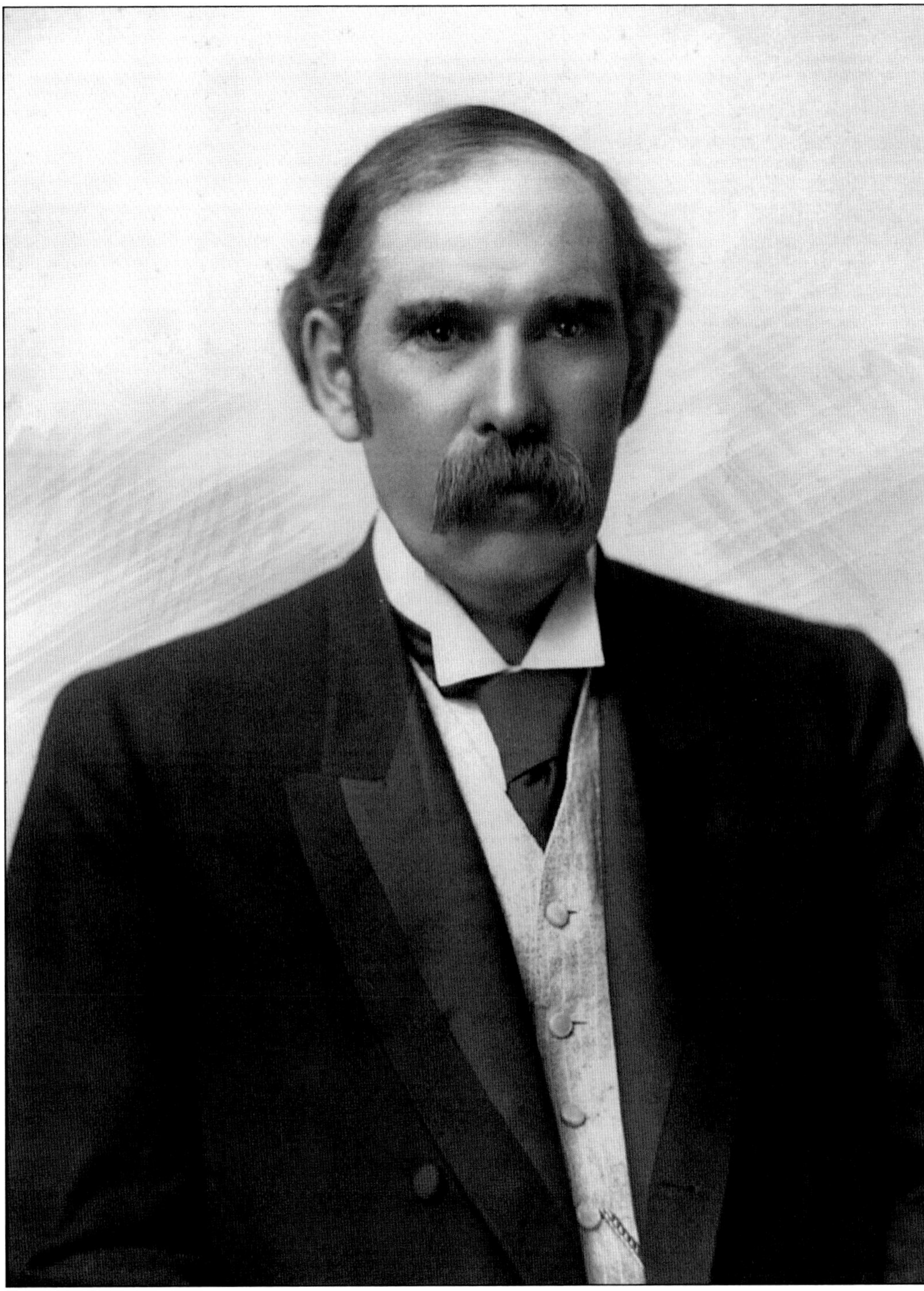

John B. Messick began practicing law in East St. Louis in 1872. He was a Civil War veteran who served as a city judge and Illinois legislator. He ended his career as superintendent of the East St. Louis Federal Courthouse. (SIUE)

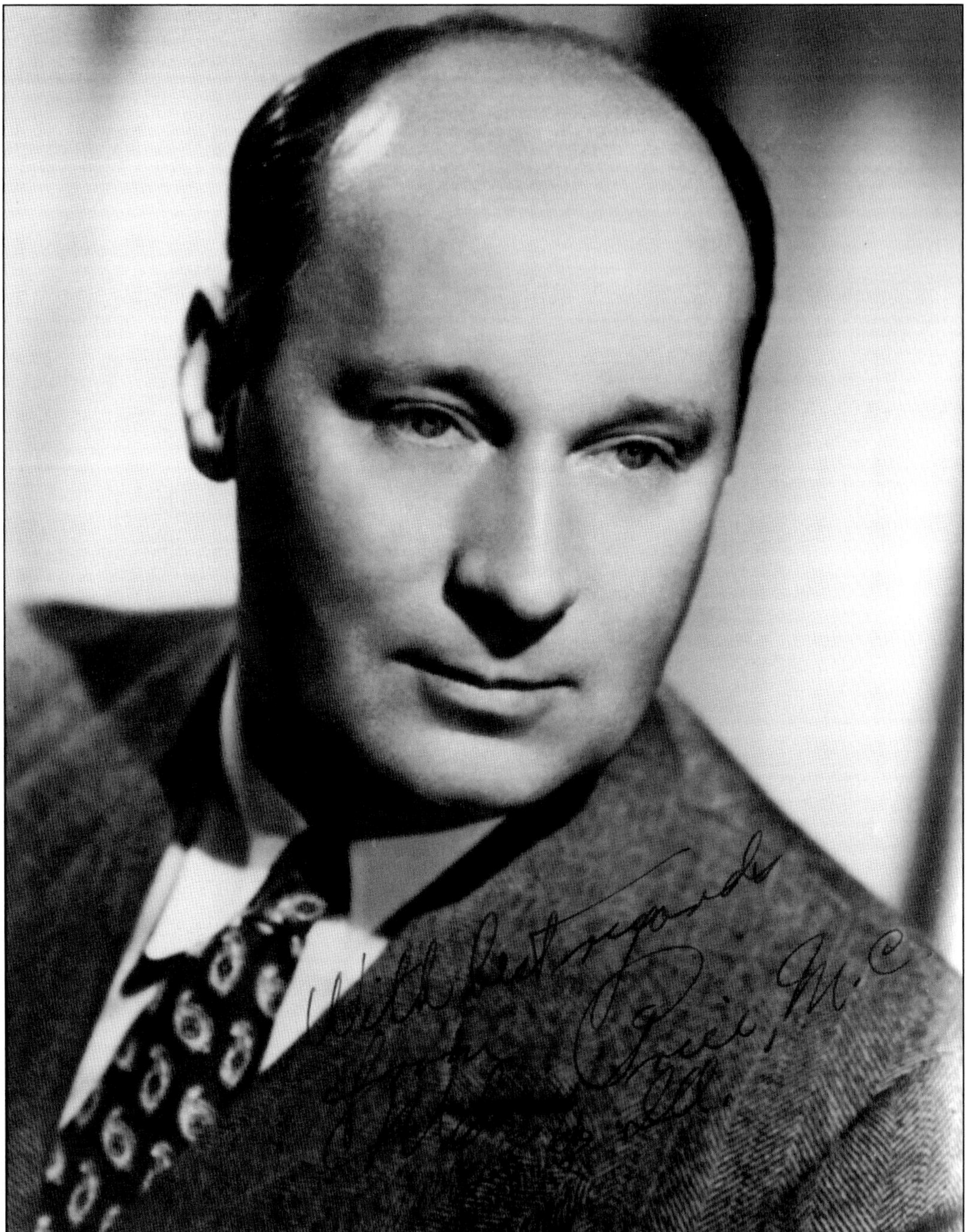

Charles Melvin Price represented East St. Louis in the US Congress for decades. He was first elected while stationed at an army base in Virginia in 1944 and was reelected 21 times. He was the chairman of the House Armed Services Committee and was one of the most powerful men in Congress. He brought considerable federal investment to his district, including large military installations in Granite City and Scott Air Force Base. He even attempted to have the Johnson Space Center built in East St. Louis. (SIUE)

Five

Leisure Time

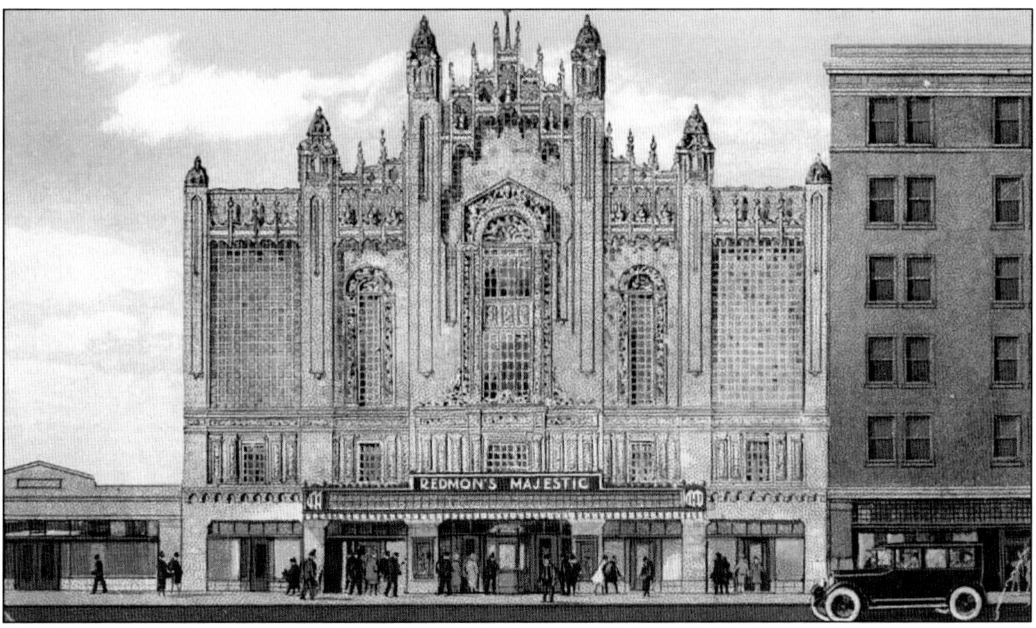

The million-dollar Majestic Theater was built in 1928 by Harry Redmon and Fred Leber on the site of the old Majestic Theater at 244 Collinsville Avenue. Sisters Dorothy and Lillian Gish saw their first silent movie at the old theater. They helped their mother, who was working at the Majestic Kandy Kitchen located next door. Over 10,000 people attended the grand opening ceremonies. It was the first theater in the city to show talkies. The theater closed in 1960 as more and more people stayed home to watch television. This image came from the invitation to opening day on Saturday, February 25, 1928. (SIUE)

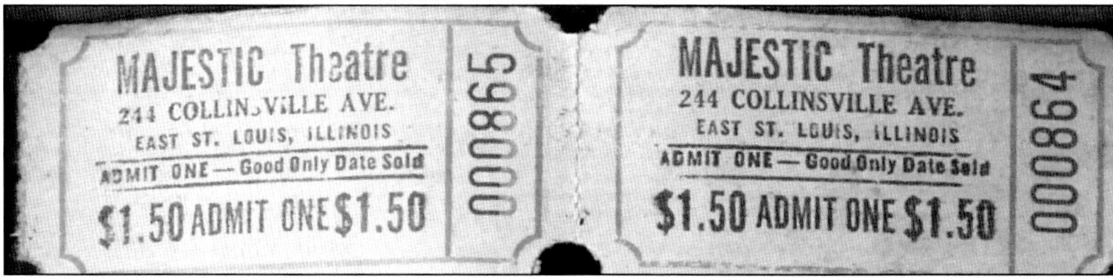

Seen here is a pair of Majestic tickets from 1960. The admission price when the theater opened was 40¢. By the time it closed, the price was $1.50. (SIUE)

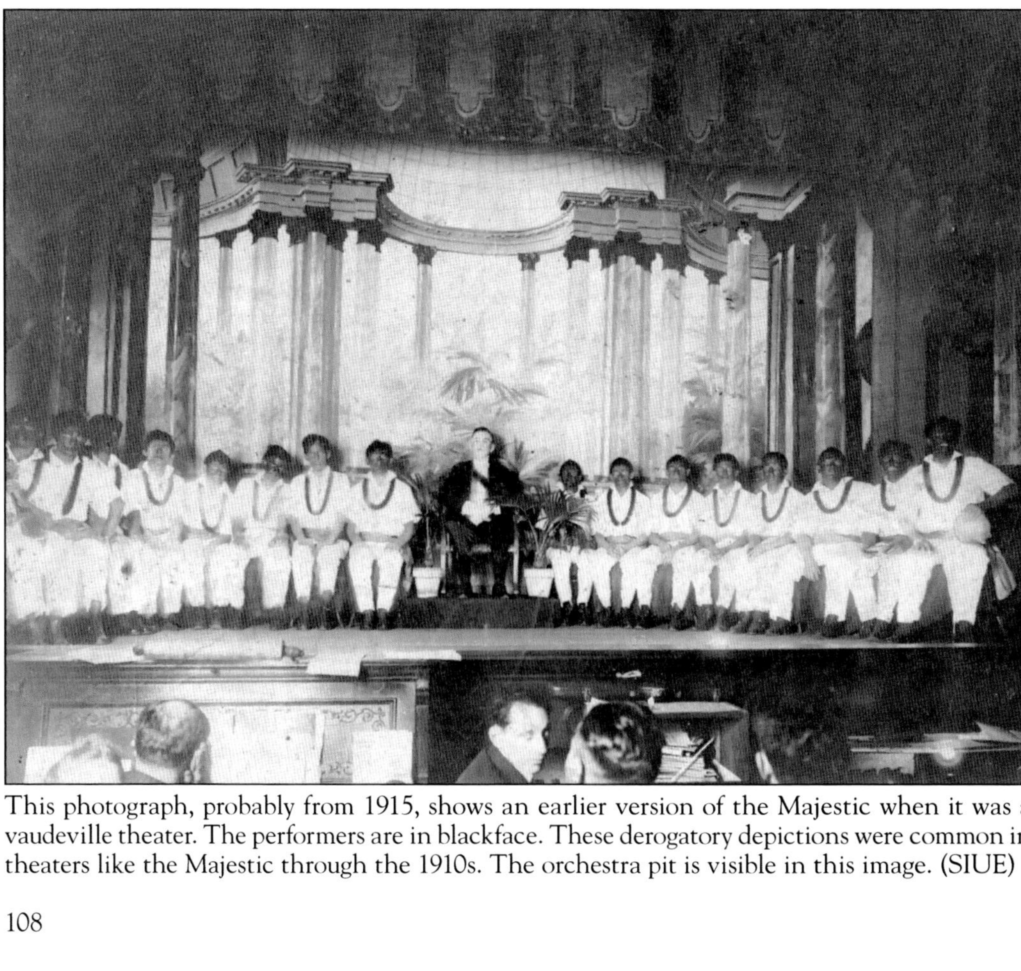

This photograph, probably from 1915, shows an earlier version of the Majestic when it was a vaudeville theater. The performers are in blackface. These derogatory depictions were common in theaters like the Majestic through the 1910s. The orchestra pit is visible in this image. (SIUE)

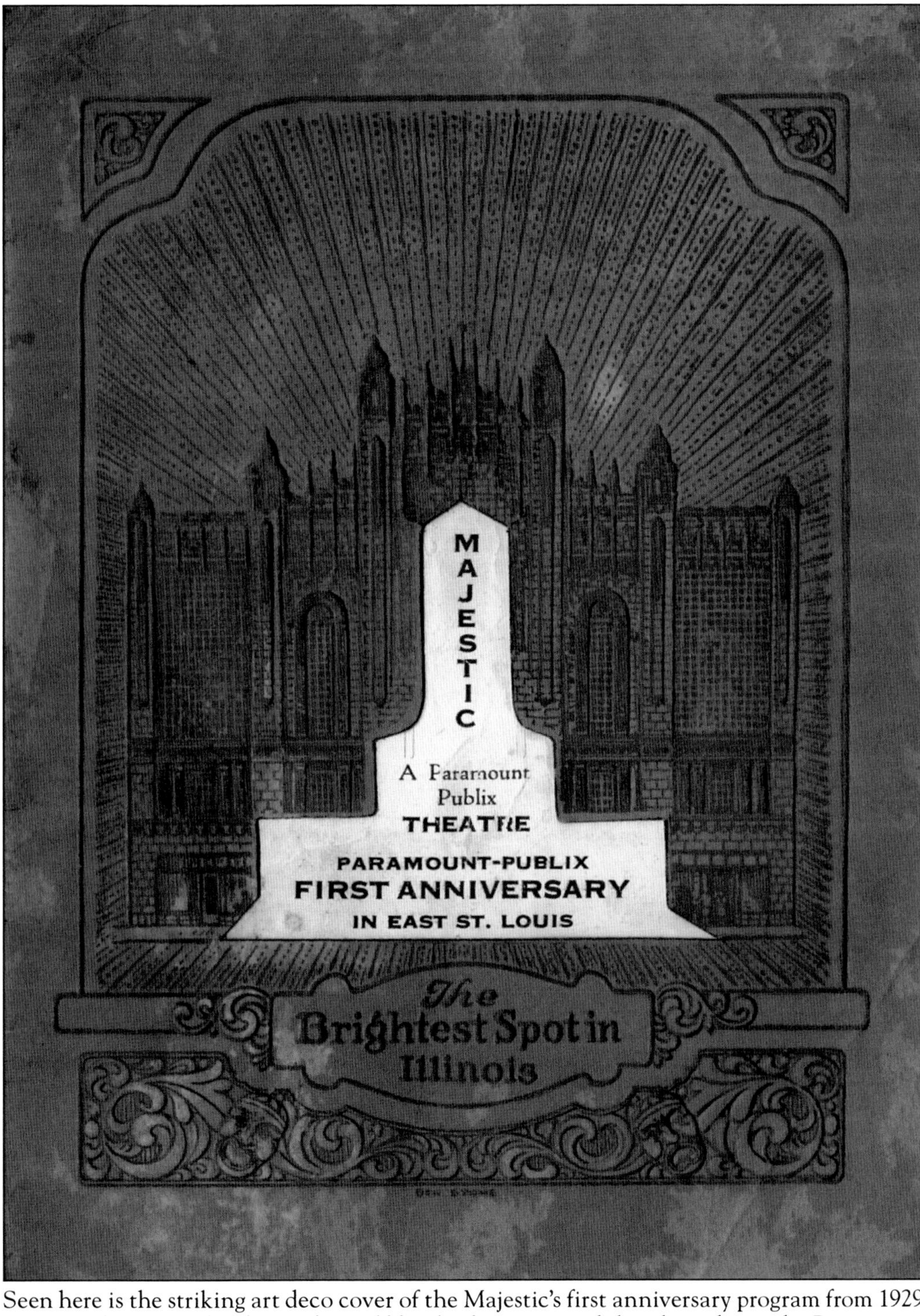

Seen here is the striking art deco cover of the Majestic's first anniversary program from 1929. Harry Redmon ran the theater himself for the first year, and then leased it to the Paramount-Publix group. The theater had a huge foyer, plush seats, and a three-tier balcony. The movie screen was 20 feet high. (SIUE)

January 3, 1958.

Mr. Duncan R. Kennedy

Dear Mr. Kennedy:

Following is number of colored people entering Majestic, East St. Louis, Sunday, December 22nd thru Saturday, December 28th:

		ADULTS	CHILDREN
Sun. 12/22	APRIL LOVE	42	6
Mon. 12/23	GOD IS MY PARTNER	9	-
Tue. 12/24		11	6
Wed. 12/25		188	75
Thu. 12/26	MR. ROCK & ROLL	38	26
Fri. 12/27	DEVIL'S HAIRPIN	75	30
Sat. 12/28		74	46
		437	189

TOTAL ATTENDANCE 3278 19% (626)

Sincerely,

Vincent F. O'Leary
Majestic Theatre
East St. Louis, Illinois

VFO'L/dh

CC: I. Wienshienk

The Majestic Theater integrated its audiences in 1958. Theater management tracked the number of African Americans who attended and issued weekly reports like this one, which are now in the archives of Southern Illinois University Edwardsville. (SIUE)

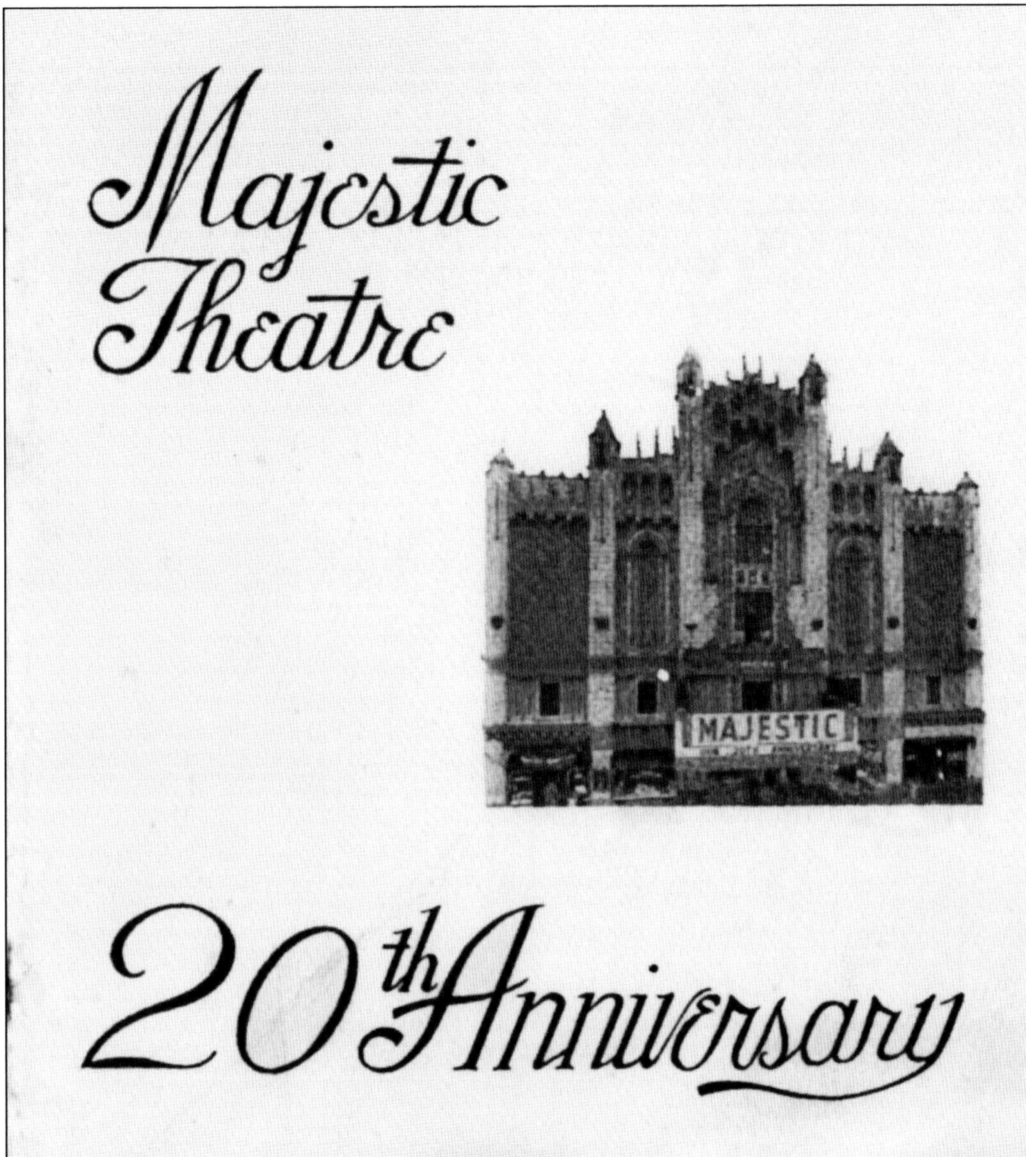

The Majestic celebrated its 20th anniversary in 1948. The theater added a sound system in 1930 to accommodate "talking" pictures. Its first 3-D film would be shown in 1952, called *Bwana Devil*. In 1954, the theater began showing Cinemascope films. This required a new screen, which was 42 feet wide—an astounding size for its day. (SIUE)

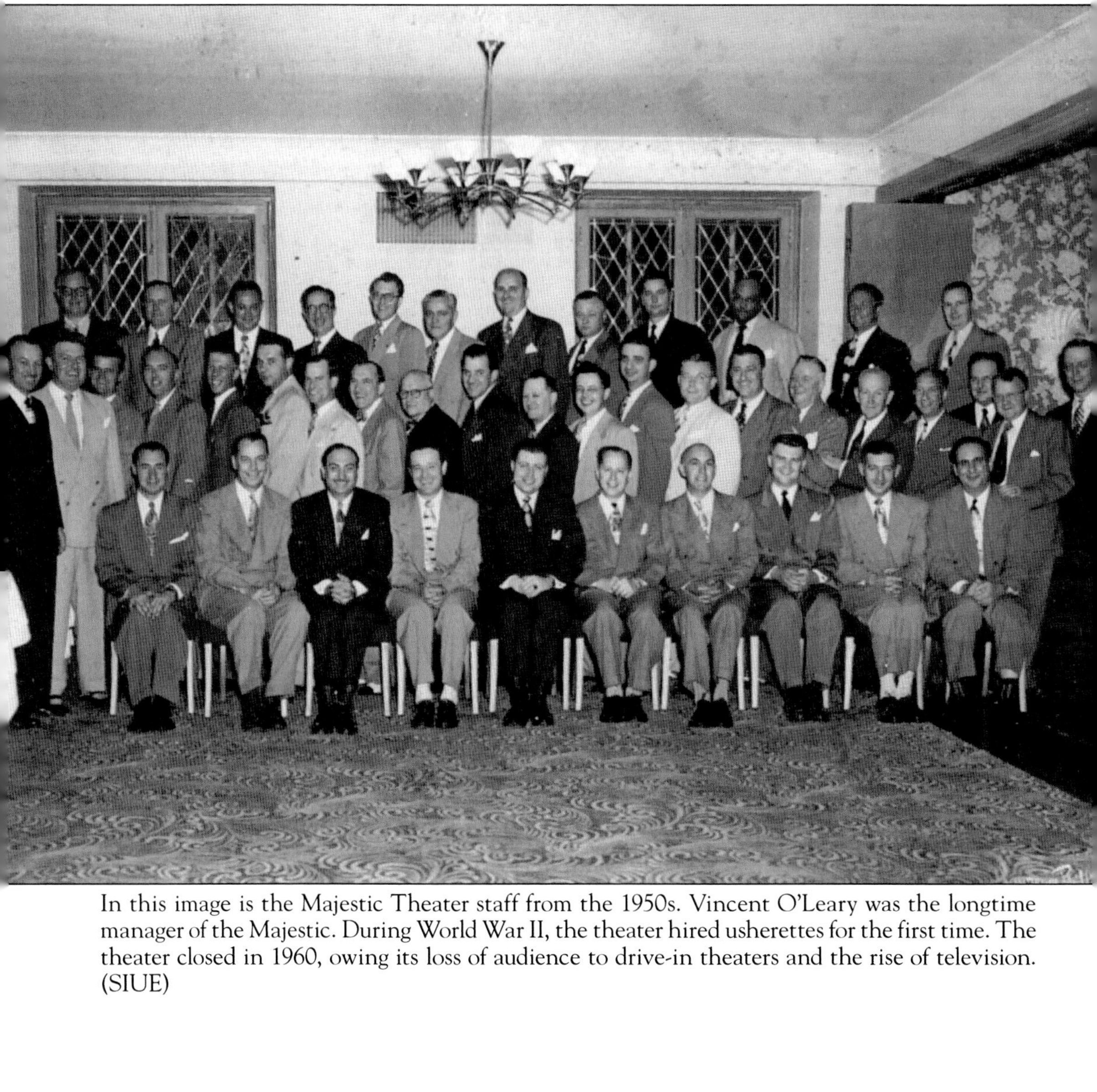

In this image is the Majestic Theater staff from the 1950s. Vincent O'Leary was the longtime manager of the Majestic. During World War II, the theater hired usherettes for the first time. The theater closed in 1960, owing its loss of audience to drive-in theaters and the rise of television. (SIUE)

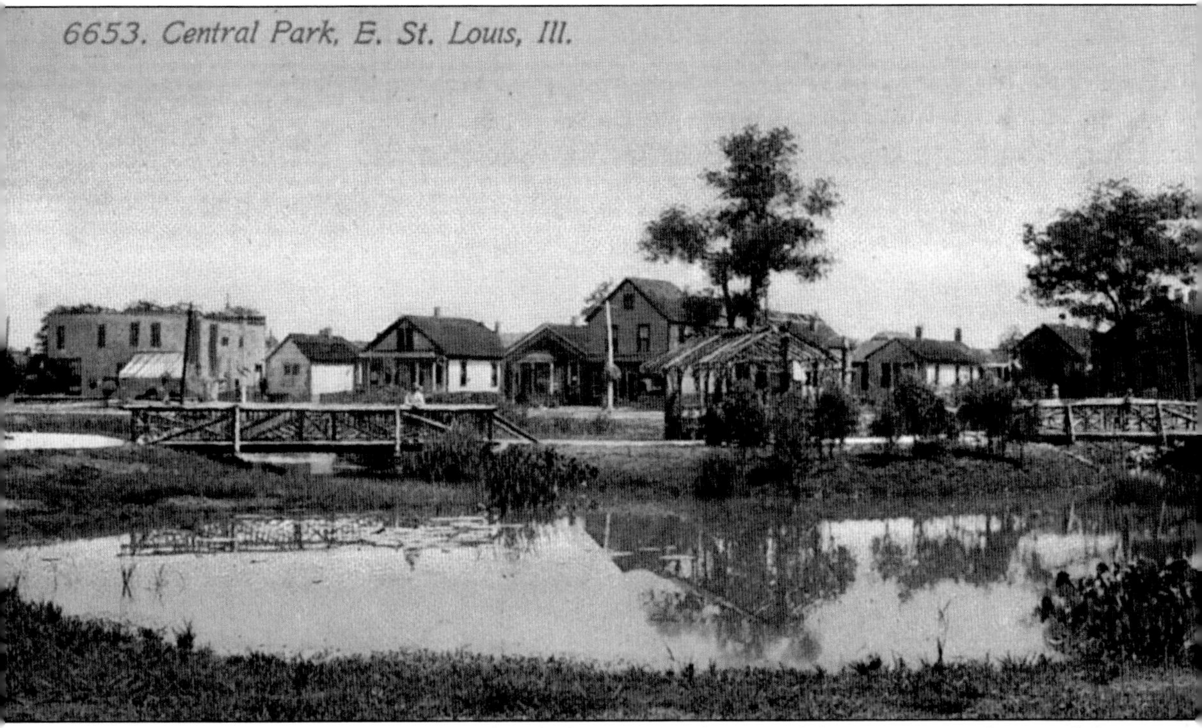

Central Park was a small neighborhood park, but it offered a peaceful water scene. The city did not have a parks department like other cities, but rather turned these responsibilities over to a Park District, which had its own governing board and collected its own taxes. Many of these special districts were patronage plums for politicians. As a boy, Congressman Mel Price had a lifeguard job with the Park District—even though he could not swim! (HF)

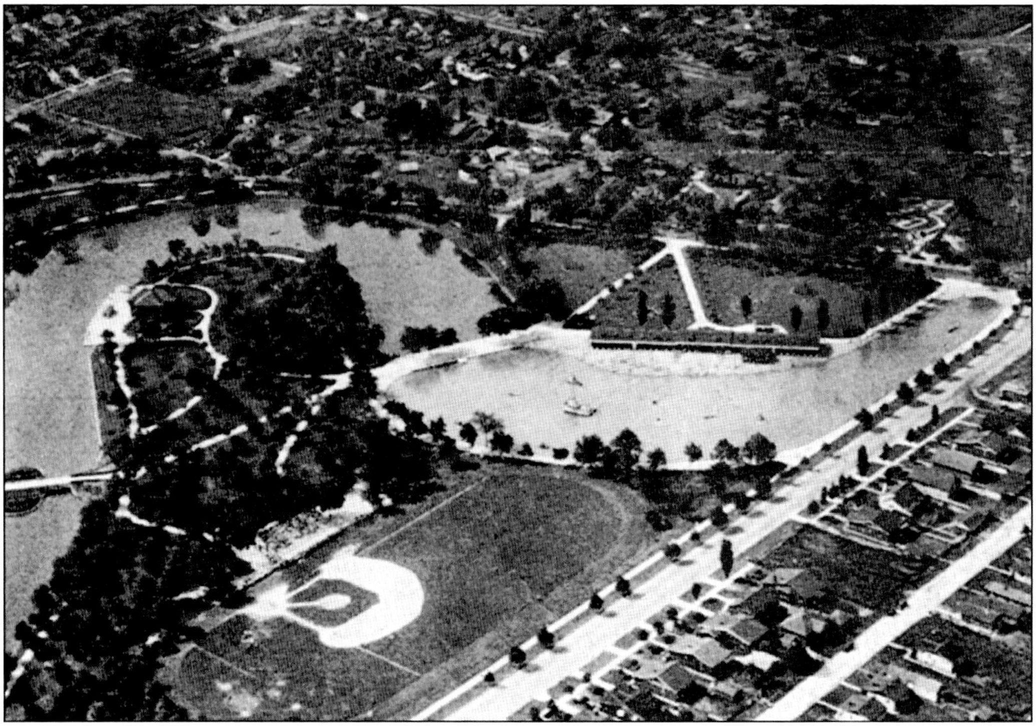

Jones Park consisted of about 130 acres and was bounded on the east by North Park Drive and on the west by Caseyville Avenue. Sam Jones, a local barrister in the post–Civil War era, donated his 55-acre farm to the city in his will with the proviso that the name never be changed. Park District officials, probably unaware of this proviso, changed the name to Kenneth Hall Park to honor a prominent state senator after his death in 1995. (HF)

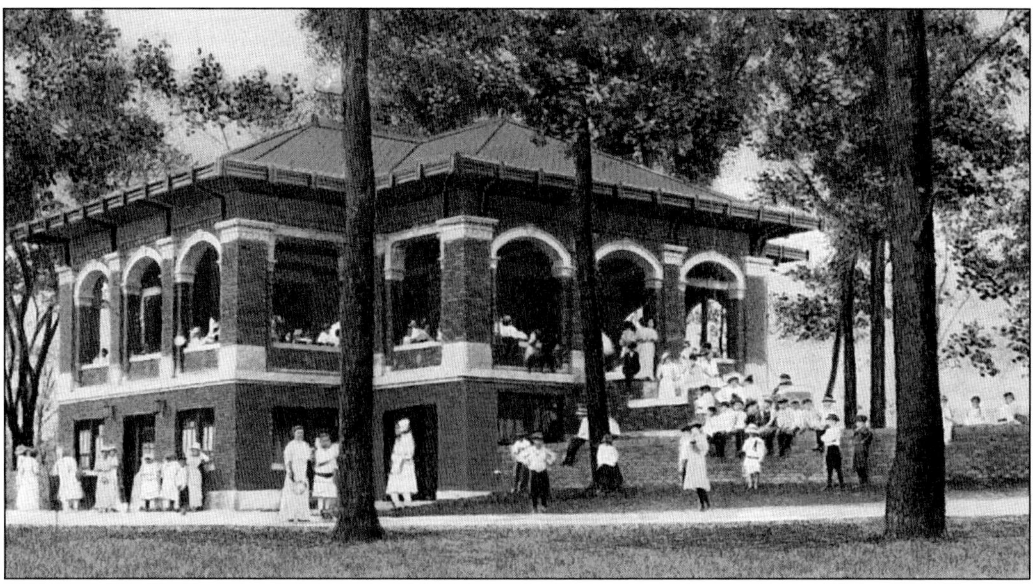

The bandstand at Jones Park was a brick structure where concerts were played on Sunday afternoons. The structure still stands today. There are several initiatives underway to restore various parts of Jones Park, in particular the gardens and greenhouses. (HF)

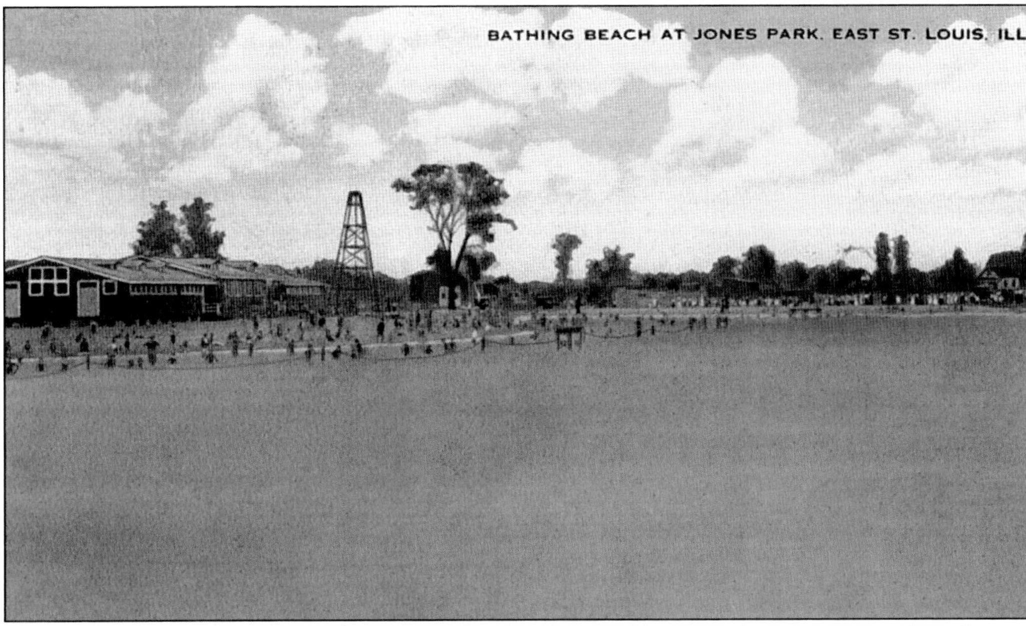

In 1913, the Park District spent $25,000 to develop the sand-bottomed swimming pool on the east end of Jones Park. The shallow end featured a sliding board, while the deep end offered a diving platform in the middle. Separate wooden bathhouses were built for men and women as places to change from street clothes into swimsuits. (HF)

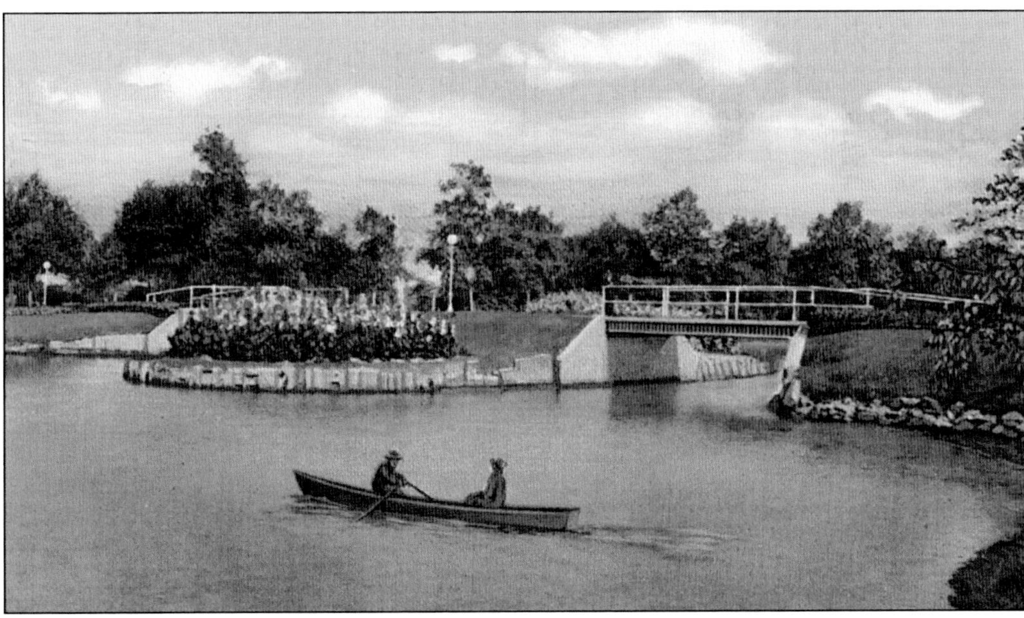

In addition to a nice lagoon for rowing, the park provided tennis courts, softball diamonds, baseball diamonds, a swimming pool, and a lighted lily pond. The members of the American Federation of Labor ended their Labor Day parade here at Jones Park, while members of the Congress of Industrial Organizations ended their parade at the adjacent Lansdowne Park. (HF)

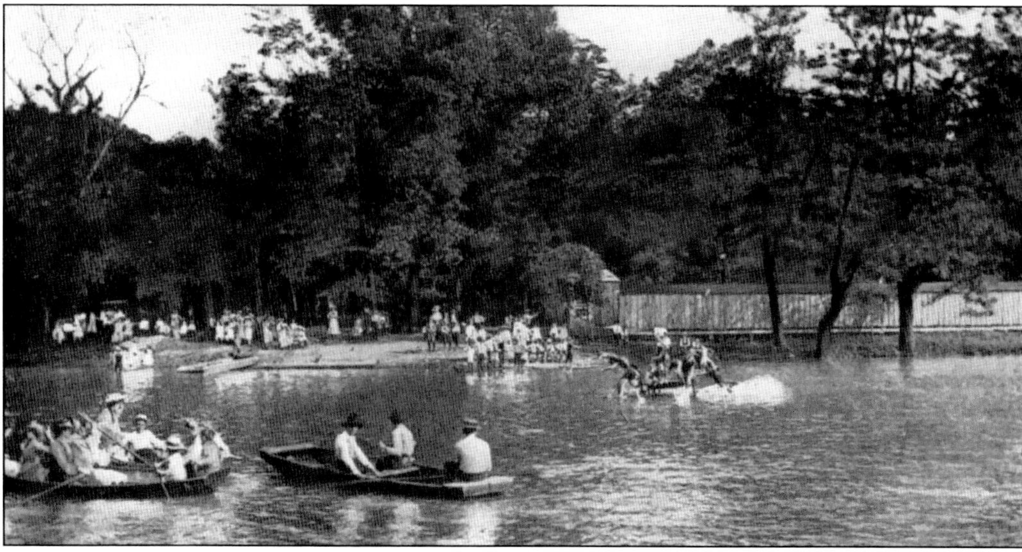

Rowboats that could be rented for 25¢ an hour were kept on the lower level. The boats could be taken out on the fishhook-shaped lagoon, which was only about four to five feet deep. (HF)

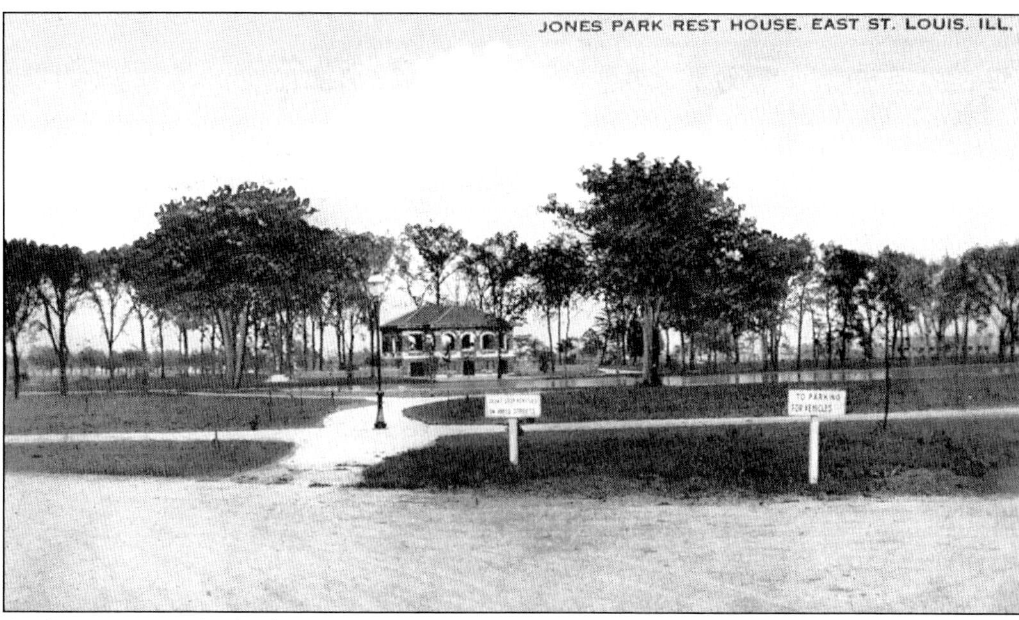

At the time it was built, the Jones Park swimming pool was the largest inland beach in America. An artesian well pumped thousands of gallons of fresh water into the swimming pool and nearby lagoon. Baseball diamond no. 1 was located just east of the bandstand and rest house. (HF)

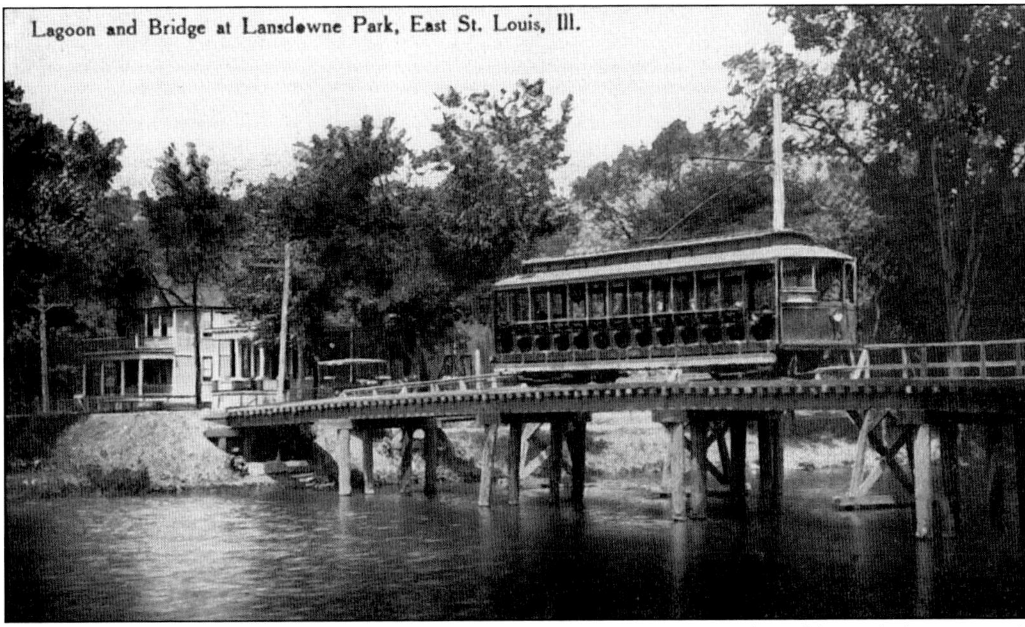

Lansdowne Park, opened in 1901, was a few blocks north of Jones Park and bounded on one side by Caseyville Avenue and Waverly Avenue on the other. Here, the Lansdowne streetcar is seen crossing through the park. (HF)

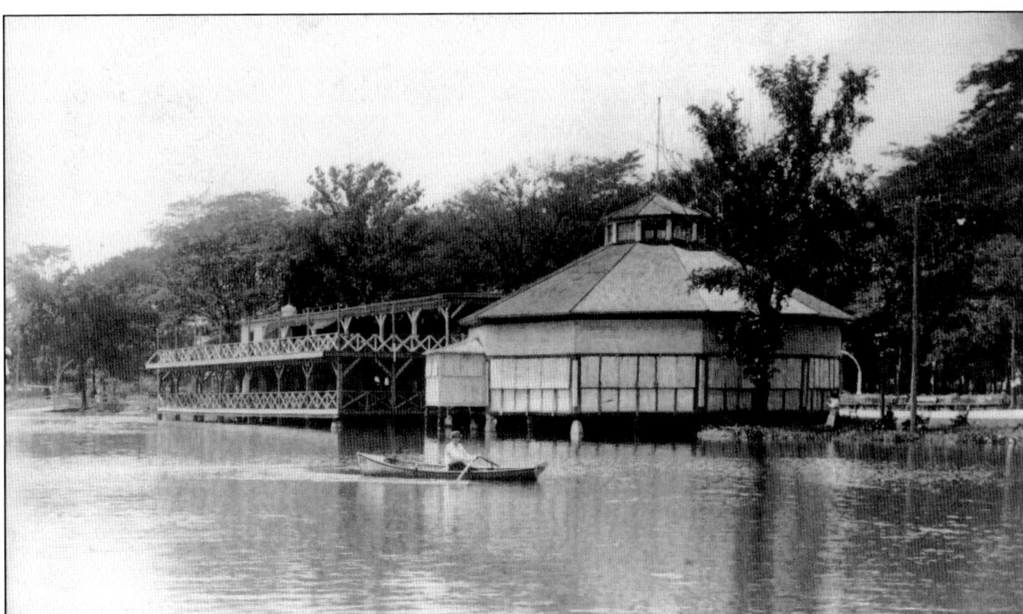

The Park District decided that two adjacent parks were an unnecessary expense, so this lagoon was eventually drained and Lansdowne Park was eliminated. Lansdowne Park featured a large dance hall, a bowling alley, and several carnival rides. (HF)

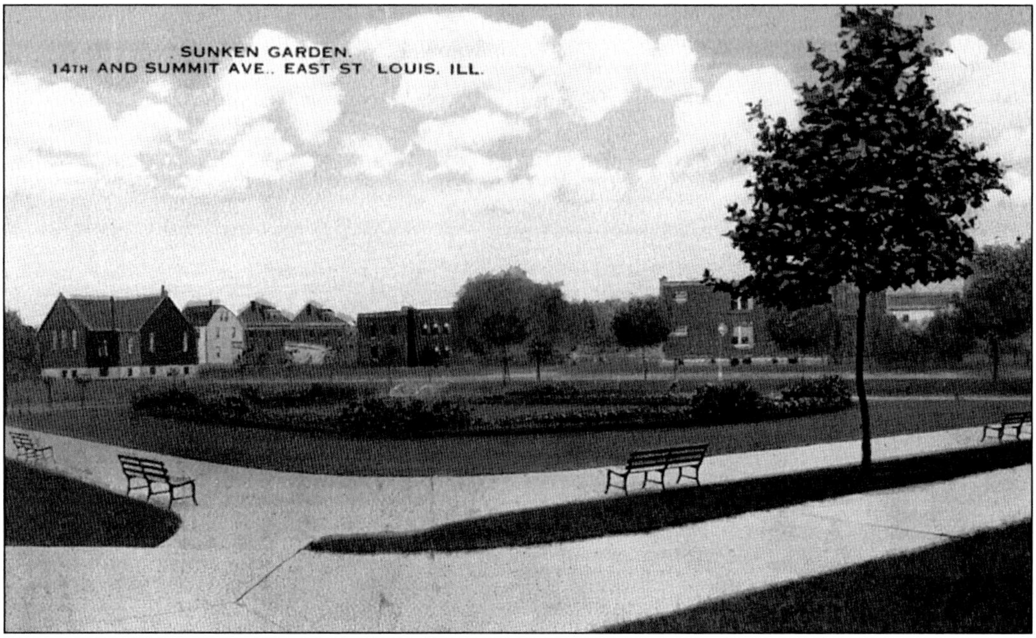

The beautiful sunken garden was in the triangle formed by Veronica, Summit and Pennsylvania Avenues. Originally, this land was part of the Phillip Wolf farm. The neighborhood is named for his daughter—Olivette Park. (HF)

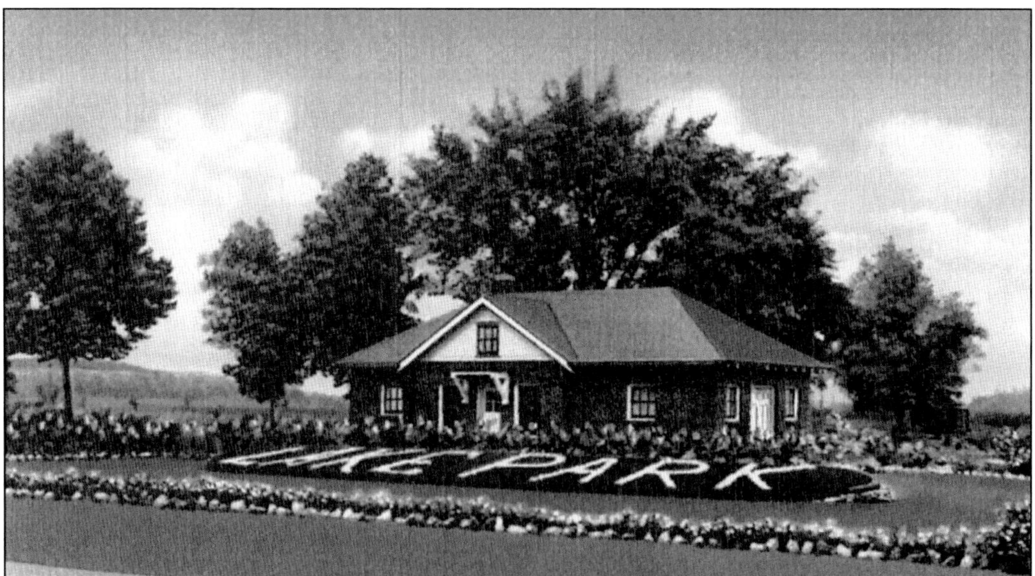

In 1914, the park board purchased 1,125 acres of marshy ground south of the Day Line Railroad tracks near the bluffs at Route 157. In 1932, the acreage was bulldozed, dredged, and graded to form three distinct lakes, making it the fourth largest municipal park in the nation. The land was eventually sold to the state for one dollar and renamed Grand Marais (French for "great swamp") State Park. Currently, the park is named in honor of Frank Holten, an East St. Louisan who was a Democratic state legislator for 40 years. (HF)

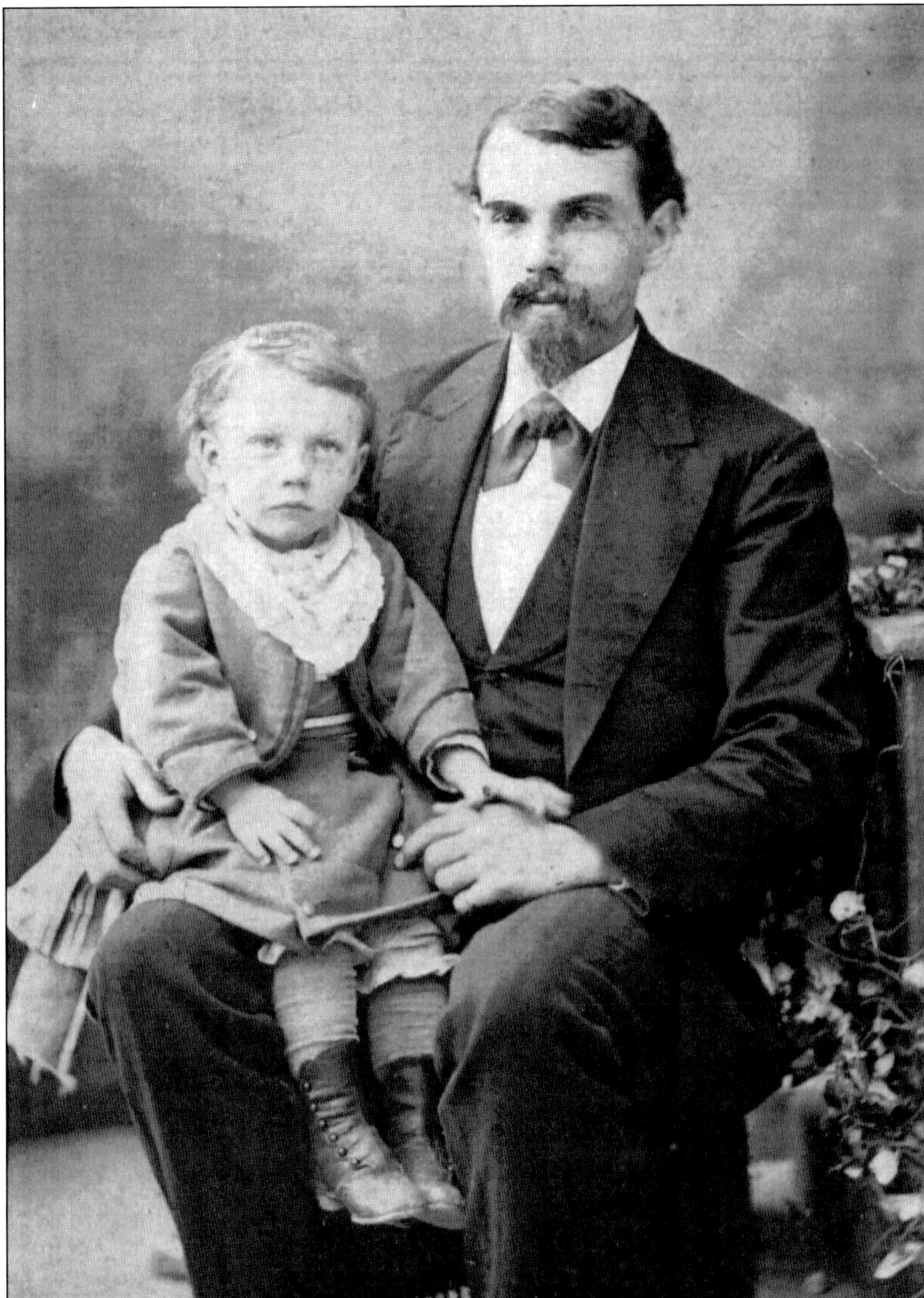

Seen here is Malbern Monroe Stephens with his daughter Lenora Frances, shortly after he entered politics in 1883. Stephens would become the city's longest-serving mayor and the only leader to bring true peace and prosperity to East St. Louis. (SIUE)

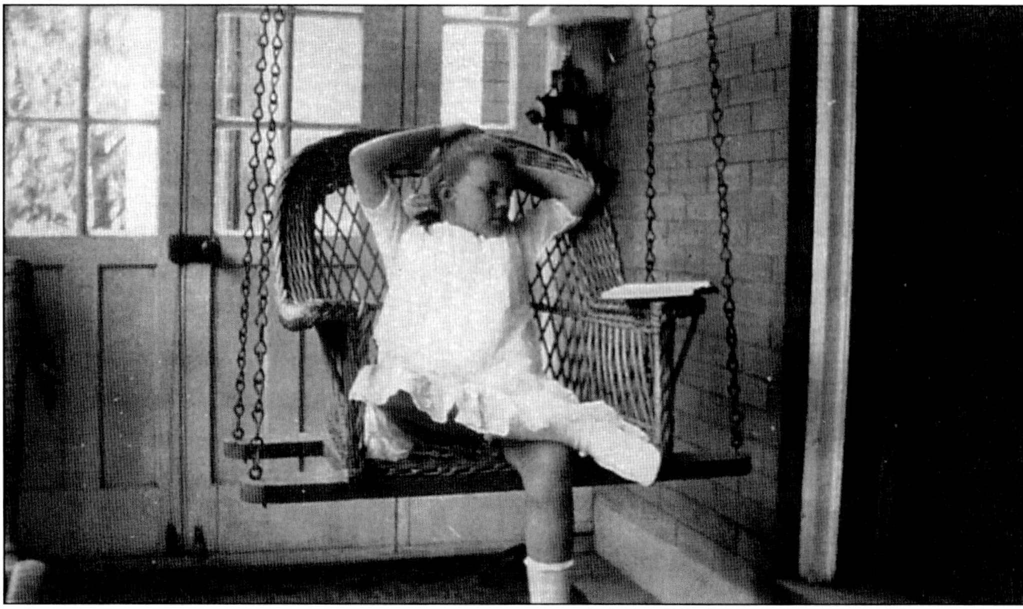

Malberna Jane Stephens was born November 16, 1907, when Malbern Stephens was 60 years old. She attended Horace Mann School and East St. Louis High School (class of 1924), and taught fourth grade until her marriage in 1927. In 1925, her design was chosen for the new police officer badges. (SIUE)

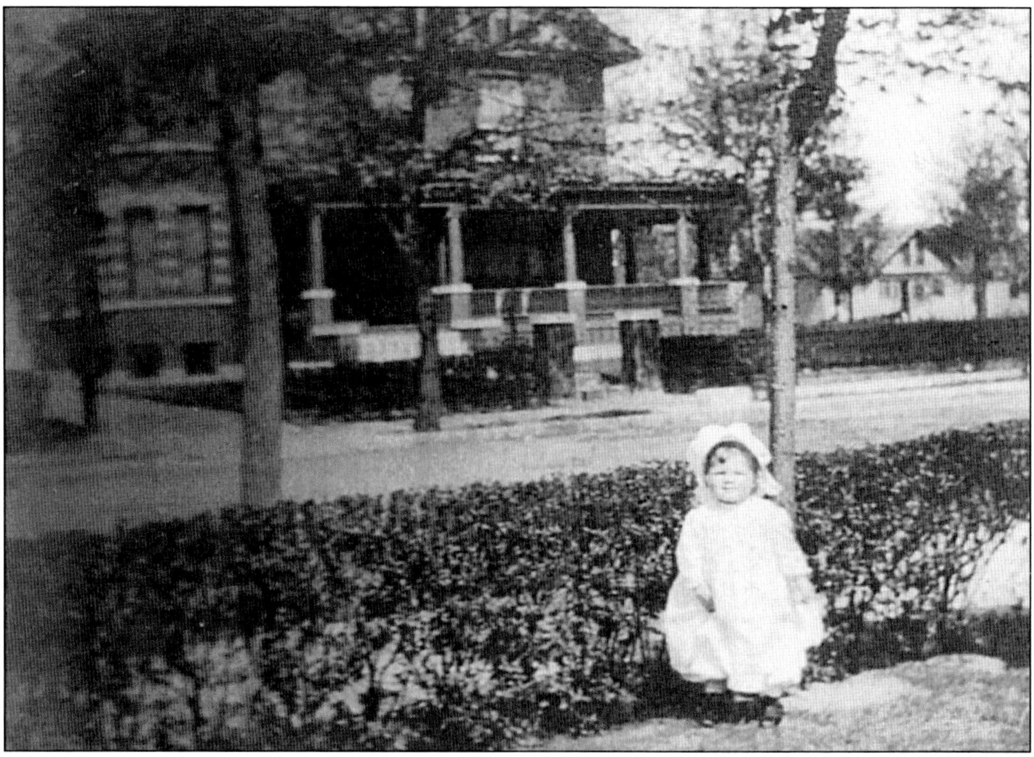

A very young Malberna poses by the hedge, showing one of the graceful homes that stood across Pennsylvania Avenue. Thomas Fekete, a prominent local real estate developer, was Stephens's neighbor to the east. (SIUE)

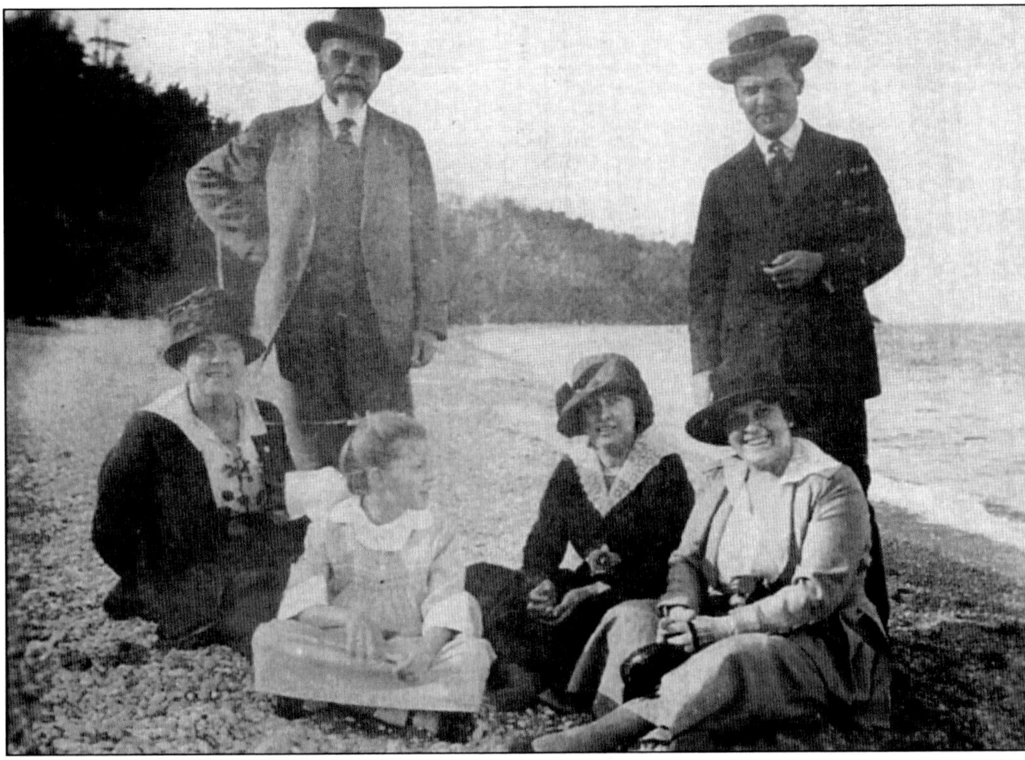

Seen here, Mayor Stephens and his family and friends enjoy an outing at an unidentified location. (SIUE)

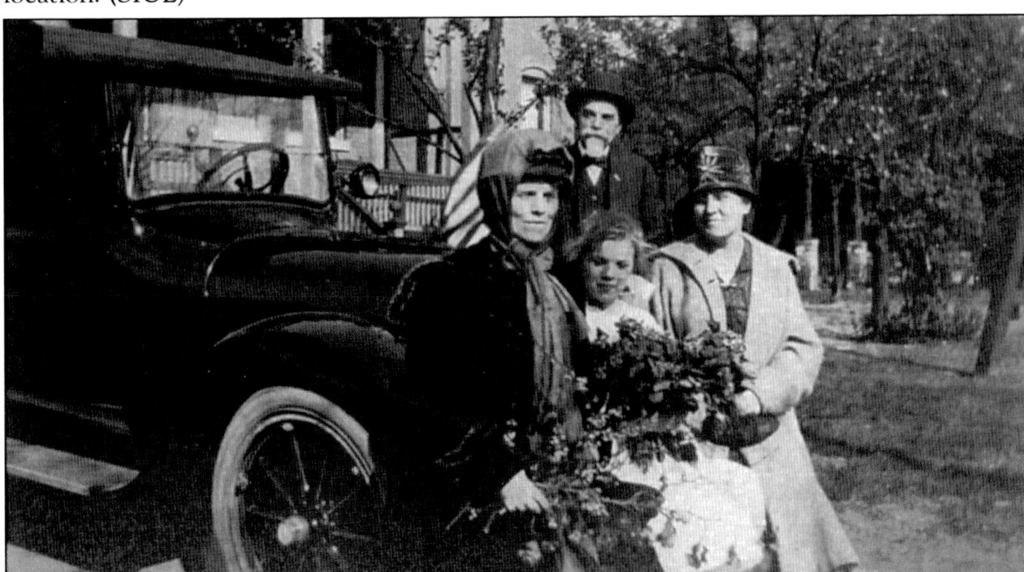

In this image, clockwise from Mayor Stephens standing in rear, is his wife, Sarah Jane Stephens; his daughter, Malberna Jane; and his mother, who moved to East St. Louis from Pennsylvania. Mayor Stephens's mother came to East St. Louis to help run the family business, which was the Stephens House Hotel. The building still stands on Collinsville Avenue near Summit Avenue, surrounded by Metrolink tracks, billboards, and Interstate 64. (SIUE)

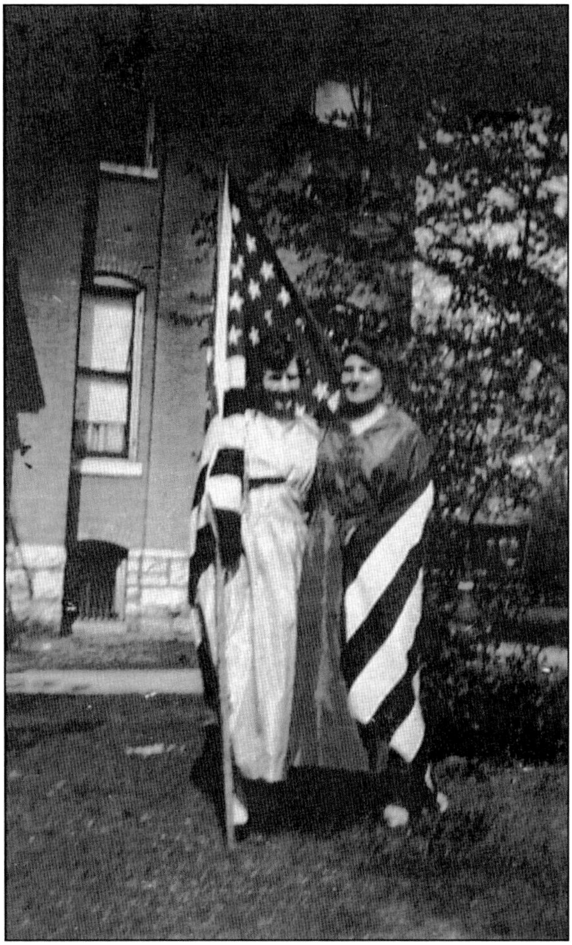

The Stephens family's nurse, Miss Stearns, seen at left, poses patriotically with Sarah Jane Stephens. Stephens's maiden name was Bolte, and her brother served as fire chief for a brief time at the turn of the last century. (SIUE)

Sarah Jane Stephens sits in the driver's seat of the family automobile in 1917. Though Stephens had a nice vehicle and opulent manse, he declared himself penniless in 1916 due to a failed investment in a New York development project. (SIUE)

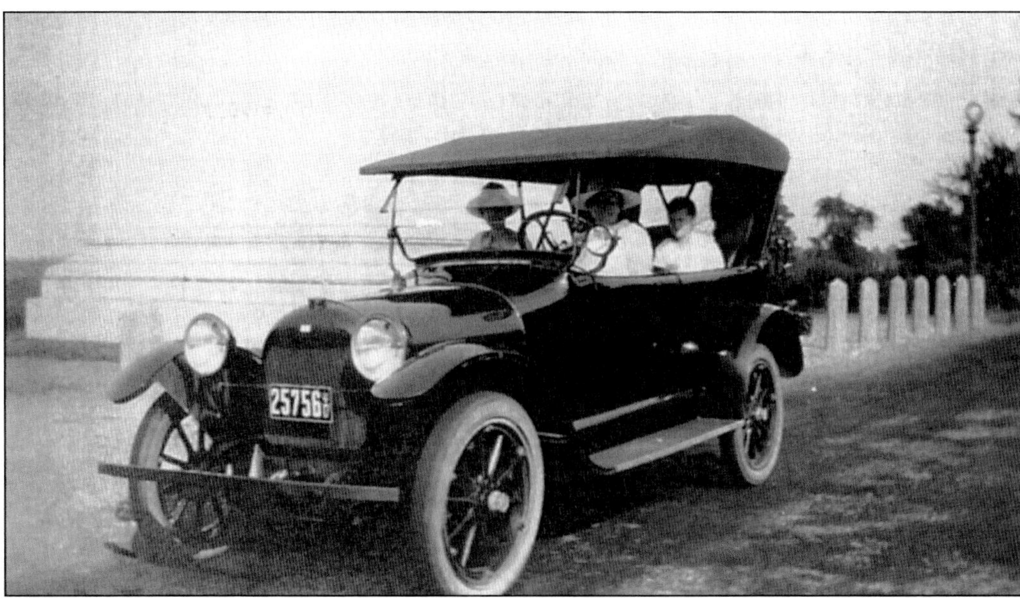

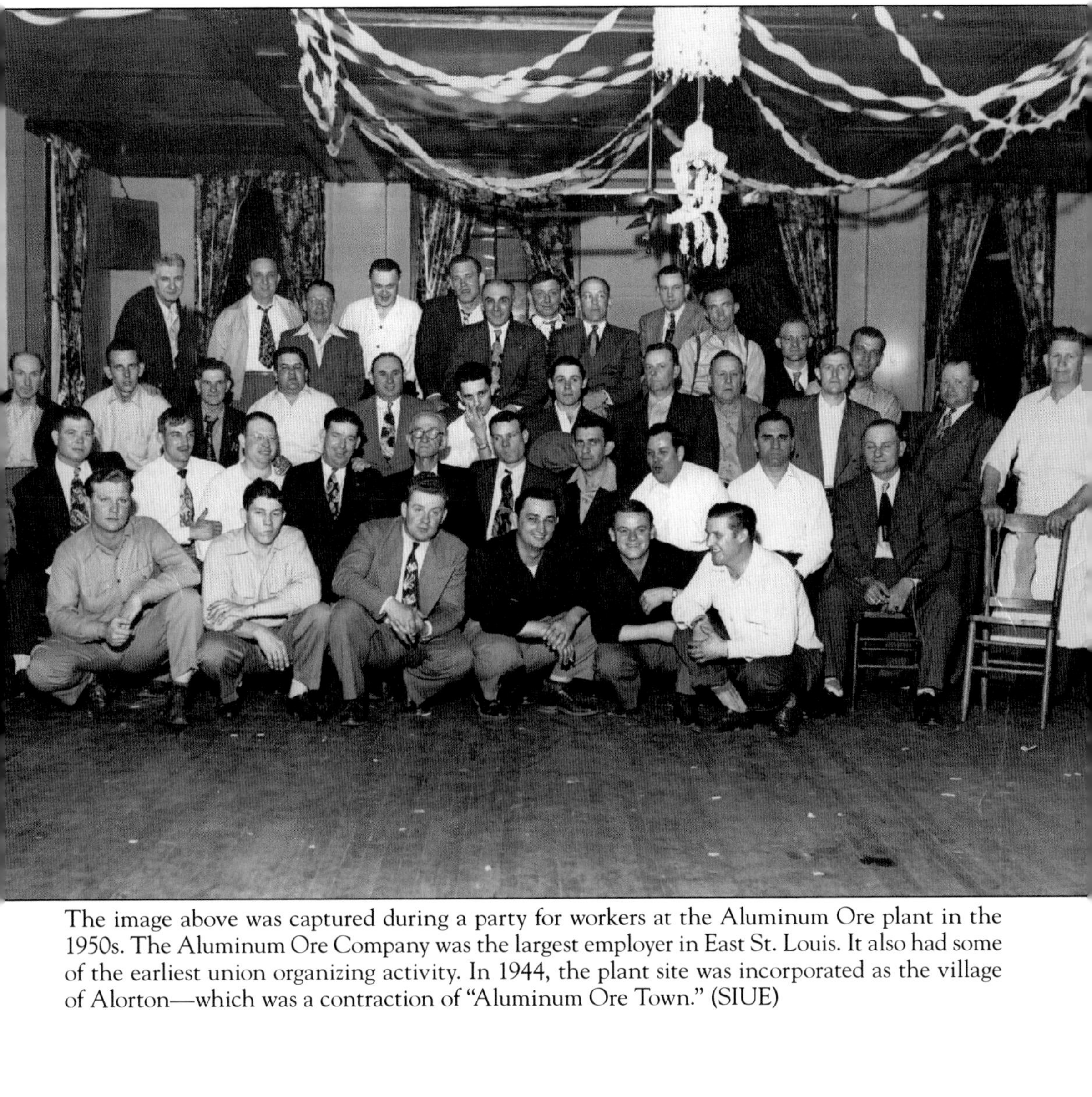

The image above was captured during a party for workers at the Aluminum Ore plant in the 1950s. The Aluminum Ore Company was the largest employer in East St. Louis. It also had some of the earliest union organizing activity. In 1944, the plant site was incorporated as the village of Alorton—which was a contraction of "Aluminum Ore Town." (SIUE)

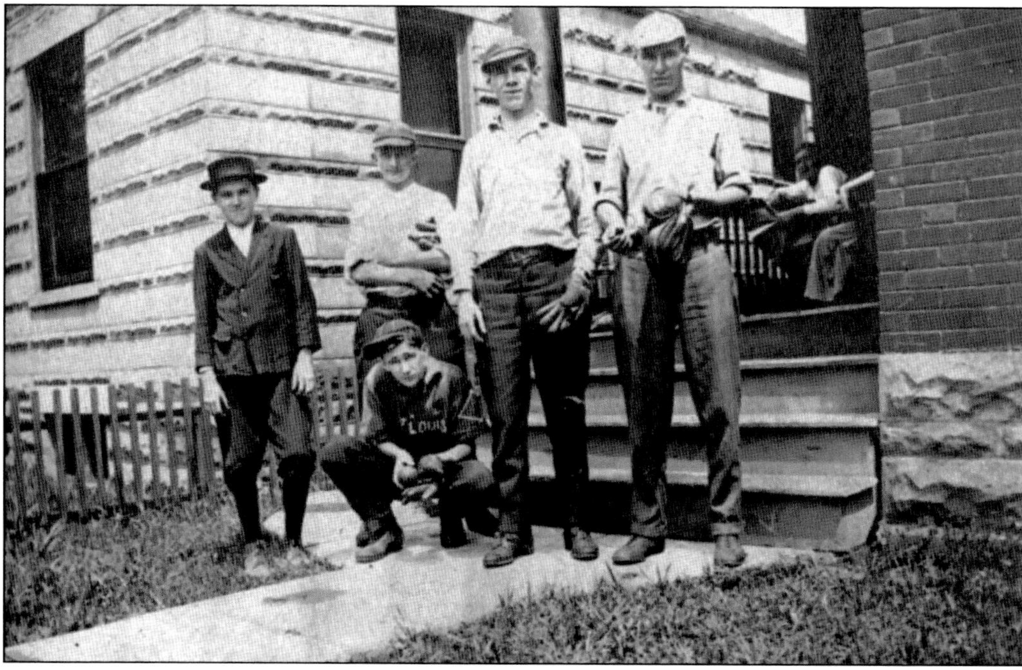

Members of an early East St. Louis baseball team pose in front of the family home. The city had many sports teams, including an early Negro League team called the East St. Louis Tigers. There is a long list of athletes from East St. Louis who went on to professional sports careers, including baseball great Hank Bauer. (SIUE)

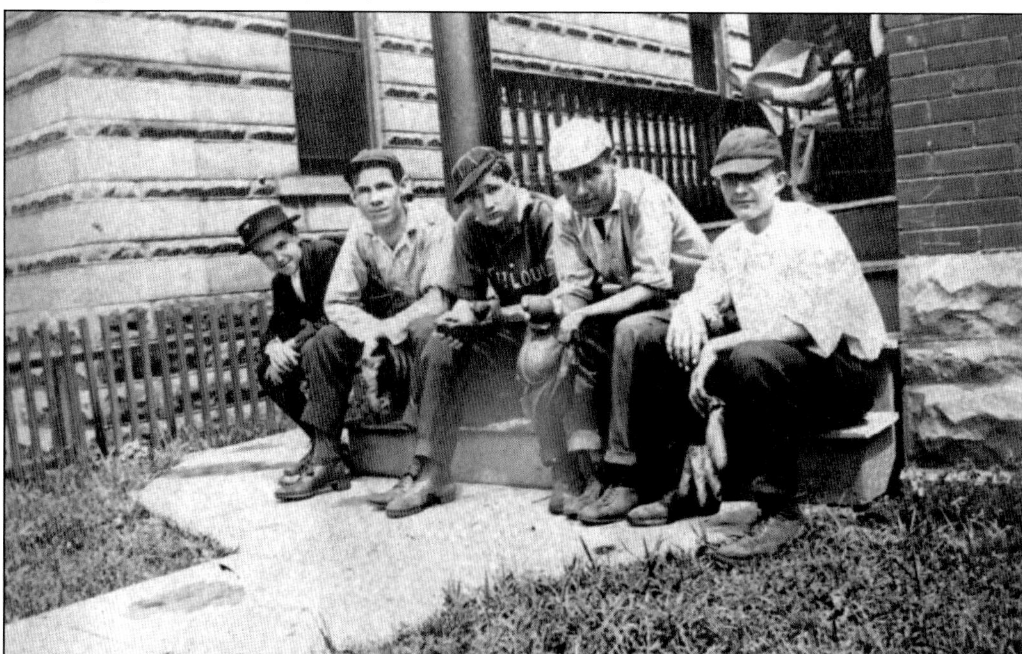

Many businesses had sports teams associated with them. It is possible that these young men played for a factory team (and the fact that children worked in the factories of East St. Louis has been well documented). (SIUE)

At near right, unidentified young couples act silly for the camera. The young woman at far right poses outside in a fine rocking chair. These photos were taken by a travelling photographer in the East St. Louis area, and were never picked up by the subjects. Travelling photographers were quite common in the early 1900s. (Both RP)

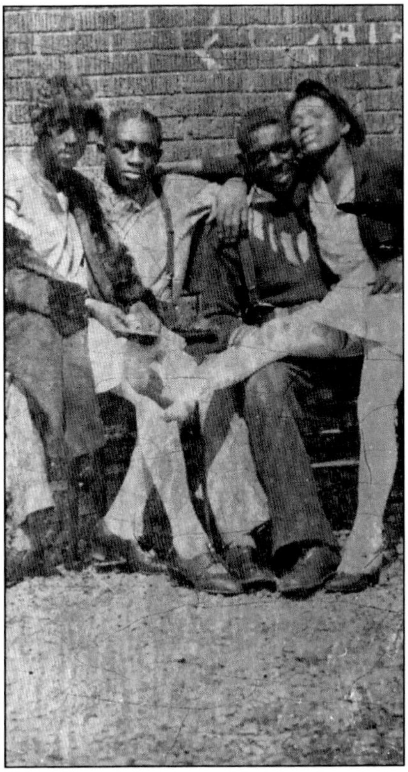

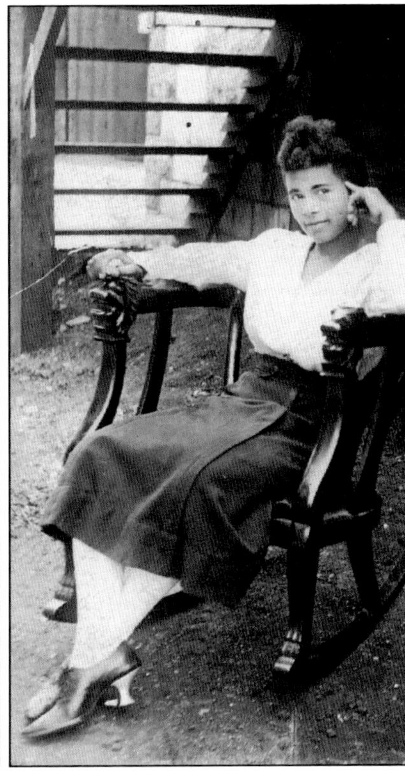

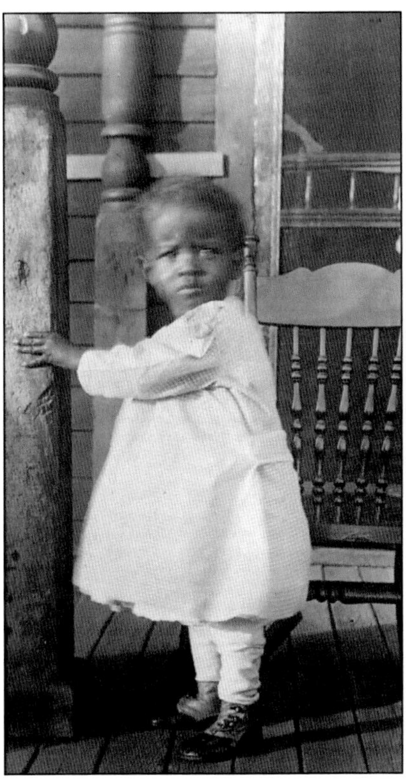

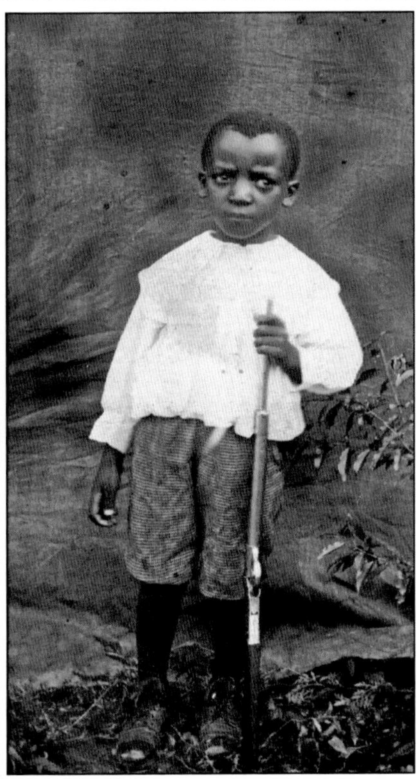

Pictures like these of daily life among African Americans do not survive in great numbers. Digital versions of this photographer's complete collection are housed in the Petty Collection of the SIUE Archives. The young child at the far left sports lovely button-up shoes. The young boy at near left poses with a gun. (Both RP)

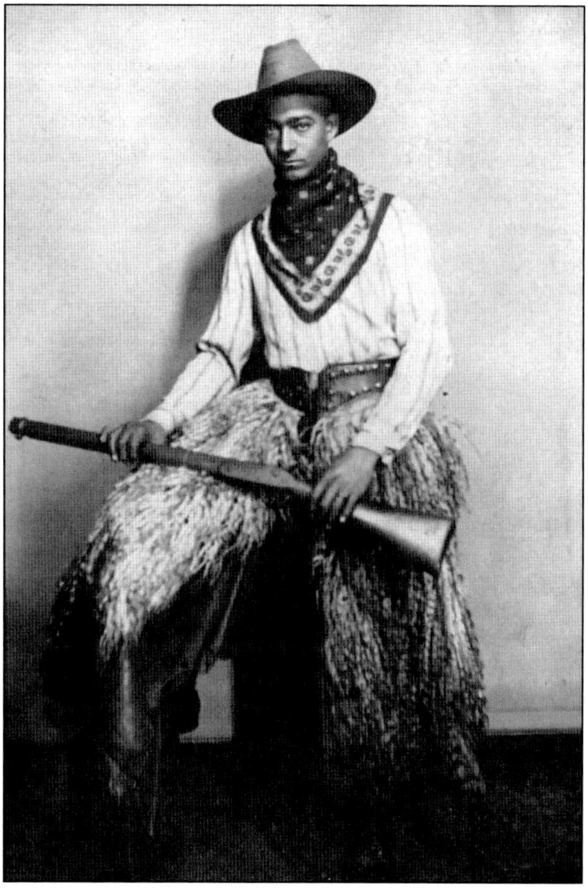

This young man strikes a pose in cowboy attire. East St. Louis had several well-known photography studios. Names included The Majestic Studio, Zahn Studio, E.J. Brockmeyer, and George Killion; all had studios on Collinsville Avenue. (RP)

The African American population of East St. Louis lived predominantly in the South End, and Bond Avenue was the main street of this community. These photos were likely taken in this vicinity. Below, a young boy in a military-inspired suit is ready to go for a ride. (RP)

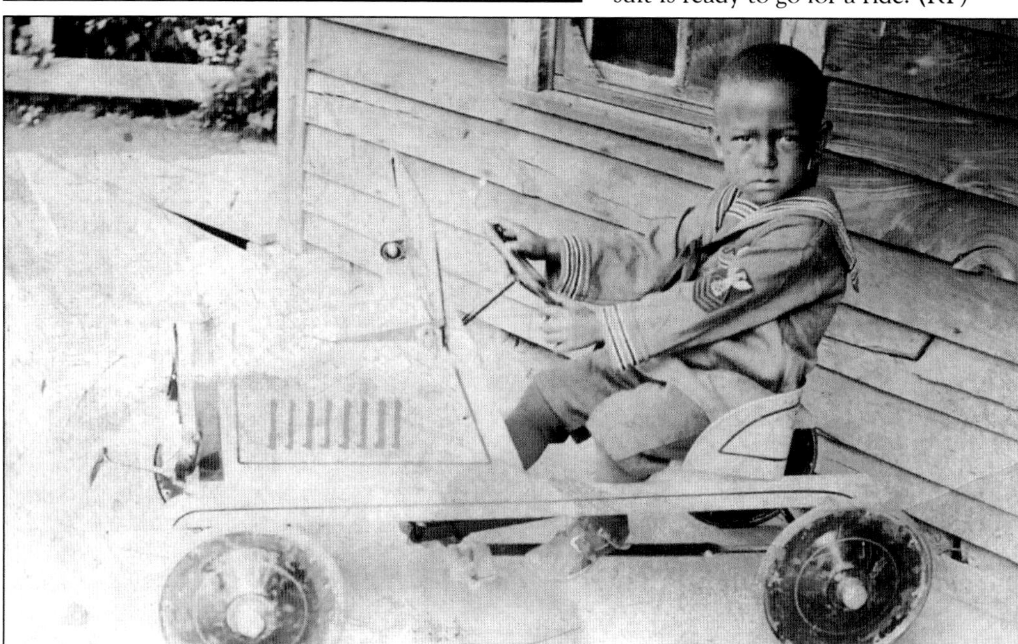

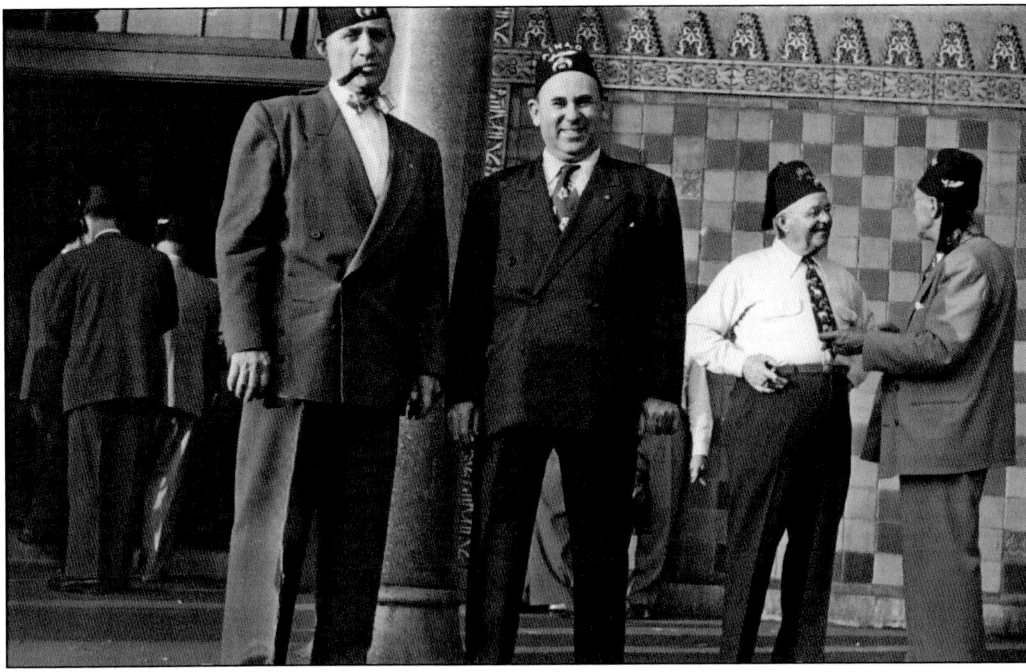

Sid Harwood (left) and Eugene Schmisseur pose at an Ainad Temple function. The Ainad Temple, a brick structure of Moorish design, was constructed in 1923 at 6th Street and St. Louis Avenue. (SIUE)

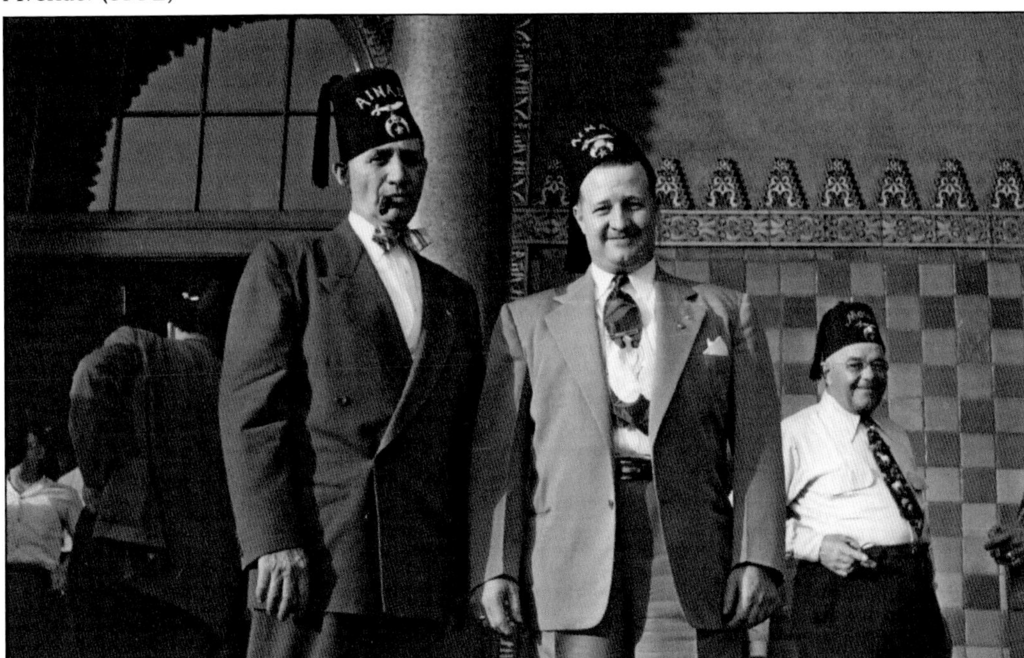

Seen above is Sid Harwood (left) and Ato Shannon at the Ainad Temple. East St. Louis High played their basketball games at the temple and held graduation ceremonies there. In 1924, the temple hosted the city's first Pageant of Progress, which became an annual October event until the site was changed in the 1930s to Grand Marais Park. (SIUE)